PASS Cambridge BEC Preliminary

Student's Book

Ian Wood
Anne Williams

Summertown Publishing

Published by
Summertown Publishing

29 Grove Street
Summertown
Oxford
OX2 7JT
United Kingdom
www.summertown.co.uk

ISBN 1-902741-25-0
ISBN 978-1-902741-253

First published 2001
Reprinted 2003,(twice), 2004,(twice), 2005,(twice), 2006, 2007, (twice)

Editor: Anne Williams
Authors: Ian Wood & Anne Williams

Revised Edition Author: Catrin Lloyd-Jones

Series Editor: Elizabeth Clifton

Produced for Summertown Publishing by the Linguarama Group Pedagogical Unit.

Cover Design by Richard Morris, Stonesfield Design

Acknowledgements

The Publishers would like to thank the following companies for their kind permission to reproduce photographs and other copyright material. Linguarama are particularly grateful to the individuals named below for their help in contributing to the content of the units.

First Great Eastern	Juliet Sharman, Communications Manager
Holiday Inn	Kevin Smith, Deputy Manager Holiday Inn, London - Nelson Dock
Raupack Ltd	Wolfgang Rauch, Managing Director
UPS	Connie Lydon, Marketing Department
Direct Line Insurance plc	George Watt, National Sales Manager

Direct Line, Direct Line Insurance and the red telephone on wheels are registered trade marks of Direct Line Insurance plc and are used with its permission.

Rank Xerox for the advertisement which appeared in **Arena,** Feb-March 1998.

Agfa Gevaert for the advertisement which appeared in **Arena,** Feb-March 1998.

Every effort has been made to trace the copyright holders.
The publishers would be interested to hear from any not acknowledged.

Printed in Malta by Gutenberg Press

Introduction

The Cambridge BEC exam

The **Cambridge Business English Certificate (BEC)** is an international Business English examination which offers a language qualification for learners who use, or will need to use, English for their work. It is available at three levels:

Cambridge BEC Higher

Cambridge BEC Vantage

Cambridge BEC Preliminary

Cambridge BEC Preliminary is a practical examination that focuses on English in business-related situations. The major emphasis is on the development of language skills for work: reading, writing, listening and speaking.

Pass Cambridge BEC Preliminary

The book contains:

- **Introduction** — An introductory unit which gives you information about the examination.
- **Core units** — Twelve double units which cover a wide range of business-related topics.
- **Exam focus units** — A section in the centre of the book to prepare you directly for the examination.
- **Activity sheets** — Pairwork activities and games at the back of the book.
- **Self-study** — A section in every core unit to provide consolidation coursework and examination practice. In order to prepare for the examination effectively, it is important also to spend study time outside your lessons.
- **Tapescripts** — The content of the audio cd.
- **Answer key** — Answers to **Self-study.**
- **Essential vocabulary** — A list of the key vocabulary in each unit. **Multilingual key vocabulary lists are available on our website at www.summertown.co.uk**
- **Irregular verb list** — A list of common irregular verbs.

Language development in *Pass Cambridge BEC Preliminary*

- Grammar

Grammar is systematically reviewed throughout the book. However, the review is brief: look out for the **Don't forget!** sections in each unit. If you need to work on basic structures, you may need to supplement the material in this book.

If you are not sure of basic verb forms, look at the **Irregular verb list** at the back of the book.

- Functions

The book reviews and provides practice to activate basic functional language such as phrases for making requests, asking for permission, making suggestions and arranging an appointment. For Cambridge BEC Preliminary you also need to be able to express such functions in writing.

- Vocabulary

Vocabulary is not tested separately in the examination but is very important. At the back of the book there is a list called **Essential vocabulary**, which lists the key vocabulary for each unit.

You will probably meet words that you do not know in the Reading and Listening Tests so it is important to have strategies for dealing with difficult words. Unit 3, the **Exam focus: Vocabulary** unit, provides ideas on helping you to guess the meaning of words. It also provides ideas about storing and building your vocabulary.

The exercises in the **Self-study** sections recycle vocabulary from the units.

- Reading

The book contains a lot of reading practice, using authentic, semi-authentic and examination-style texts. Do not panic if you do not understand every word of a text; sometimes you only need to understand the general idea or one particular part.

However, you need to read very carefully when answering examination questions; sometimes the most obvious answer on the first reading is not correct and you will change your mind if you read the text again.

- Listening

Listening is also an important skill for the examination and most units contain listening activities. You can find the **Tapescripts** to the audio cd at the back of the book.

- Writing

  In the examination you have to write short notes, e-mails and memos and also letters and longer memos. The examination expects you to pay attention to the task and the word limit. If you have good spoken English, it does not necessarily mean that you can write well. To be successful, you need training and practice.

- Speaking

  Unit 15 helps you to prepare for the Speaking Test. In addition, there are speaking activities in every unit.

Examination preparation in *Pass Cambridge BEC Preliminary*

- Introduction

  The **Introduction** presents the content of the examination and focuses on important examination dates. You will also do a quiz to get to know the book and start to think about how to study for the examination.

- The core units

  The core units contain general and examination-style activities. For example, *multiple-choice* and *matching* are both typical examination-style exercises.

- Exam focus

  Four **Exam focus** units in the book give you information about how to succeed in each of the examination tests. They are yellow to help you to identify them.

Unit 6	Exam focus: Reading	Unit 12	Exam focus: Listening
Unit 9	Exam focus: Writing	Unit 15	Exam focus: Speaking

- Exam practice

  The final exercise in the Self-study section of each unit is **Exam practice**. As it is yellow, you can see clearly that it is examination practice. The final unit of the book, Unit 18, provides four pages of examination practice.

Contents

Introduction

Cambridge Business English Certificate Preliminary

All Cambridge BEC Preliminary candidates receive a statement of results showing their overall grade (Pass with Merit, Pass, Narrow Fail or Fail) and their performance in each of the four papers. Look at the following extract from a sample statement.

Exceptional	Reading			
Good			Listening	Speaking
Borderline		Writing		
Weak				

Successful candidates also receive a certificate showing their overall grade. Each paper represents 25% of the total mark.

An overview

The following table gives an overview of the different parts of the examination, how long they take and what they involve.

	Test	Length	Contents
1	Reading & Writing	90 minutes	Reading: 7 parts Writing: 2 parts (e-mail, memo or note, formal letter)
2	Listening	40 minutes	4 parts Approx.12 mins of listening material played twice plus time to transfer answers
3	Speaking	12 minutes	3 parts (personal information, short talk and collaborative task) 2 examiners and 2 or 3 candidates

Important Cambridge BEC Preliminary dates

Your teacher will give you some important dates at the start of your course. Write these dates in the boxes below.

Cambridge BEC Preliminary examination

Your teacher will give you the dates of the written papers but can only give you the date of the Speaking Test after your entry has been confirmed by Cambridge.

- PAPER 1 Reading & Writing Test
- PAPER 2 Listening Test
- Speaking Test (to be confirmed) Between ______ and ______

Entry date

This is the date by which the examination centre must receive your exam entry.

- Entries must be confirmed by

Grades and certificates

Cambridge sends out results approximately seven weeks after the examination. Successful candidates receive their certificates about four weeks after that.

- Results should be available by

Introductions

1 Introduce yourself to the people in your class. Find out the following information from them.

Name ....
Company ....
Position ....
Why is he/she doing Cambridge BEC? ....

Name ....
Company ....
Position ....
Why is he/she doing Cambridge BEC? ....

Name ....
Company ....
Position ....
Why is he/she doing Cambridge BEC? ....

Name ....
Company ....
Position ....
Why is he/she doing Cambridge BEC? ....

❷ Now find someone in your class who ...

- has already taken an English examination.
- knows someone who has a Cambridge BEC Preliminary certificate.
- uses English regularly at work.
- has been to the UK or USA on business.
- has an English-speaking colleague.
- reads the same newspaper/magazine as you.
- has the same interests as you.

Studying for Cambridge BEC Preliminary

❶ Work in pairs. Look at the diagram below and complete it with ideas for studying for Cambridge BEC Preliminary.

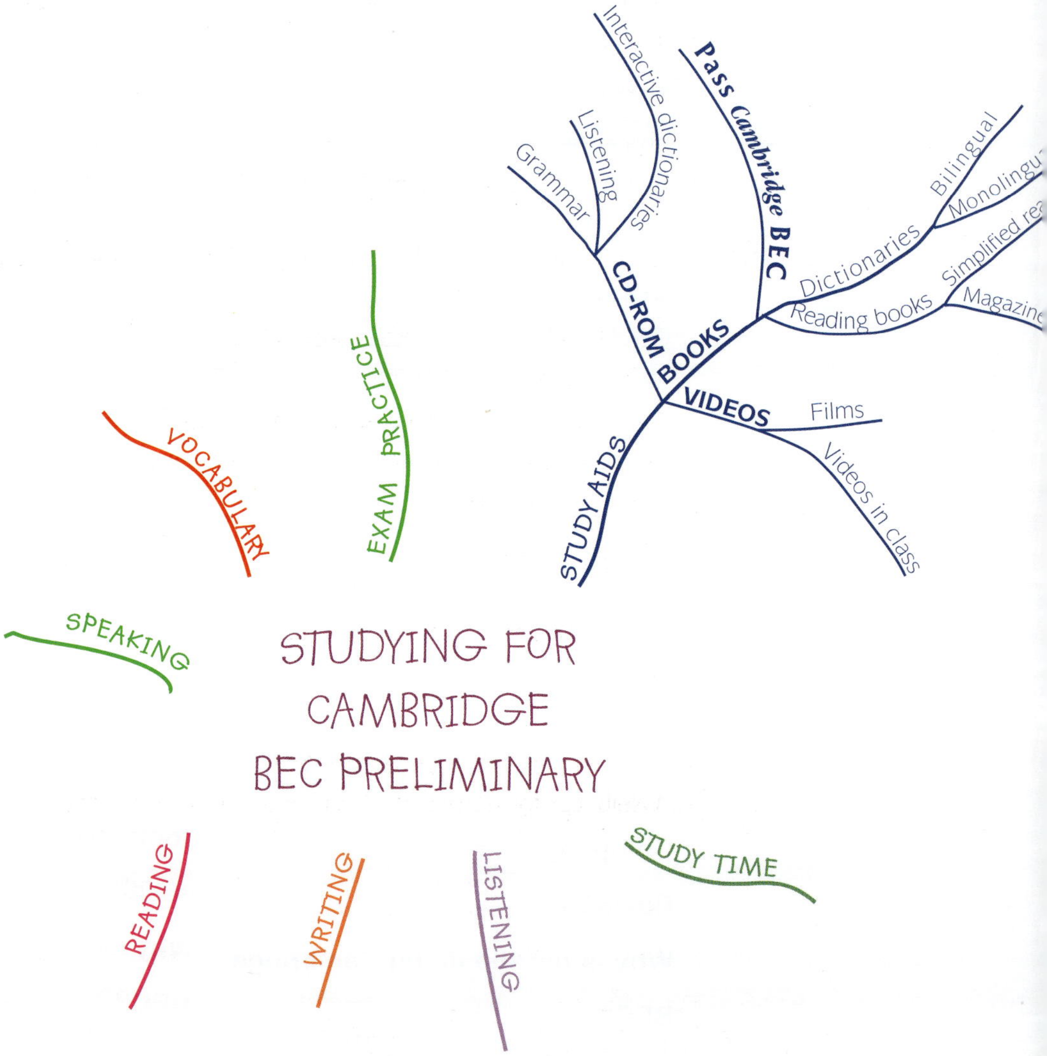

❷ Work in pairs. How useful are the following?

	useless	useful	very useful
1 Using a bilingual dictionary	❑	❑	❑
2 Using an English-English dictionary	❑	❑	❑
3 Having the teacher correct all my mistakes	❑	❑	❑
4 Doing pairwork with other students	❑	❑	❑
5 Keeping vocabulary in a list	❑	❑	❑
6 Writing new words on cards	❑	❑	❑
7 Listening to a lot of cassettes	❑	❑	❑
8 Reading tapescripts	❑	❑	❑
9 Recording myself to check pronunciation	❑	❑	❑
10 Doing a lot of grammar practice	❑	❑	❑
11 Doing a lot of examination practice	❑	❑	❑
12 Reading through class notes regularly	❑	❑	❑
13 Reading for pleasure	❑	❑	❑
14 Keeping a learner diary	❑	❑	❑

Quiz: Pass Cambridge BEC Preliminary

❶ Where would you find the following in this book? Write the unit or page numbers.

1 Terms and conditions of employment
2 A picture of a very famous car
3 Information about the companies on this page
4 A game where you have to get to work before 9am
5 Advice on how to write memos
6 Information about the use of the present perfect
7 A list of irregular verbs
8 Information about hotels in Prague
9 A crossword
10 A job advertisement
11 An article about drug development
12 Useful tips for each of the Cambridge BEC Preliminary tests

Holiday Inn®

UPS®

First Great Eastern

Unit 1a

Job descriptions

Duties

Listening 1 **1** The Chamber of Commerce is an organisation for business people. Listen to six new members. Number the business cards in the order the people speak.

Listening 2 **2** Helen Marsden and Robin Seaton talk about their jobs. Before you listen, decide what their duties are. Then listen and check your answers.

3 Listen again and complete the notes below.

Helen Marsden: Job description

1 Works for a company that produces vaccines and sells them to doctors

2

3

4 Deals with the health authorities in central Europe

5

6

Robin Seaton: Job description

1 Recruits people

2

3

4 Interviews the applicants with the department manager

5 Contacts successful and unsuccessful candidates

6

7

Don't forget!

Present simple

- The third person singular form takes **-s**.
  *She work**s** in marketing.*
- Negatives are formed with **don't** or **doesn't**.
  *I **don't** work with other people.*
  *He **doesn't** travel on business very often.*
- Questions are formed with **do** or **does**.
  ***Do** you work in an office?*
  ***Does** she work at head office?*

Reading

4 Look at the business cards again. Who is each question for?

1 How many sales meetings do you attend each month?
2 What advertising do you want to organise for this product?
3 Why do we need to update our current network?
4 When do you want to discuss the balance sheet?
5 Could you give me some advice on investing money?
6 Do you want me to interview the short-listed candidates?
7 How do you plan to increase output at the factory?
8 What kind of after-sales service do you provide for this software?
9 When do you want the successful applicant to start?
10 Do I need to keep a record of the number of packs we produce a day?

Reading tip: You do not need to know every word to understand the meaning of what you read. Concentrate on the words that you do know!

Speaking **5** Find out about people in your group. Find someone who …

- organises things. What does he/she organise?
- attends meetings. What sort of meetings does he/she attend?
- deals with different nationalities. Which ones and why?
- provides a service. What service?
- travels a lot. Where to and why?

Talking about your job

Vocabulary **1** Match the sentence halves about Beth Lambert.

1	I work as	questions people have about their accounts.
2	I'm responsible for	an accountant with RTLP.
3	My job also involves	produce financial reports.
4	I deal with	checking companies' accounts.
5	As part of my job I have to	Reading, not far from London.
6	I am based in	giving financial advice.

Speaking **2** Work in pairs. You are going to write an article about your partner's job for the Chamber of Commerce newsletter. Interview your partner about his/her job and take notes. Start your questions with the words below.

Do you …?	Are you …?	Where …?	Who …?
When …?	What …?	Why …?	How often …?

1 Match the verbs with the nouns. Then look back through the unit and check your answers.

1	give	a problem
2	provide	a record
3	interview	a conference
4	deal with	advice
5	attend	a service
6	keep	a meeting
7	organise	an applicant

2 Think of another noun to go with each verb.

1 give ....
2 provide ....
3 interview ....
4 deal with ....
5 attend ....
6 keep ....
7 organise ....

3 Complete the table below.

Noun	Verb
discussion	discuss..............
product	....
sale	....
....	organise
interview	....
applicant	....
advertising	....

4 Now complete the following sentences with the correct form of the words from the table above.

1 We're going to _______________ ten applicants for the position of accountant.

2 Could you _______________ the room for the meeting tomorrow?

3 Are we going to _______________ our new sports shoes on the radio or only on television?

4 There were forty _______________ for the job but we short-listed only five of them.

5 My company sells financial _______________.

6 We had a very interesting _______________ about increasing output at the factory.

7 Peter works in the _______________ department. His job involves a lot of travelling to visit clients.

5 **Exam practice**

- Read the text below from the 'New Members' section in the Chamber of Commerce newsletter.
- Choose the correct word from **A**, **B** or **C** to fill each gap.
- For each question, mark the correct letter **A**, **B** or **C**.

Meet Thomas Kingsley

Thomas Kingsley works for Meridian Finance in East London. He works **(1)** ..... a sales executive. He **(2)** ..... with a large number of small and medium-sized businesses in the London area. He **(3)** ..... them on the best financial products for their needs.

He is only in **(4)** ..... office in the morning when he discusses clients **(5)** ..... the Sales Manager. Then he travels around London to see his clients. He informs them **(6)** ..... new products on the market. He keeps a **(7)** ..... of any changes in the clients' information so that he can offer advice if necessary. He **(8)** ..... his paperwork and arranges **(9)** ..... from home or from his car between appointments.

If any members would like **(10)** ..... advice on insurance or any financial product, please do not **(11)** ..... to phone Thomas or one of his colleagues **(12)** ..... 0207 236 4925. They will be happy to help you if they can!

1	**A** as	**B** like	**C** in
2	**A** organises	**B** provides	**C** deals
3	**A** advise	**B** advises	**C** advised
4	**A** his	**B** her	**C** its
5	**A** with	**B** to	**C** from
6	**A** about	**B** on	**C** to
7	**A** notice	**B** record	**C** reference
8	**A** does	**B** produces	**C** deals
9	**A** meets	**B** meet	**C** meetings
10	**A** an	**B** a	**C** some
11	**A** hesitate	**B** stop	**C** think
12	**A** to	**B** on	**C** under

Working conditions

Comments about work

Reading 1 The staff at Amberley Advertising have a comments box. Read the comments and answer the questions.

1 Why is one employee unhappy about taking calls?
2 What kind of supply problems does the office have?
3 What are the problems with pay?
4 What stops people from doing their job efficiently?
5 One person makes a suggestion as well as a comment. What is it?

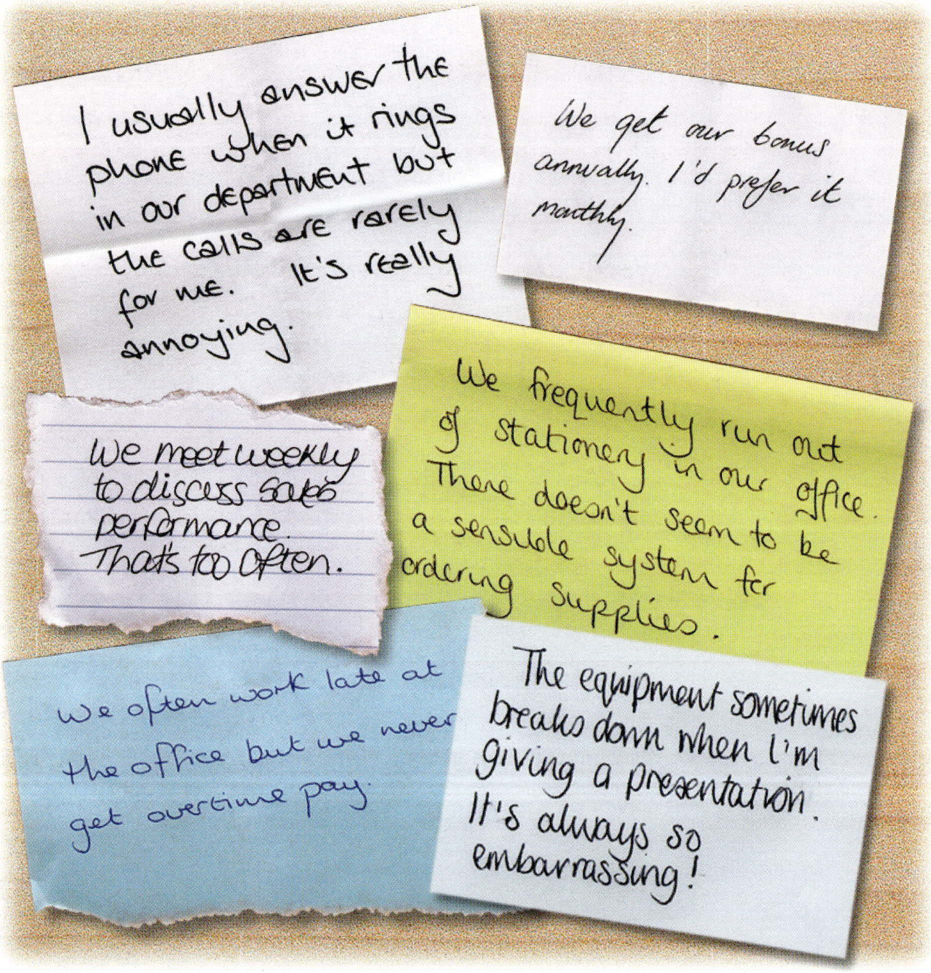

Vocabulary 2 Put the words into the correct order on the line below.

How often?

never, sometimes, always, usually, often, rarely, occasionally, frequently

never ——————————————————————————— always

Work in pairs. Compare your order with your partner.

Grammar **3** Look at the comments on the previous page. What do you notice about the position of the adverb in each one? Complete the information below.

Adverbs of frequency: word order

- Words such as **always**, ______________, ______________, **frequently**, ______________, **occasionally**, **rarely** and ______________ usually come before the verb.
- However, these words come ______________ the verb **to be**.
- Words such as **hourly**, **daily**, ______________, ______________ and ______________ come after the verb, often at the end of the sentence.

Speaking **4** Work in pairs. Find something that you both do:

frequently	occasionally	annually	weekly

5 Work in pairs. Look at the comments again. How would you deal with them?

Terms and conditions of employment

Vocabulary **1** Match the following words with the correct meaning.

1	shift	work clothes that people wear to keep their own clothes clean
2	salary	rules people have to follow
3	to review	a period of work which starts when another one finishes
4	overalls	money a person receives for work
5	regulations	the person you are directly responsible to
6	overtime	holiday from work
7	leave	to look at something again in order to change it
8	line manager	to give somebody something he/she needs
9	break	extra hours a person works
10	to provide	time to have a rest and possibly something to eat or drink

Reading **2** **Read this page of Fibretech's conditions of employment. What type of work is it?**

FIBRETECH PLASTICS

Terms and conditions of employment

These terms and conditions should be read before you sign your contract.

Salary

Your starting salary is ....£14,000...... This is reviewed annually.

Hours

The normal hours of work are eight hours a day, Monday to Friday. A shift system is in operation. The shifts are:
A 06:00 - 14:00 B 14:00 - 22:00 C 22:00 - 6:00.

There are three shift groups and the following system is in operation.

Week one:	Group one	Shift A	Group two	Shift B	Group three	Shift C
Week two:	Group one	Shift B	Group two	Shift C	Group three	Shift A
Week three:	Group one	Shift C	Group two	Shift A	Group three	Shift B

For your first shift, week commencing ....8/6.........., you will be in Group ....3............ and Week ....3.......... will be in operation. On the first morning report to your line manager ..John Knight...

Health and Safety

Please read the safety regulations attached. If you have any questions, contact the Health and Safety Officer, whose name is at the top of the regulations sheet. If you have any health problems, please inform the Senior Nurse, ..Jane Thomas.. If you cannot work because of illness, please telephone the factory before your shift is due to start.

Annual leave

During your first year of employment you are allowed twenty days' leave. This should be arranged with your line manager.

Overtime

If you work more than forty hours a week, you will be paid at the current overtime rate. Your line manager will keep a record of the overtime you work. If you work on public holidays, you will be paid at the current rates. If you prefer, time can be taken instead of extra pay for public holidays and overtime.

Clothing

The Supplies Department provides overalls. Inform Supplies of your size two days before you need them. You can also order any other special equipment you need for your job from Supplies.

Choose the correct option to complete the sentences.

1 This employee will start work at
A 06.00.
B 14.00.
C 22.00.

2 Employees consult their line manager about
A health problems.
B their annual holidays.
C a salary review.

3 If employees work on public holidays, the company will give them
A only extra money.
B only days off.
C extra money or days off.

4 The company provides
A special clothing.
B no special clothing.
C a uniform.

Speaking **3** **Work in pairs. Discuss your conditions of employment. Use the ideas below.**

hours	overtime	leave	clothing	health and safety

Which things are the same for you and your partner?

1 Write two things at work which:

- you can run out of.

____

- you discuss with your line manager.

____

- you keep a record of.

____

- you find really annoying.

____

2 **Complete the sentences with the prepositions below. You can use the prepositions more than once.**

about at in with of

1 You should arrange your holiday _______ the line manager.

2 I need to consult my boss _______ that.

3 If you work more than 40 hours, you will be paid _______ the current overtime rate.

4 If you want, you can have time off instead _______ overtime pay.

5 We need to keep a record _______ the hours you work every month.

6 A shift system is _______ operation.

7 I don't work late _______ the office very often.

8 We have a lot of problems _______ pay.

9 Please write all meetings _______ the diary.

10 They are having a meeting next week _______ the new sales reps.

3 **Choose three of these areas. Write about your own conditions of employment.**

hours overtime leave
clothing health and safety

4 **Exam practice**

Questions 1 - 5

- Read the memo and e-mail.
- Complete the form below.
- Write each word, phrase or number in **CAPITAL LETTERS**.

MEMO
To All Line Managers
From James Bensen, Accounts

Overtime Payment

Please could you let me have any staff overtime details dating from 30/10/01 to 29/11/01 as soon as possible so that the salaries can be calculated. Please remember to state if the worker would prefer to be paid or have leave.

Thanks very much.

To: jamesbensen@fibretech.co.uk
From: johnknight@fibretech.co.uk
Subject: Overtime payment

Jason Martin, Quality Control Assistant in Production, has done 32 hours' overtime this month, i.e. four extra shifts. He would like to have time off.

OVERTIME PAYMENT

Worker's name: **(1)** ....

Hours worked: **(2)** ....

Period ending: **(3)** ....

Pay/Leave: **(4)** ....

Department: **(5)** ....

Company history

The history of Volkswagen

Speaking 1 How much do you know about Volkswagen? Work in pairs and do the quiz below.

1 The company was first registered in
A 1912. B 1938. C 1947.

2 The company produced its first car in
A 1920. B 1938. C 1947.

3 The company exported the first Beetle to the USA in
A 1949. B 1957. C 1976.

4 How many Beetles have been produced?
A 3 million. B about 12 million. C over 20 million.

5 The company opened a Chinese joint venture in
A 1977. B 1982. C 1994.

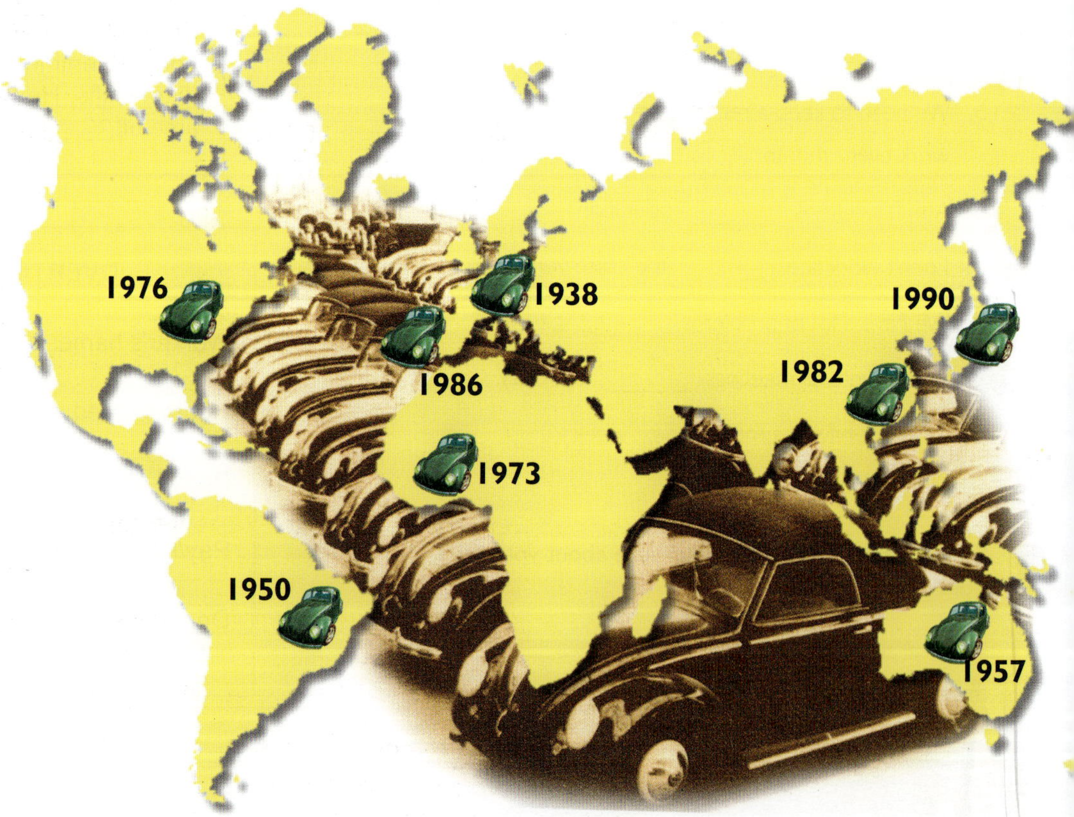

Reading ❷ Read about the history of Volkswagen to find the answers to the quiz.

Volkswagen

a history

Ferdinand Porsche started work on the 'people's car' with money he received from the German government in 1934. First of all he travelled to America to learn about car production. Then in 1938 he returned to Germany, founded Volkswagen GmbH and started production with his new American machinery in Wolfsburg, Lower Saxony.

Commercial production stopped during the war and the factory and its 9,000 workers fell into British hands in 1945. After the war the British helped the local economy by ordering 20,000 cars but decided not to take over the company as they did not think it had a future. Instead, Heinrich Nordhoff took over as Managing Director and the Volkswagen success story began.

Within five years annual production went from 20,000 to 230,000 cars and the company founded its first South American subsidiary, Volkswagen do Brasíl S.A. In 1949 the first exports to the USA arrived in New York, where they were described as 'beetle-like' and the VW Beetle legend was born. Thirty-two years later the 20 millionth Beetle rolled off a Volkswagen de Mexico production line. In 1960 Volkswagen became a public limited company valued at DM600m.

The company continued its globalisation by setting up its own production facilities in Australia (1957), Nigeria (1973) and Japan (1990) while expanding into the USA (1976) and Spain (1986) by buying car manufacturers. The company also set up a joint venture in China (1982). Political events at the end of 1989 gave VW the opportunity to move into central Europe, where it soon began production in the former East Germany and expanded into the Czech Republic.

Today Volkswagen AG is Europe's largest car-maker with 242,770 employees and a turnover of $65bn. With new versions of two of the world's most successful cars, the Beetle and the Golf, the future for VW looks every bit as bright as its past.

❸ Choose the correct option to complete the sentences.

1 Porsche produced the first Volkswagen car
   A ten months after he received government money.
   B three years after he received government money.
   C four years after he received government money.

2 During the war the company
   A stopped producing cars completely.
   B stopped producing cars for sale to the public.
   C continued producing cars as before.

3 The British did not take over the company because
  A they did not think it would survive.
  B they did not have enough money.
  C Heinrich Nordhoff had already bought it.

4 Between 1945 and 1950 production increased
  A every year by 20,000.
  B from 20,000 to 230,000.
  C by 20,000 to 230,000.

5 Volkswagen expanded globally by buying other car companies
  A and forming partnerships.
  B and building its own car plants.
  C and also building new car plants and forming partnerships.

Vocabulary 4 **Find words in the text which mean the same as the following.**

1 buy more than 51% of a company ....
2 a company partly, or wholly, owned by another company ....
3 a company partly, or wholly, owned by shareholders ....
4 worldwide expansion ....
5 organising and building a factory ....
6 income of a company ....

Past simple

- All regular past simple verbs end in **-ed**. For a list of useful irregular verbs, see the back of this book (page 157).
- Negatives are formed with **didn't**.
  *The British **didn't** think Volkswagen would survive.*
- Questions are formed with **did**.
  *When **did** the company produce its first car?*

Speaking 5 **Work in pairs. Find out five things about the history of your partner's company.**

Company profile

Vocabulary 1 **Match the company descriptions with the definitions.**

1 A subsidiary	is owned by shareholders.
2 A public limited company	is at least 51% owned by another company.
3 A parent company	only administers other companies in a group.
4 A wholly-owned subsidiary	has a controlling stake in another company.
5 A holding company	is completely owned by another company.

Speaking 2 **Work in pairs. Your teacher will give you some cards. Read about the eight companies in the MNE group and form an organigram of the group structure.**

3 **Work in pairs. Find out about your partner's company today. Use the ideas below.**

size	turnover	locations	products	markets	subsidiaries

1 **Complete the history of the clothing company Gap, Inc. Put the verbs in brackets into the correct past simple form.**

It started in San Francisco in 1969 when Donald G. Fisher (1 *try*) ______________ to buy a pair of jeans. He (2 *visit*) ______________ store after store but only (3 *find*) ______________ jeans departments that (4 *be*) ______________ disorganised and difficult to shop in. So in August that year Fisher and his wife Doris (5 *decide*) ______________ to open a well-organised store that (6 *sell*) ______________ only jeans.

The company soon (7 *expand*) ______________ rapidly throughout the USA and in 1974 it (8 *begin*) ______________ selling its own-label products. Ten years later it (9 *had*) ______________ 550 stores and in 1983 it (10 *buy*) ______________ Banana Republic, a mail-order business. In 1985 Gap President Mickey Drexler (11 *have*) ______________ a bad experience buying clothes for his children so he (12 *set up*) ______________ GapKids in 1986. The following year the company (13 *go*) ______________ international with a store in London.

In 1991 the company (14 *announce*) ______________ that it would sell only its own-label merchandise. Gap, Inc. now has stores in Canada, France, Germany, Japan and the UK and turnover of over $5bn a year.

2 **Write the following time expressions in the correct group below.**

December	23 July
Friday	1992
10.30	summer
Christmas	Tuesday morning
the weekend	the 1980s

in	at	on
December		

3 **Delete the verbs which do not go with the nouns.**

a company: stop, found, take over, set up

a subsidiary: own, produce, found, open

production: continue, stop, begin, make

4 **Exam practice**

- **Look at the list of industries A - H below.**
- **For questions 1 - 5, decide which industry A - H each person works in.**
- **For each question, mark the correct letter A - H.**
- **Do not use any letter more than once.**

A	Financial services
B	Manufacturing
C	Telecommunications
D	Leisure
E	Retail
F	Construction
G	Pharmaceutical
H	Publishing

1 We have a chain of supermarkets all over Britain.
2 The company specialises in video-conferencing facilities.
3 We invest our clients' money on the stock market.
4 Our company is involved in major engineering projects.
5 I manage the local sports centre.

5 **Exam practice**

- **Your company has just received new company brochures from the printers.**
- **Write a note to the Sales Manager:**
  - * telling her the brochures have arrived
  - * saying which department they are in
  - * asking her to collect her copies immediately.
- **Write 30 - 40 words.**

Company activities

Investing in central Europe

Reading **1** Look at the diagram showing car company investment in central Europe. Answer the questions.

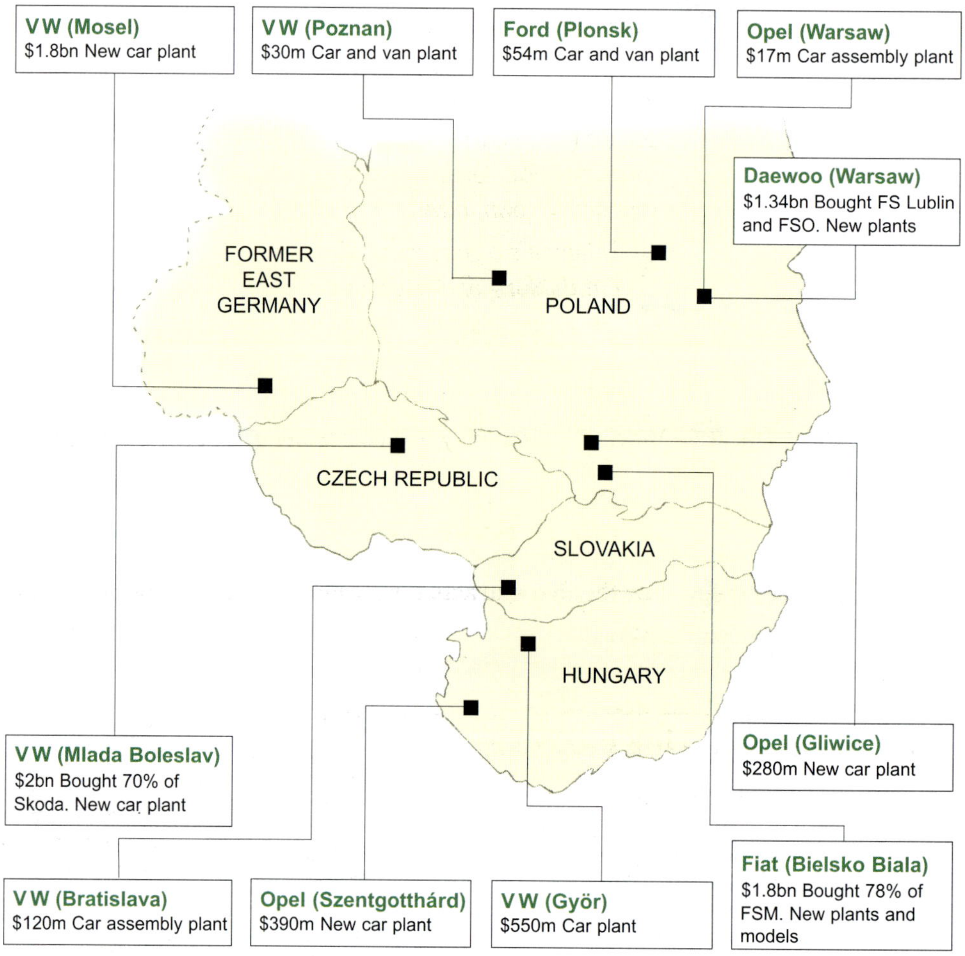

1 Who is investing the most in Poland?
2 Who is building a new car plant in the former East Germany?
3 Who is investing in five central European countries?
4 Which country is receiving the highest total investment?
5 Which country is receiving the least investment?

Grammar **2** When do we use the present simple (*I work*) and present continuous (*I am working*)? Write each description in the correct group at the top of the opposite page.

general facts	something happening now	routines
states	temporary situations	changing situations

Present simple	Present continuous
general facts	

Don't forget!

Stative verbs

We do not use the continuous form to express the following:
opinions (*think, believe*)
senses (*see, hear*)
emotions (*like, love*)
ownership (*own, have*)

! ***I think** it's a good idea.* (opinion)
***I'm thinking** of changing my job.* (process of thinking)

Speaking **3** Work in pairs. Why are companies investing so much in central Europe?

Driving eastwards

Reading **1** Put the five extracts below into the correct order to complete the newspaper article.

Driving eastwards

By Paul Taylor

Istvann Mateew, a 32-year-old production engineer, works at Audi's engine plant in Györ, western Hungary. He earns about $400 a week *but* he would earn around eight times as much for doing the same job in Germany. Low wages are just one of the attractions for the world's leading car companies that are investing in eastern and central Europe.

1

Companies such as VW and Fiat have other reasons for investing so heavily in the east. With low-cost Asian imports in western Europe, they believe that cheaper production in the east is *not only* a way of developing new markets *but also* necessary for protecting those at home. *Moreover*, the big investors are already looking beyond to the former Soviet Union and the huge profits they hope to make there.

However, in spite of all these advantages, not all car-makers are ready to buy or build production facilities in the east. Some manufacturers expect wages and costs to rise quickly. *Although* there are signs that wages are climbing, it will be years before salaries reach western levels.

In addition to the cheap labour, generous state investment grants have *also* brought car-makers to central Europe. What really attracts them, however, is the fact that sales are growing by up to 41 per cent in countries like Poland and the Czech Republic. With low growth at home, the world's largest car-makers think their money is better spent abroad.

Volkswagen, for example, is spending $1.8bn on new car and engine plants in the former East Germany. *Furthermore*, VW has spent over $2bn buying and modernising Skoda, the leading Czech car-maker. Similarly, Fiat has acquired 80 per cent of FSM, the largest car-maker in Poland, *and* is spending $830m on developing two new models by 2002.

2 Say whether the following sentences are 'Right' or 'Wrong'. If there is not enough information to answer, choose 'Doesn't say'.

1 Low pay is the biggest attraction for investors.
A Right B Wrong C Doesn't say

2 Central European governments are trying to attract inward investment.
A Right B Wrong C Doesn't say

3 Central European markets are growing faster than western markets.
A Right B Wrong C Doesn't say

4 Fiat intends to buy the remaining 20% of FSM.
A Right B Wrong C Doesn't say

5 Wages in the east will soon be equivalent to those in western Europe.
A Right B Wrong C Doesn't say

6 The big car-makers are interested in selling cars only in central Europe.
A Right B Wrong C Doesn't say

Vocabulary

3 Look at the words in *italics* in the text. Write the words in the correct group below.

Addition	Contrast
and	but

4 Now use the words to connect the following ideas.

1 production is cheaper in central Europe / car plants are expensive to build
Production is cheaper in central Europe but car plants are expensive to build.
Although production is cheaper in central Europe, car plants are expensive to build.

2 Opel is opening a new car plant in Poland / it is opening a plant in Hungary

3 wages are lower in central Europe / workers are more flexible

4 wages are increasing in eastern Germany / wages are 15-25% lower than in the west

5 VW has bought companies in central Europe / VW has built new factories there

6 wages are lower in central Europe / not the only reason companies are investing there

Speaking

5 Work in pairs. Draw a map showing your company's markets. Explain to your partner what is happening in these places at the moment.

1 Complete the sentences with the present continuous form of the verbs below.

grow invest build develop earn modernise

1 Siemens ______________ some new offices in London.
2 We ______________ a new product at the moment.
3 Markets in central Europe ______________ rapidly and are now more attractive to large companies.
4 They ______________ the offices this month so it's very hard to concentrate with all the noise.
5 The department ______________ a lot of money in new computers at the moment.
6 Most workers ______________ more money than before.

2 Put each verb in brackets into the present simple or continuous.

1 They (*work*) ______________ a lot of overtime at the moment.
2 The company usually (*spend*) ______________ a lot on foreign investment.
3 We (*think*) ______________ about moving into central Europe.
4 Normally a car maintenance engineer in central Europe (*not / earn*) ______________ as much as an engineer in Germany.
5 They (*build*) ______________ a new car plant in Poland this year.
6 Ford (*not / invest*) ______________ a lot in central Europe right now.
7 Central European markets (*grow*) ______________ fast.
8 Some car-makers (*think*) ______________ that the other companies (*take*) ______________ a big risk investing so much in central Europe.
9 Central European governments (*want*) ______________ to attract investment so they (*offer*) ______________ generous investment grants at the moment.
10 Although wages (*climb*) ______________, it will be a long time before they reach western levels.

3 Match the names, nationalities and activities. Then write complete sentences.

Aeroflot is a Russian airline.

1	Aeroflot	USA	chocolate manufacturer
2	Nokia	Switzerland	airline
3	Reuters	Russia	food group
4	Timberland	France	software distributor
5	ABN Amro	Finland	bank
6	Daewoo	Britain	electronics company
7	Godiva	Korea	clothes manufacturer
8	Swatch	Netherlands	press agency
9	Softbank	Belgium	car manufacturer
10	Danone	Japan	watch manufacturer

4 **Exam practice**

- Read the newspaper article below about Japanese car companies.
- Choose the correct word from **A**, **B** or **C** to fill each gap.
- For each question, mark the correct letter **A**, **B** or **C**.

Japanese car-makers increase European production

Japan's third largest car manufacturer, Honda Motors, has announced plans to build a third model in England. The model, a small car to compete **(1)** ..... the Ford Fiesta in the UK, will be produced at its Swindon plant in south-west England and not at a new location in central Europe. The move will **(2)** ..... Swindon's output to 250,000 cars a year.

The expansion **(3)** ..... the decision in January by Nissan, Japan's second biggest car-maker, to build a third model at **(4)** ..... Sunderland plant in north-east England.

The car-makers' plans come **(5)** ..... a time when Japan's biggest car company, Toyota, is considering **(6)** ..... its third European model at a new plant in northern France **(7)** ..... than expanding its present production facilities in England. Toyota is already looking at a possible location in a **(8)** ..... near the Belgian border. The area has a very high rate of unemployment, so generous government **(9)** ..... would be available to the company to create new jobs.

Toyota's strategy is to **(10)** ..... the French market, where sales for all Japanese car-makers have been weak due **(11)** ..... strong competition from Renault and Peugeot-Citroën. Toyota **(12)** ..... the plans were still being studied and that a decision would be made early next year.

1	**A** for	**B** to	**C** with
2	**A** rise	**B** raise	**C** build
3	**A** results	**B** follows	**C** means
4	**A** its	**B** it's	**C** his
5	**A** on	**B** at	**C** in
6	**A** building	**B** build	**C** built
7	**A** other	**B** instead	**C** rather
8	**A** country	**B** land	**C** region
9	**A** grants	**B** fund	**C** profits
10	**A** start	**B** leave	**C** enter
11	**A** to	**B** of	**C** at
12	**A** told	**B** said	**C** spoke

Exam focus: Vocabulary

Vocabulary in the examination

You are not tested directly on vocabulary in the examination. However, you need to be able to deal with words you do not know in the Reading and Listening Tests. You also need to build your vocabulary so that you can read and listen successfully in the examination.

Understanding words

1 **During the Cambridge BEC Preliminary examination you will have to guess the meaning of words from their type and the context. Match the following types of words with the examples.**

1 verbs	sharp, interesting
2 nouns	buy, produce
3 prepositions	a, the
4 articles	which, that
5 connectors	industry, company
6 adjectives	on, with
7 adverbs	but, although
8 relative pronouns	slowly, soon

What type of word can fill each of the following gaps? Now complete the sentences.

1 There was a ________________ rise in the number of unemployed.
2 I spoke to someone ________________ the Marketing Department.
3 I expect the orders to arrive ________________.
4 Here are the brochures ________________ you asked for.
5 Barbara works for ________________ same company as me.
6 I like the job ________________ the money isn't very good.
7 The company invests a lot of money in ________________.

2 **Try to guess the meaning of the words in italics from the information in the rest of the sentence.**

1 I would like to live in the city centre. Every day I have to *commute* to work and the train can be very slow!
2 The bank offers very cheap *mortgages* for people buying their first house.
3 We're going to *launch* the new product next week with TV advertisements.
4 Would you like me to *staple* all the pages together? Then if you drop them, it won't matter.
5 The company has cut jobs *despite* making large profits last year.
6 We've had a lot of telephone *enquiries* about the new product.
7 You don't need to worry about the expense of a taxi. The hotel has a *courtesy* bus which will take you to the airport whenever you want to go.

Storing new vocabulary

Speaking 1 As you learn new words on your course, it is important to store them effectively. You will need to find these words quickly, add to them and practise them. What are the advantages and disadvantages of storing new words in the following places?

- In your course book in the unit where you learn them
- On a separate sheet of paper
- In a separate vocabulary book in alphabetical order
- On cards
- On a computer

2 Look at the following ways of storing vocabulary. Which do you use?

Diagrams

Diagrams clearly show relationships that have some kind of hierarchy.

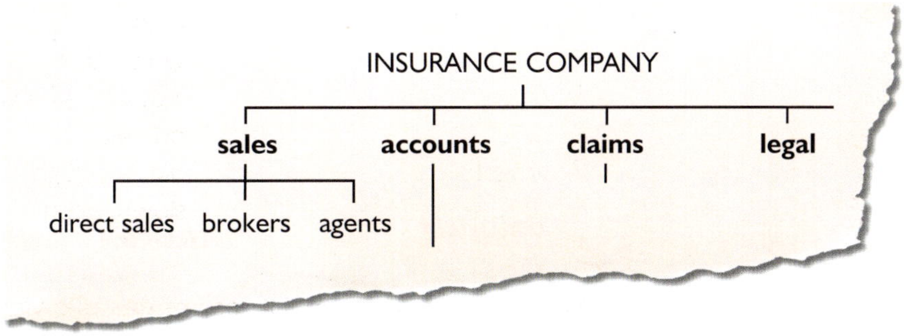

Tables

These are particularly good for showing how words are used together. By using tables, you learn vocabulary in groups rather than single words. Write example sentences to make the table even more effective.

	a meeting	a conference	a training session	an appointment
have	✔	✔	✔	✔
hold	✔	✔	✔	
attend	✔	✔	✔	
arrange	✔	✔	✔	✔

Keywords

You can show which words combine with a keyword. You also need to write example sentences.

Scales

Groups of words that all measure the same thing can be stored together in order. The scale does not provide context so you need to write example sentences.

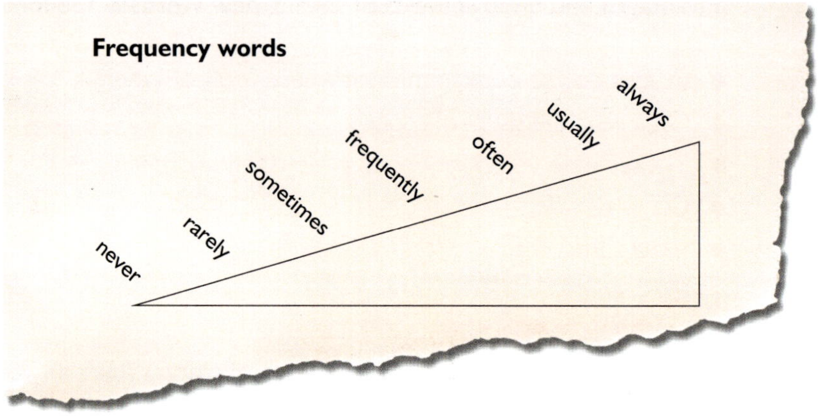

Word fields

If a group of words is connected with the same topic, store them in a word field. Decide what the topic word is and place the other words around it. It does not matter what type of word they are. Then write example sentences.

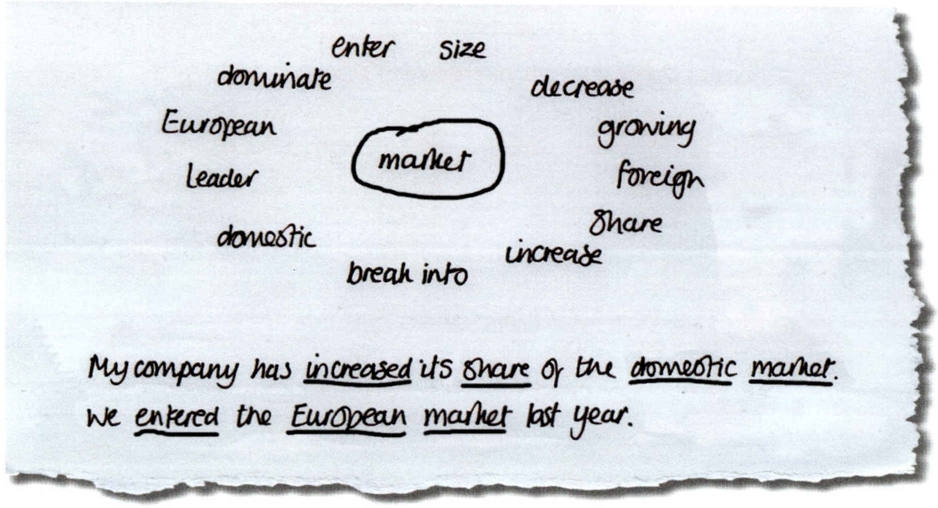

3 **Work in pairs. Now look at the groups of words below. What is the best way of storing them?**

1 slightly, steadily, sharply, dramatically
2 commission, contract, target, results, figures, executive
3 send a package, send documents, send a shipment, send a letter, post documents, post a letter
4 group, holding company, division, subsidiaries, offices
5 pension, salary, leave, hours, duties
6 a long time ago, recently, currently, in the near future, long term
7 chairman, sales director, regional sales managers, sales executives, agents, head of production, production manager, shift managers
8 merchant bank, bank loan, bank transfer, bank manager, investment bank

Vocabulary cards

1 Cards can be an effective and flexible way of learning vocabulary. You can read them on the way to work if you travel by bus or train. Look at the example below and make cards for the following words. Use a dictionary to help you.

equipment	steady	available	receipt

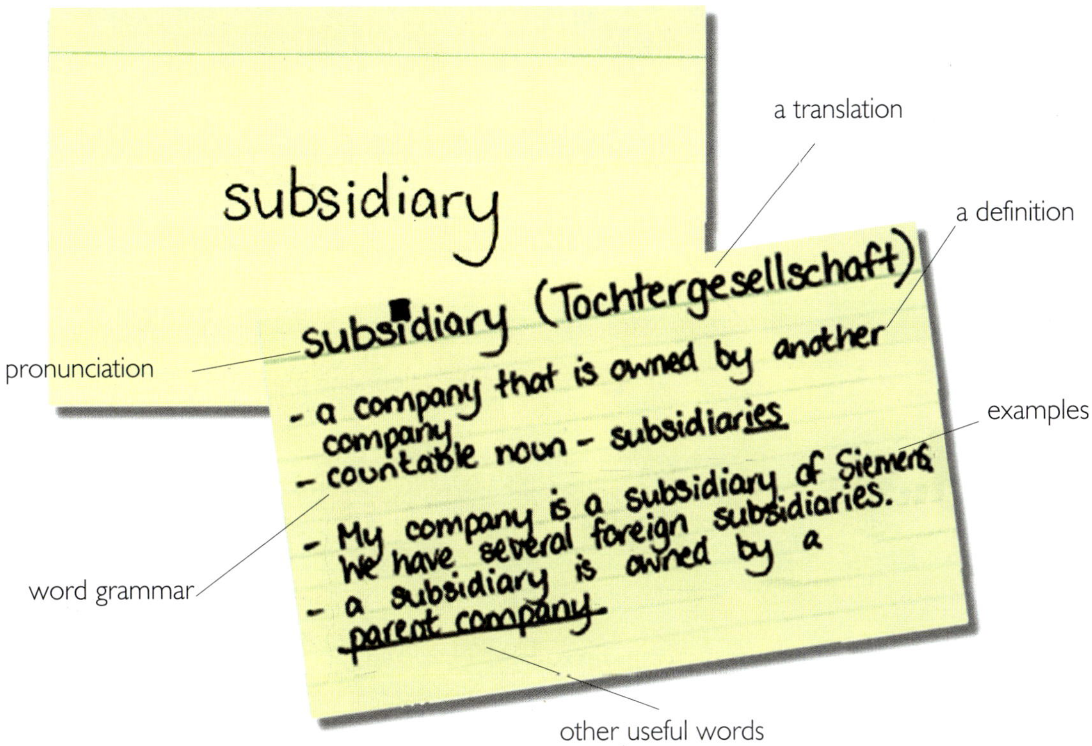

Building your vocabulary

1 Many words have several forms (*produce, production, producer, productive* and *productively*). Look at the following ways of changing the forms of words.

Change	Add	Example
Noun to verb	*-ise*	glohal**ise**, standard**ise**
Verb to noun	*-tion/sion/ment*	confirma**tion**, employ**ment**
Verb to person/company/machine	*-er/or*	manufactur**er**, invest**or**
Adjective to noun	*-ity/ty*	probabil**ity**, loyal**ty**
Adjective to adverb	*-ly/ily*	normal**ly**, stead**ily**
Adjective to its opposite	*un-/im/in*	**un**interesting, **im**probable
To add the meaning "do again"	*re-*	**re**launch, **re**write

2 Work in pairs. How many different forms of the words below can you think of? Use a dictionary to check your answers.

possible	develop	operate	safe
general	organise	private	employ

Now write example sentences for two forms of five of the words.

Unit 4a

Telephoning

Getting through

Listening 1 **1** Clare MacPherson is a receptionist for Baker and Kerr, a manufacturer of cosmetic products. Clare takes six calls. Listen and number the descriptions of the calls.

A The receptionist connects the caller.

B The caller leaves a message.

C The caller will phone again soon.

D The caller will phone again later.

E The caller was cut off and phones again.

F The caller waits for a short time then the receptionist connects her.

2 Look at the telephone phrases below. What are the possible responses?

1 Who's calling?
2 Can I take a message?
3 Can I have extension 184, please?
4 Can I speak to William Grogan, please?
5 Do you know when he'll be free?
6 I'm returning her call.
7 Is Keith available?
8 We were cut off.

Now listen to the conversations again. How do the speakers respond?

Don't forget!

Immediate decisions with will

We use **will** to express an immediate decision, offer or promise.
(In spoken English **will** becomes **'ll**.)
I'll *call back in about ten minutes.*
I'll *put you through.*

3 Match the telephone phrases below with the responses.

1 I'm afraid the line's busy.	It's OK. I'll phone back later.
2 Can I have extension 236, please?	It's OK. I'll hold.
3 I'm afraid he isn't in the office.	Sorry, I'll try to reconnect you.
4 Could you tell Sarah that I called?	I'll put you through.
5 It's Dave Rogers again for Joe West. We were cut off.	OK. I'll give her your message.

Reading 4 Work in pairs. Look at the maze below. Use the language in the squares to make a telephone conversation. To start, find the correct square. Then follow the conversation to the end. Move in any direction except up.

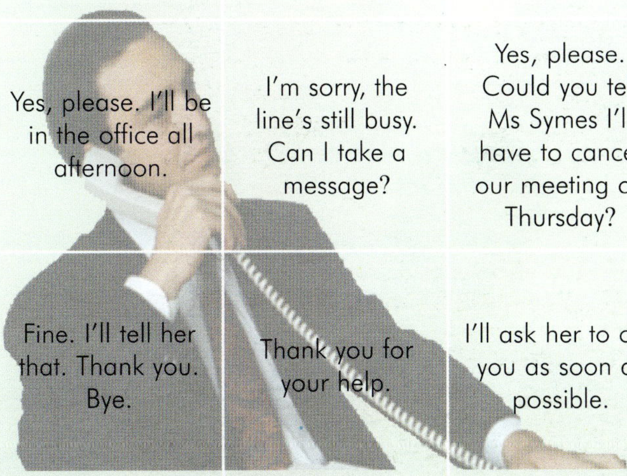

Good morning. Anna Jones speaking.	Good morning. Davis and Sons. Can I help you?	Hello. My name's Pete Brown. Can you put me through to Craig Wilson, please?	Good morning. Walton's. Can I help you?	Yes. Can you put me through to Ellen Symes, please?
Extension 471, please.	Hello Anna. It's Marion again. We were cut off.	I'm afraid he's in a meeting. Can I take a message?	Do you know when he'll be free?	Who's calling, please?
I'm sorry. Could you repeat that?	I'm calling about a problem with the delivery dates.	Could you repeat the name of the company, please?	Alan Murphy from RSL Finance.	He should be available in about an hour.
Hold the line, please. I'll put you through to Sales.	RSL.	The line's busy at the moment. Would you like to hold?	Right. I'll call back later. Thank you.	Did you say 'F' for Freddie or 'S' for Sugar?
Yes, I'll tell him that. Shall I ask him to call you back?	I'm sorry. He won't be free until this afternoon.	OK.	I'm afraid I can't hold. Could you take a message, please?	It's 'S' for Sugar.
Yes, please. I'll be in the office all afternoon.	I'm sorry, the line's still busy. Can I take a message?	Yes, please. Could you tell Ms Symes I'll have to cancel our meeting on Thursday?	Could you repeat your name, please?	Alan Murphy.
Fine. I'll tell her that. Thank you. Bye.	Thank you for your help.	I'll ask her to call you as soon as possible.	**Fine, Mr Murphy. I'll give her your message.**	Yes, I'll tell Ms Lewis it's urgent. Thank you. Bye.

Speaking 5 Work in pairs. Choose two squares from the maze. Make them into a conversation.

Reasons for calling

Listening 2 1 Clare takes another call. Listen and complete the message.

PHONE MESSAGE

Message for Sharon Thomson

Name of caller ....

Company ....

Message ....

....

....

2 Listen again. Write the phrases that the speakers use ...

- to ask for spelling ________________
- to give the reason for calling ________________
- to check what the other speaker said ________________

Speaking 3 Work in pairs. Student A: Look at the Activity sheet on page 125. Student B: Look at the Activity sheet on page 129.

1 Look at the telephone conversation below. Put the conversation into the correct order.

Receptionist

- ❑ Thank you, Mr Abraham. I'll give Mr Green the message.
- ❑ I'm afraid the line's busy. Can I take a message?
- ❑ You're welcome. Bye.
- ❑ Good morning, Priory Hotel.
- ❑ And what's the message, please?
- ❑ Could you spell your surname, please?
- ❑ Did you say 7.15 or 7.50?

Caller

- ❑ Yes, please. Could you tell him Alan Abraham called?
- ❑ Thank you very much.
- ❑ Could you tell him I've booked a table at Marcel's restaurant for 7.15 this evening and I'll meet him there?
- ❑ A-B-R-A-H-A-M.
- ❑ Hello, could you put me through to Mr Green in room 105, please?
- ❑ 7.15. Quarter past seven.

2 Robin Hobson applies for a job at Baker and Kerr. He telephones to arrange an interview. Read the conversation and fill the gaps.

Clare	Baker and Kerr. Can I help you?
Caller	Hello. I'd like to speak to Louise Sanderson, please.
Clare	I'm afraid she's out of the office this morning. (1) ______________________?
Caller	Yes, please. My name's Vic Hobson.
Clare	(2) ______________________?
Caller	H-O-B-S-O-N.
Clare	(3) ______________________ B-S or P-S?
Caller	B for book - S. (4) ______________________ the position as sales executive.
Clare	Yes?
Caller	Ms Sanderson left a message on my voice-mail asking if I could come for an interview at 2pm on 16 May. (5) ______________________ that I'll be able to come then?
Clare	So, that's 2 o'clock on 16 May.
Caller	That's right.
Clare	Fine. (6) ______________________.
Caller	Thank you. Bye.

3 **Exam practice**

- **Look at questions 1 - 5.**
- **In each question, which phrase or sentence is correct?**
- **For each question, mark the correct answer A, B or C.**

1

> Sally phoned. She said your e-mail was deleted by accident. Could you send it again?

The e-mail message
A did not arrive.
B was sent to the wrong address.
C was destroyed.

2

> Ms Haan called. Our order's been delayed due to problems with a supplier.

The order has
A arrived late.
B not arrived yet.
C been cancelled.

3

> Tuesday, 6pm
> Alex
> Sebastian Page returned your call from yesterday. He'll try again in the morning.

Sebastian Page is going to
A call Alex tomorrow.
B wait for Alex to call back later.
C call Alex again later today.

4

> UPS called to say they'll collect the parcel at 3 o'clock this afternoon.

The delivery service
A will pick the parcel up today.
B intends to deliver the parcel at 3pm.
C came for the parcel at 3pm.

5

> Chris
> Call Annette Pohl. She's on her way to a meeting so try her mobile on 0486 366 57.

Annette Pohl is in
A her office.
B a meeting.
C her car.

Unit 4b

Internal communication

Memos, notes and notices

Reading **1** Danos is a manufacturer of office furniture and supplies. Look at the examples of the company's internal communication below and find the following information:

- the company's markets
- some of the company's activities
- where it is based.

Henry
Meeting with Veronique Leboeuf cancelled. Could we meet on the 14th anyway?
Paula.

MEMORANDUM

DANOS OFFICES

To: All National Sales Managers
From: Henry Wallace
Sales Director
Date: 10 July 2001

INTERNATIONAL SALES CONFERENCE

Our International Sales Conference will take place from 30 October to 1 November in Rome. I will send details of the hotel later. Please go ahead and book your flight to Rome now. Please note that you need to arrive in Rome by 15.00 on the Friday and stay until 16.30 on the Sunday. It is essential that everybody books an APEX flight or equivalent. Please contact me in case of any difficulty.

SALESPERSON OF THE YEAR

The decision for Salesperson of the Year has been almost impossible as there have been so many excellent performances. However, because of her work in turning round a long-term fall in sales, the prize goes to:

Paula Stuart
(Madrid office)

Congratulations to Paula, who wins a holiday in Florida.

Sue,
Can't find name or tel no. of customer who phoned about new seating range. If you've got it, could you give it to me ASAP?
Thanks,
Mike

MEMORANDUM

DANOS OFFICES

To: Managers
From: Sarah Longman
Accounts Dept
Date: 4 July 2001

Salary sheets for the third quarter should arrive at Manchester Head Office by the following dates:

For August:	Thursday 23 July
For September:	Thursday 21 August
For October:	Tuesday 23 September

NB Please send salary details by GUARANTEED DELIVERY.

2 Answer the questions below.

1 When is the next International Sales Conference?
2 What is the prize for Salesperson of the Year?
3 When do salary details for August have to arrive at Head Office?
4 Who is the Head of the Sales Department?
5 Who is meeting on 14 July?
6 What has Mike lost?

3 Read the documents on the opposite page again. What are the differences between memos, notes and notices?

Functions **4** Look at the memos and notes again. Find phrases to express requests and obligation/necessity. Put them in the groups below.

Requests	Obligation/necessity
please (send ...)	you need to (arrive ...)

Speaking **5** Work in pairs. Find out what kind of written communication your partner uses at work. How efficient is internal communication where he/she works?

Writing memos

Listening 1 **1** Sarah Longman calls Henry Wallace to talk about expenses. Listen and take notes.

Writing memos

It is not necessary to use very formal language when writing memos. We often make requests with simple forms such as **Please** ... and **Could you** ...?

Please *inform* ***Could you*** *please inform*	*the secretary by 24 November.*

Writing **2** Now use your notes to write the memo Henry needs to send his salespeople.

Writing e-mails

Speaking **1** Work in pairs. Say the e-mail and website addresses below. Use the following words to help you.

@ = at	. = dot	: = colon	/ = forward slash
\ = backslash	- = dash	_ = underscore	

1 http://www.ikea.com
2 morgan_i_t@zig-zag.de
3 www.thebritishmuseum.ac.uk/
4 c_jones\71@dfe.org.nz

2 Now take turns in saying and writing down other e-mail and website addresses.

Writing **3** E-mails can be quite short and may contain contractions and other characteristics of spoken English. Look at the e-mail and Henry's note below and use them to write an e-mail to Sue. Write 30 - 40 words.

Writing tip:
When you write e-mails always think about your relationship with the person you are writing to.

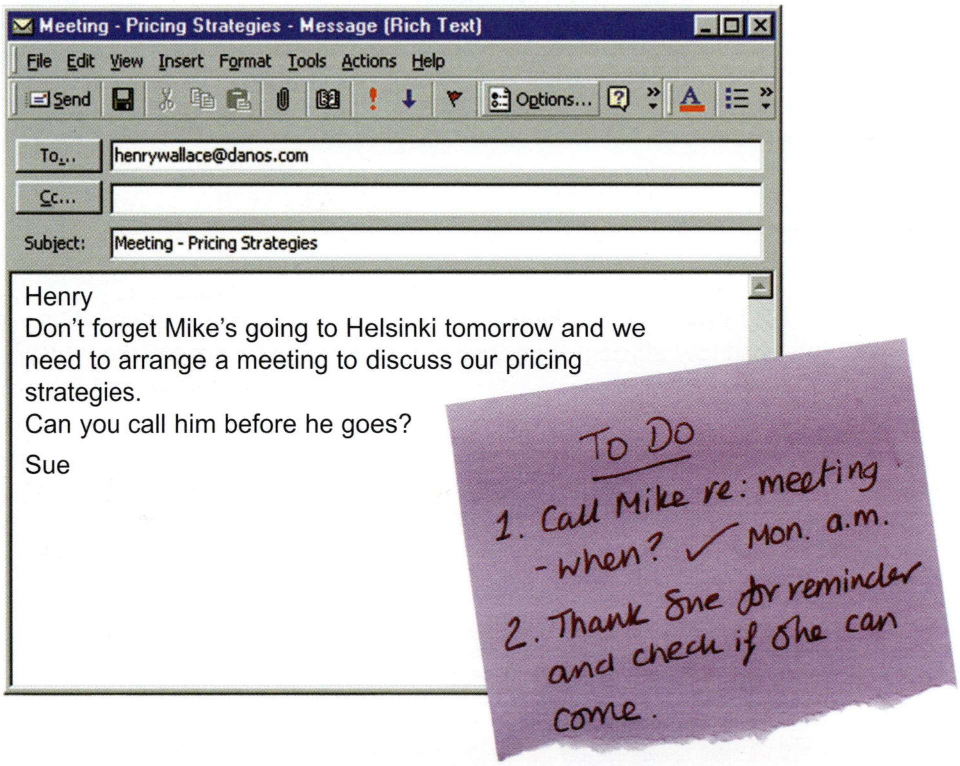

Listening 2 **4** Karen Mitchell receives a phone call from John Woods, the Head of Human Resources. Listen and take notes. Then write an e-mail for Karen to send to Steve Cooper.

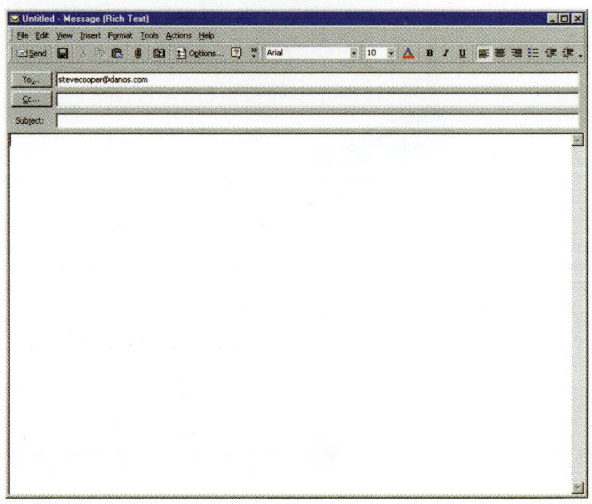

1 Look at the memo below from John Woods to all Training Officers. Rewrite it as a personal note from John to Karen Mitchell. Write 30 - 40 words.

To: All Training Officers

From: John Woods
Human Resources Manager

Date: 14 January 2001

There will be a meeting on Tuesday 21 January to discuss the training schedule. Please prepare your proposals by 18 January and make sure that everyone has a copy in advance.

Thank you

Karen

____
____
____
____
____
____

John

2 Use the note and diary page below to write a memo to all staff in the Marketing Department. Write 30 - 40 words.

Alex

Could you organise a meeting on Tuesday with all the Marketing Department to discuss our new brochure and then send a memo to inform them about it?

Look at my desk diary for the best time. We'll hold the meeting in the boardroom and I think it'll take about an hour.

Thanks

Tuesday 8 June

09.00	Meeting with Paul Ross
	9.30-10.30
10.00	
11.00	
12.00	Lunch with Stuart Fraser
	12-1.30
13.00	

MEMO

To: Marketing Dept

From:

____
____
____
____
____
____
____
____

3 **Exam practice**

- Elizabeth Sharp is going to be the new Human Resources Manager at your company.
- She is going to visit your office to learn more about the company.
- Write an e-mail to all staff:
  * explaining who she is
  * saying when she will be in the office
  * asking staff to introduce themselves to her.
- Write **30 - 40 words**.

To: All staff

From:

____
____
____
____
____
____
____
____
____

Unit 5a

Facts and figures

An annual report

Reading **1** Look at the extracts from the Millennium Software 1998 Annual Report. Are the sentences on the opposite page 'Right' or 'Wrong'? If there is not enough information to answer, choose 'Doesn't say'.

Chairman's Statement

Last year saw both the continued development of trends within the industry and some unexpected results. The domestic British market saw further steady growth but could be overtaken by US sales next year. As in 1997, sales in the USA rose sharply with the successful release of three new computer games. However, hopes of the European market showing the same rate of growth were affected by a strong pound.

Computer games increased their domination of sales in 1998 with the football game *The Golden Boot: France 98* selling over 100,000 units in World Cup year. Other sports titles are now amongst the company's top brands.

The company also enjoyed a sharp rise in sales of educational products. Our new range of interactive multimedia products, *Schoolware,* launched in late 1997, is now a top-selling brand. Further *Schoolware* titles to be launched this year should ensure continued growth in this market.

Sales figures for 1998 show very clearly the changing face of the company's activities. Millennium Software is now a producer of entertainment and educational products. In order to adapt to these markets, the company will have to expand by increasing its product range and reducing its development times.

Moreover, the company faces new challenges in distribution. Large retail chains with pan-European buying power are becoming increasingly dominant in the distribution of computer software. These superstores now offer competitive prices and a narrow product range based on top-selling titles. With computer shops, they now account for nearly two thirds of sales.

David Matthews

David Matthews, Chairman

4 | **Annual Report 1998**

1998 distribution

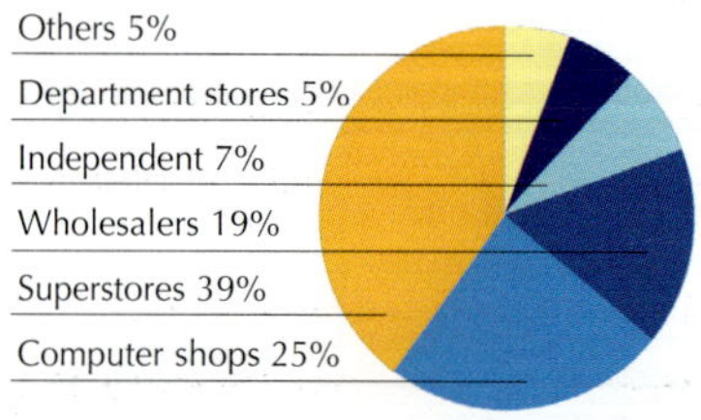

Top selling Millennium titles 1998

Title	Units
The Golden Boot	112,000
Road Rage III	63,000
Tournament Golf 98	51,000
Law & Order II	48,000
Virtual Ninja	39,000
Club Manager 98	22,000

Sales per games machine as %

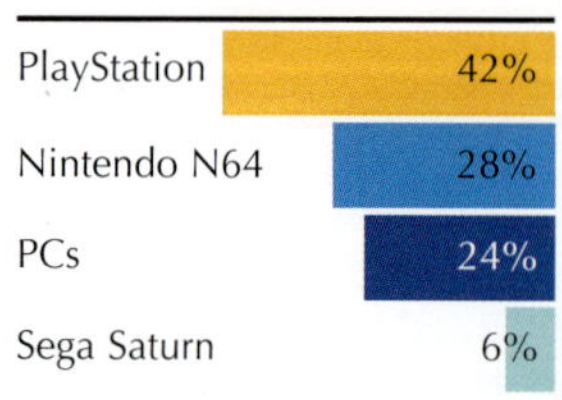

1 Superstores sell more Millennium software than computer shops.
A Right B Wrong C Doesn't say

2 PCs are the most popular games machine for Millennium games.
A Right B Wrong C Doesn't say

3 Sales increased sharply in the company's home market last year.
A Right B Wrong C Doesn't say

4 *The Golden Boot* sold more copies in France than Britain.
A Right B Wrong C Doesn't say

5 The company is developing its range of multimedia educational software.
A Right B Wrong C Doesn't say

6 In future the company will have to produce new games more quickly.
A Right B Wrong C Doesn't say

7 Superstores sell a wide range of computer software.
A Right B Wrong C Doesn't say

Speaking **2** **Work in pairs. What will be in the Chairman's Statement in the next Annual Report of your partner's company?**

Describing graphs

Reading **1** **Read the sentences below about Millennium Software's performance. Write a letter from the diagrams next to each sentence.**

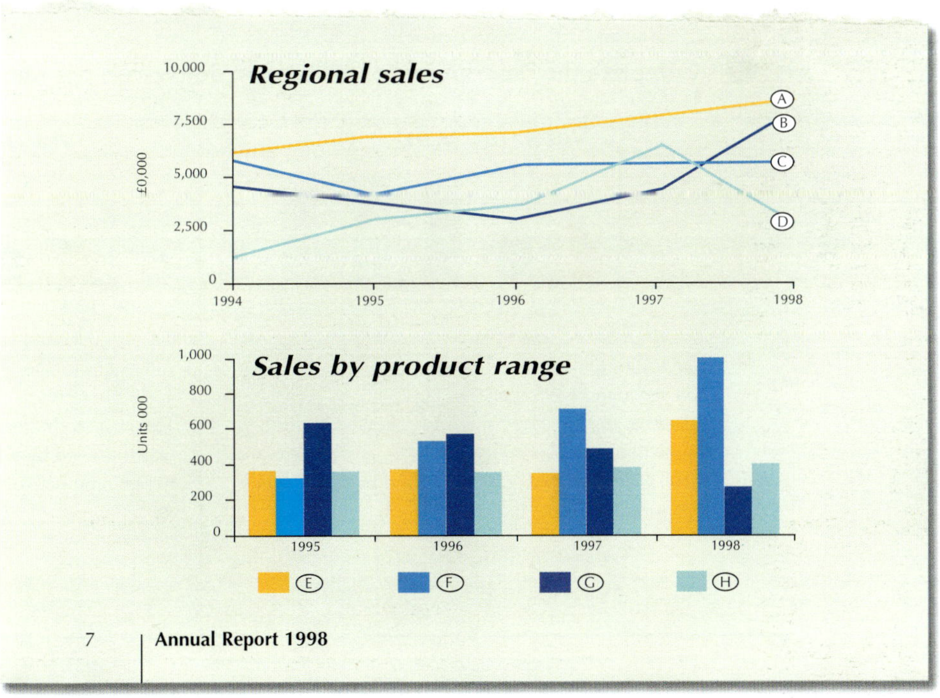

1 After a fall in 1995, sales in Asia recovered and then levelled off. C
2 There was very strong growth in sales of computer games from 1995 to 1998.
3 Sales in Britain improved steadily throughout the period from 1994 to 1998.
4 Sales in the USA fell slightly in 1995 and 1996 before a strong recovery in 1997, followed by a sharp rise in 1998.
5 Sales of educational software remained steady until 1997 but increased sharply in 1998.
6 There was a steady decrease in sales of office software from 1995 to 1998.
7 Sales in continental Europe grew from 1994, peaked in 1997 and then dropped sharply.
8 Sales of communications software remained steady throughout the period.

Vocabulary **2** Complete the table below.

Verb		Noun
Infinitive	Past simple	
fall	....fell....	...a fall...
drop	....	....
....	....	a decrease
increase	....	....
rise	....	....
....	....	growth
improve	....	....
....	recovered	....
peak	....	....

Grammar **3** Look back at the adjectives and adverbs in the unit. Complete the information below.

Don't forget!

Adjectives and adverbs

- Adjectives give information about ______________.
  *There was a **sharp rise** in sales of computer games.*
- Adverbs give information about ______________ or ______________.
  *Sales of computer games **rose sharply** last year.*
  *Educational software is becoming **increasingly important**.*

4 Complete the descriptions of Millennium Software's net sales and net income.

Net sales (£m)

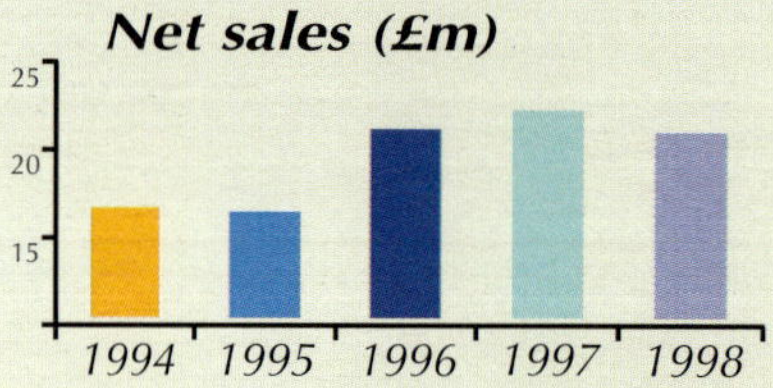

Net sales remained (1) ______________ at £17m in 1994 and 1995 then rose (2) ______________ in 1996 to reach £21m. This was followed by further growth as sales (3) ______________ at £22m in 1997. However, as a strong pound began to affect exports to Europe, net sales fell (4) ______________ in 1998.

Net income (£m)

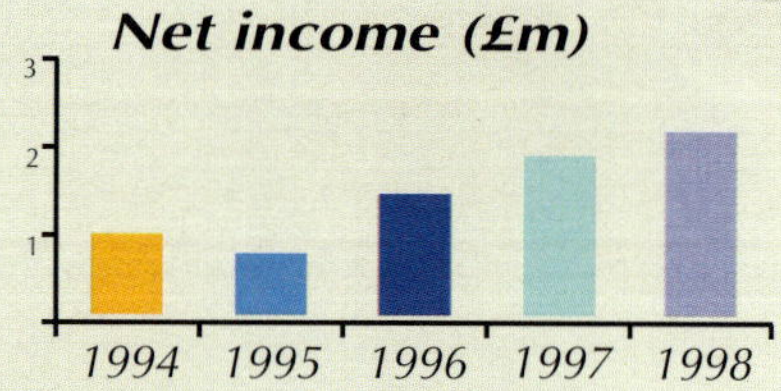

After net income (5) ______________ by £0.25m in 1995, there was a strong (6) ______________ in 1996 due to increased sales and reduced costs. This was followed by a further (7) ______________ in net income of £0.7m over the next two years: it grew (8) ______________ from £1.4m in 1996 to £2.1m in 1998.

6 | **Annual Report 1998**

5 Underline the prepositions in Exercise 4. Then complete the following sentences.

Operating costs

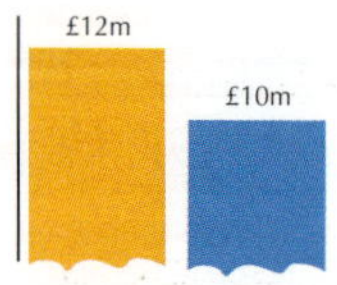

1 There was a fall _______ operating costs.
2 Operating costs fell _______ £12m _______ £10m.
3 Operating costs fell _______ £2m.
4 There was a fall _______ £2m.

Speaking **6** Work in pairs. Student A: Look at the Activity sheets on pages 125-126. Student B: Look at the Activity sheets on pages 129-130.

1 Use the words below to label the pictures.

peak	remain steady	fall
rise	level off	recover

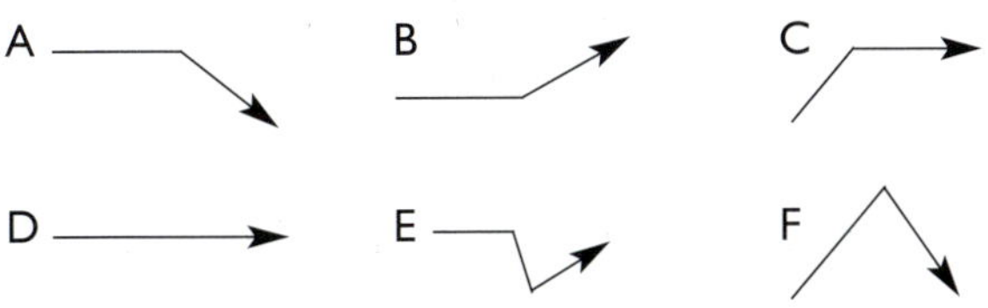

2 Complete the sentences with one of the following prepositions.

in	at	by	from	of

1 Last year there was a drop _______ net sales _______ 9%.

2 Market share increased _______ 3%, up to 8%.

3 Net sales peaked _______ £22m in 1997.

4 European sales went _______ £4.2m to £3.0m.

5 Sales levelled off _______ £5m in 1998.

6 Costs rose _______ £3.3m. This was a rise _______ 10%.

7 Office software sales fell _______ 10% in 1997.

8 A strong pound meant a fall _______ exports in 1998.

3 Match the following words.

1 retail	brand
2 product	chain
3 net	income
4 top-selling	report
5 annual	launch

4 Write a short description of the graph below.

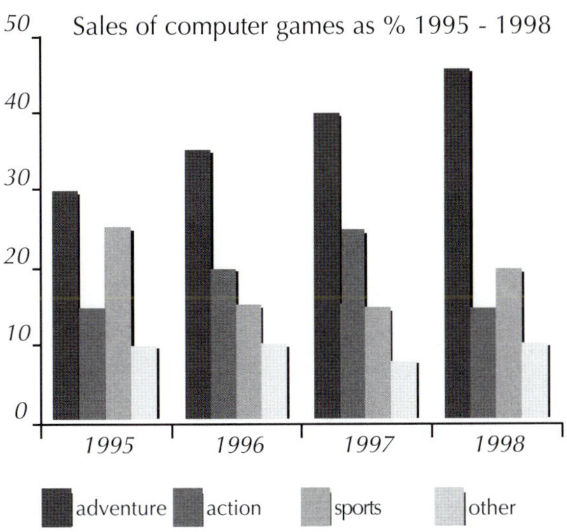

5 **Exam practice**

- Look at the charts below. They show the orders for eight different companies over three years.
- Which company does each sentence **1 - 5** describe?
- For each sentence mark the correct letter **A - H**.
- Do not use any letter more than once.

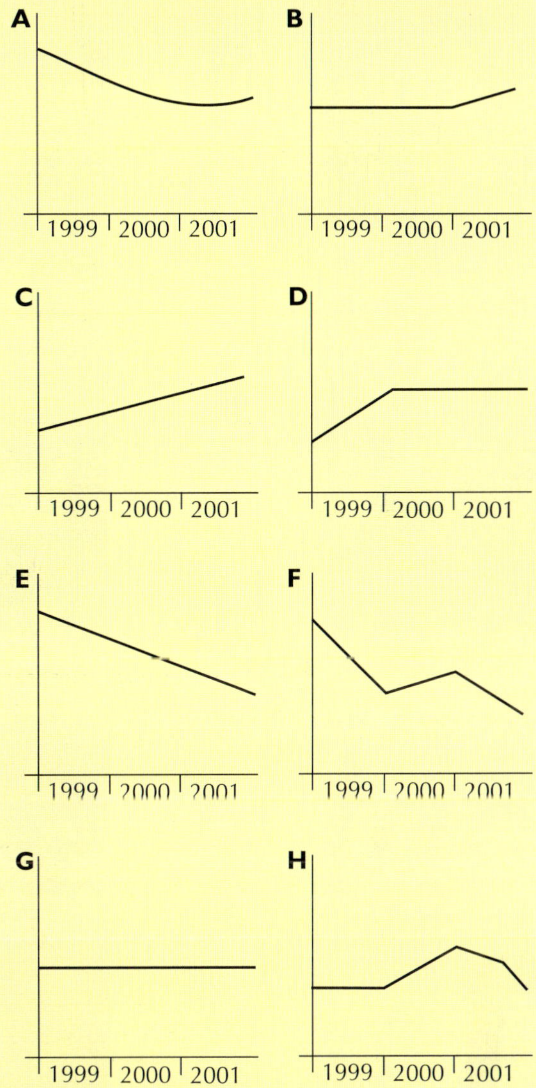

1 After a sharp drop in 1999, orders recovered for twelve months and then fell again in 2001.

2 Orders rose sharply in 2000 but peaked at the end of the year and then fell back to their 1999 levels.

3 Orders remained steady between 1999 and 2001.

4 The order books showed strong growth throughout the three year period.

5 After decreasing steadily for two years, orders finally levelled off and began a recovery in 2001.

Performance

Measuring performance

Listening 1 **1** First Great Eastern is one of 25 private rail companies operating in Britain. The company's Communications Manager, Juliet Sharman, makes a presentation to possible investors. Listen and complete the information below.

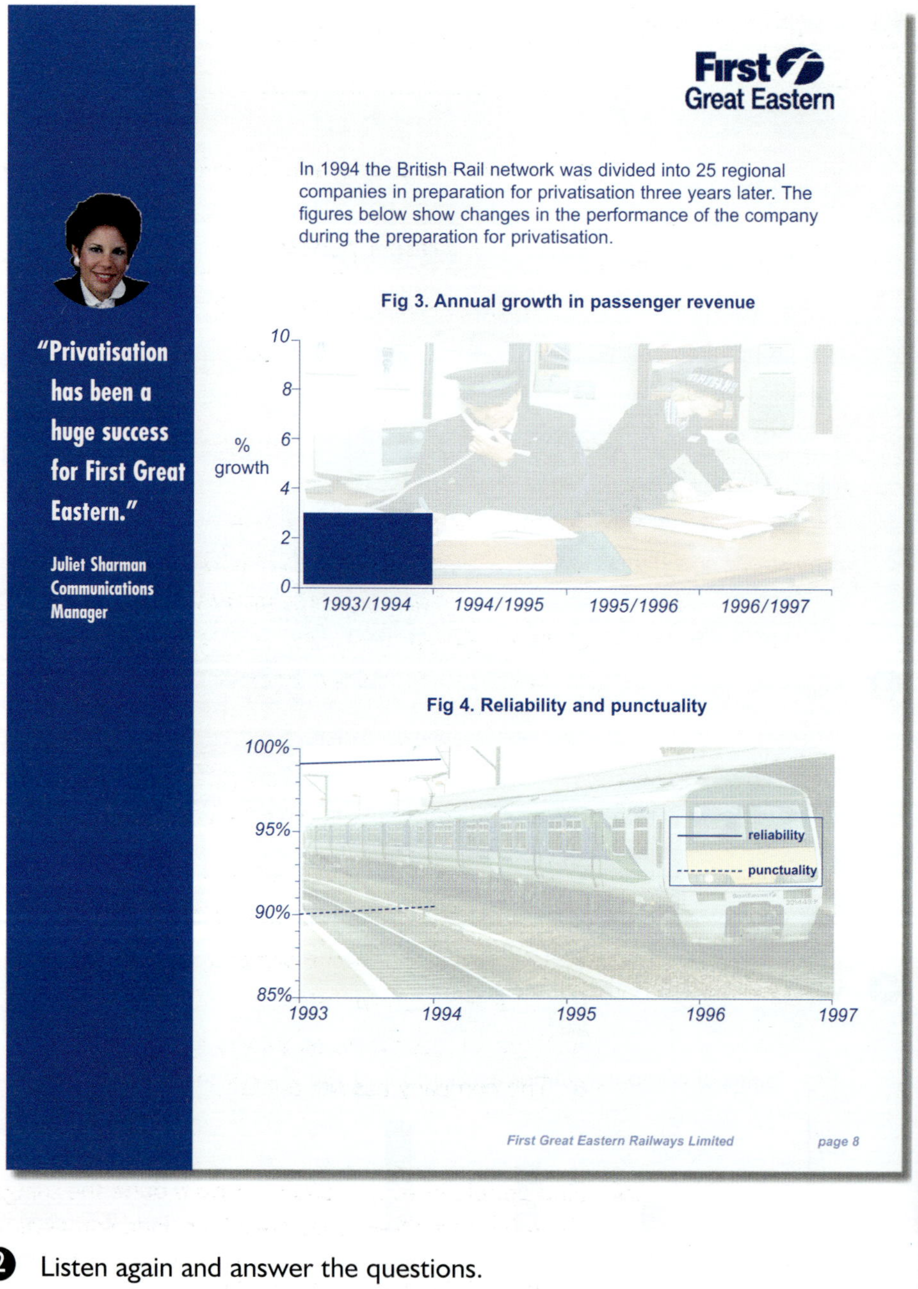

2 Listen again and answer the questions.

1 When did First Great Eastern become a private company?
2 What is the name of its parent company?
3 How did the company increase revenues in 1995/96?
4 Why have some privatised rail companies been in the newspapers recently?
5 Why has Juliet not given the punctuality figure for 1997?

Grammar

3 Look at the tapescript on page 135. Find an example of each of the following:

- an action at an unfinished or indefinite time

  ____

- a situation that started in the past and is still continuing

  ____

- an action that happened at a definite time in the past

  ____

- a change that affects the present situation

  ____

Now write descriptions in the correct groups below.

Present perfect	Past simple
unfinished or indefinite time	

Don't forget!

For and since

- **For** is used with periods of time such as days, months and years.
  *I've worked here **for** three months now.*
- **Since** is used with points in time such as **Monday**, **July**, **1996**.
  *We've lived here **since** 1995.*

4 Match the sentence halves about First Great Eastern.

1 Revenue growth was slow	the last two years.
2 The company has been private since	before privatisation.
3 FirstGroup bought the company	so far this year.
4 Reliability improved steadily	1997.
5 Revenue has increased sharply over	between 1993 and 1995.
6 The company has not published any figures	when the network was privatised.

Speaking

5 Find people in your group who have done the things below.
Then ask three follow-up questions. Find someone who has ...

- been to a conference this year.
- changed jobs this year.
- worked in a foreign country.
- done some kind of training this year.
- been promoted in the last five years.

Speaking tip:
To keep a conversation going, follow up all **yes**/**no** questions with more open questions (**when**? **why**? **how**? etc.).

Explaining results

Listening 2 **1** Juliet Sharman finishes her presentation and the investors ask her questions. Listen and complete the notes below.

First Great Eastern

- Punctuality in 1996?
- Investment plans?
- Profits in the future?

Liverpool Street Station, Lor

2 Listen again and choose the correct option to complete the sentences.

1 The railway track that First Great Eastern uses belongs to
  A the company.
  B another private company.
  C the Government.

2 The company is spending £9m in order to
  A improve the condition of the track.
  B build new stations and improve punctuality.
  C improve customer service and reliability.

3 The company's biggest costs are paying
  A other companies for the track and trains.
  B the Government so it can operate services.
  C for new stations and facilities.

Don't forget!

Reasons and consequences

- We can talk about reasons with the following:
  Reliability fell ***because of/due to*** *problems with the track.*
  That's why *we're improving our service.*
- We can talk about consequences with the following:
  Our costs are fixed ***so*** *we have to increase passenger volumes.*
  There will be less financial support. ***Therefore****, we have to increase revenue.*
  The investment will ***lead to/result in*** *better customer service.*

Speaking **3** Work in pairs. Write five results or changes that have happened in your company on a piece of paper. Give the paper to your partner. Find out the reasons for the results and changes.

1 Re-arrange the words to make presentation phrases.

1 you'll / the / notice
You'll notice the ...

2 I'd / at / with / a / like / begin / look / to
____

3 as / can / you / see
____

4 the / clearly / shows / graph
____

5 I'd / at / like / to / you / look
____

6 I'd / to / your / like / to / draw / attention
____

2 Complete the presentation. Put the verbs in brackets into the present perfect or past simple.

Good afternoon everyone. Welcome to the presentation of the company's half year sales results. As you can see, this year (1 *be*) ________ very successful so far and the company (2 *already/achieve*) ________ many of its targets for the year. Our sales people (3 *work*) ________ very hard and the department (4 *perform*) ________ very well. The success is especially pleasing when you think back to the problems we (5 *have*) ________ last summer. Sales (6 *be*) ________ down by 10% and things (7 *not/look*) ________ good at all. We (8 *make*) ________ some difficult decisions last year, which a lot of people (9 *not/be*) ________ happy with. However, since then we're happy to say that performance (10 *improve*) ________ sharply.

3 Write sentences linking the following ideas.

1 the £9m investment → better customer service
The £9m investment led to better customer service.

2 new trains → more reliable service
____

3 the number of delays increased ← track problems
____

4 we can't raise prices → we have to increase volumes
____

5 customer satisfaction has improved ← better facilities
____

6 reduced ticket prices → an increase in passenger volumes
____

4 **Exam practice**

- Look at the graphs below. They show a comparison of the quarterly sales figures for 2000 and 2001 for eight different companies **A - H**.
- Which company does each sentence **1 - 5** describe?
- For each sentence, mark the correct letter **A - H**.
- Do not use any letter more than once.

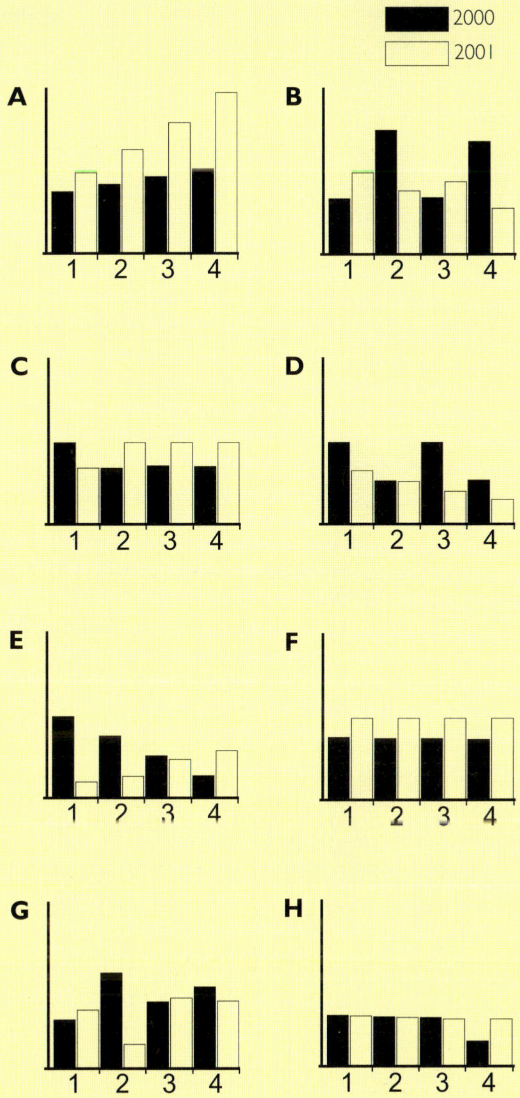

1 Sales fluctuated dramatically in 2000, whereas 2001 saw a steady decline in sales.

2 Sales rose steadily throughout the two-year period, but the increase was more dramatic in 2001.

3 Although sales in 2000 reached a peak in the second quarter, this was the worst period for sales in 2001.

4 Sales remained steady for most of the two-year period despite a sudden fall at the end of 2000.

5 Sales started slowly in 2001, before recovering in the third quarter, in contrast to the previous year when sales declined steadily.

Exam focus: Reading

The Reading Test

The Cambridge BEC Preliminary Reading Test has seven questions. Questions 1-5 test general comprehension. Question 6 specifically tests your knowledge of grammar and vocabulary. Question 7 tests your ability to process information accurately.

Part	Input	Task
1	5 short notes, messages, adverts, timetables etc.	Multiple-choice
2	Notice, list, plan etc.	Matching
3	Graphs, charts, tables	Matching
4	Letter, advert, report etc. (150 - 200 words)	Right, Wrong, Doesn't say
5	Newspaper article, advert etc. (300 - 400 words)	Multiple-choice
6	Newspaper article, advert etc. (125 - 150 words)	Multiple-choice gap-filling
7	Short memos, letters, notices, adverts, etc.	Form-filling, note completion

Length: The Reading questions should take about 60 minutes of the Reading and Writing Test.

How to succeed

Here are some important tips for doing the Reading Test.

- Read all instructions **carefully**.
- Read through the whole text once before looking at the questions.
- Read through all the questions before answering Question 1.
- Read Question 1 again and then look quickly through the text for the answer.
- Underline the answer in the text - it will make checking quicker.
- The questions are in the same order as the answers. If you are confident that an answer is right, begin looking for the next answer from that point in the text, not from the beginning.
- Leave difficult questions and return to them later if you have time.
- Only write **one** answer for each question.
- **Never** leave a question unanswered. If you are running out of time or really have no idea, guess.
- Use any time you have left to check your answers.

Part One

Reading tips
1 Read **all** three options before answering.
2 Be careful of negative forms.

Questions 1 - 5

- Look at questions **1 - 5**.
- In each question, which phrase or sentence is correct?
- For each question, mark the correct letter **A**, **B** or **C**.

1

> I am sorry but the parts will not be available until 25 January.

The parts can be delivered
A immediately.
B before 25 January.
C after 25 January.

2

> Mr Ranson called while you were on the phone - he'll try again this afternoon.

Mr Ranson
A promised to call back.
B left a message.
C was put through.

3

> Congratulations to Vanessa Clark on her promotion to Brand Manager.

Vanessa Clark works in
A production.
B marketing.
C finance.

4

> Sales were good but distribution problems led to a slight drop in profits.

The company had problems with
A producing enough goods.
B delivering enough goods.
C selling enough goods.

5

> ❑ Tick if you wish to make an immediate purchase.

You have to tell the company if you want
A to buy the product.
B more information.
C a product demonstration.

Part Two

Reading tips
1 Read **all** the information before answering.
2 Do the easy questions quickly and then see which possible answers are left.

Questions 6 - 10

- Look at the list below. It shows the contents of a company's Annual Report.
- Decide in which part of the report **(A - H)** you would find the information **(6 - 10)**.
- For each question, mark the correct letter **(A - H)**.

Stella Group Plc

Annual Report

A Chairman's Statement
B National Sales Reports
C Review of Subsidiaries
D Changes in Key Personnel
E Group Organigram
F Auditor's Report
G Profit and Loss Account
H Balance Sheet

6 A statement of the company's income and expenses.

7 The names of new executives and board members.

8 A look at the performance of smaller companies that Stella owns.

9 A list of what the company owns and owes.

10 A statement by the company that checked the financial reports.

Exam practice

Part Three

Reading tips

1 Look at the graphs and try to predict vocabulary describing direction (*rise, fall*) and the strength of movement (*steadily, sharply*).
2 Read **all** the sentences before answering.
3 Be careful of words such as *but, despite* etc.

Questions 11 - 15

- Look at the graphs below. They show unemployment in eight different regions compared to the national average.
- Which region does each sentence **11 - 15** describe?
- For each sentence mark the correct letter **A - H**.
- Do not use any letter more than once.

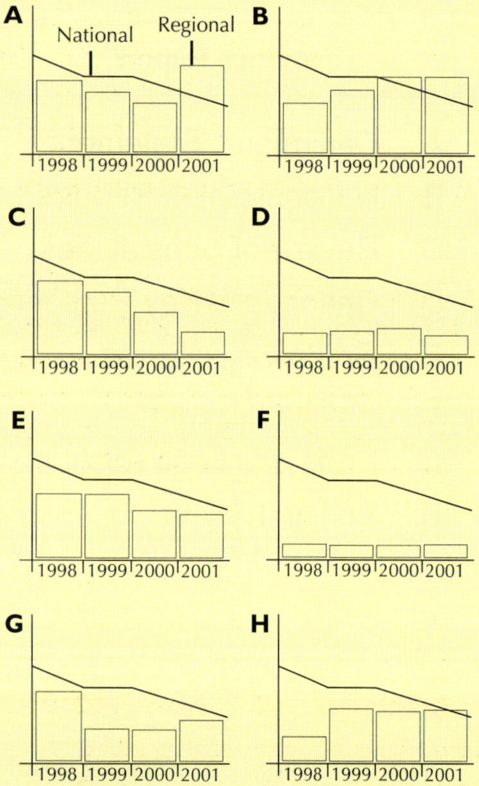

11 After an initial fall, unemployment figures remained steady before showing a slight increase, in contrast to the national situation.

12 Unemployment fell steadily throughout the period and remained below the national average.

13 Despite a drop in the national average, the rate of unemployment remained steady for two years before falling in 2000.

14 Although there was a fall in the national average, unemployment in this region rose sharply at the end of the period.

15 After rising steadily, unemployment finally began to reflect the national situation and decreased.

Part Five

Reading tips

1 Read through **all** the text first.
2 Read **all** questions before answering.
3 Begin with question **16** and work through the text.
4 **Never** leave a question unanswered.
5 When you have finished, check **all** your answers.

Questions 16 - 21

- Read the Chairman's Statement below and answer questions **16 - 21** on the opposite page.

Chairman's Statement

Despite the appearance of a new competitor on the market the company continued to grow and increase its market share throughout 2000. Partly in response to this new threat but, more importantly, as part of a strategy for growth, several key decisions were taken this year. The most significant new developments included a range of vitamin rich children's drinks and low calorie diet drinks, which both proved very popular.

The company is still best known for its range of refreshing fruit drinks and, not surprisingly, these were our biggest sellers once more. There were two new additions to the range last year, *Squish!* and *Liquid Sunshine*, both of which have a distinctive Caribbean flavour. The first sales figures suggest that our expensive TV advertising campaign was very successful and that these products will soon be as popular as the rest of the fruit drink range.

Growth in the keep-fit and health markets meant our energy drinks did well in 2000. Sales of one brand, *Booster!*, were second only to fruit drinks in April. The strength of this particular market also explains the success of our new diet drinks.

There were, however, big differences in the performance of our older products. The company's oldest product, mineral water, continued to enjoy a healthy share of a very profitable mass market. It seems our customers are still happy to stay with the brand despite the increasing number of competitors' products. Unfortunately, the same cannot be said of our *Ice-T* and *Chocomania* drinks. Sales showed an initial increase in the summer after we re-launched both products but customers soon bought other brands and total annual sales for both product ranges were disappointing.

The company also said goodbye to its own brand of cola, launched in 1998. After two unsuccessful years of trying to break into the huge cola market, 2000 looked like being another poor year. The company finally accepted that it had made a wrong decision and stopped production in September of that year.

Questions 16 - 21

- For questions **16 - 21**, choose the correct answer.
- For each question, mark the correct letter **A**, **B** or **C**.

16 What was the main reason the company decided to launch its new product ranges?
A It faced increased competition.
B It wanted to enter new markets.
C It initiated a policy of expansion.

17 The new fruit drinks cost a lot of money to
A develop.
B produce.
C launch.

18 The best selling drinks in April were
A energy drinks.
B fruit drinks.
C diet drinks.

19 The company's brand of mineral water has a
A small share of a small market.
B large share of a small market.
C large share of a large market.

20 Sales for Ice T and Chocomania
A rose and then fell again.
B increased steadily.
C were disappointing all year.

21 When did the company stop producing its own brand cola?
A 1998.
B 2000.
C 2002.

Part Six

Reading tips
1 Read through **all** the text first.
2 What type of word could fill each gap?
3 Write possible answers in the gaps in pencil on the exam paper. Then look to see if these words are among the answers.
4 Look again at the gaps you are not happy with.
5 **Never** leave a gap unanswered.
6 When you have finished, **read** the complete text.

Questions 22 - 33

- Read the newspaper article below about a new alliance in the packaging industry.
- Choose the correct word from **A**, **B** or **C** below.
- For each question, mark the correct letter **A**, **B** or **C**.

The Big Number

The country's demand for telephones, mobile phones, faxes and the Internet is growing at an increasingly fast rate. In fact, it is growing **(22)** ..... quickly that our telephone numbering system needs re-organising **(23)** ..... some major changes will have to **(24)** ..... made.

These changes, **(25)** ....., will make the system simpler and easier to use. It is **(26)** ..... an important task that all the UK phone companies are working together to make **(27)** ..... changes. The changes will **(28)** ..... only make hundreds of millions of new numbers, but they will **(29)** ..... bring order and flexibility to the system for years to come.

(30) ..... main changes are due to happen **(31)** ..... now and the year 2002, which will give you **(32)** ..... of time to prepare. You will find details of the number changes on our website, **(33)** ..... you can visit any time at www.numberchange.org, or call our freephone helpline on 0808 224 2000.

22 A so	**B** that	**C** too
23 A and	**B** with	**C** before
24 A been	**B** be	**C** being
25 A despite	**B** however	**C** although
26 A much	**B** such	**C** so
27 A this	**B** there	**C** these
28 A if	**B** not	**C** but
29 A furthermore	**B** additionally	**C** also
30 A The	**B** Those	**C** Their
31 A from	**B** between	**C** until
32 A plenty	**B** many	**C** lot
33 A when	**B** who	**C** which

Product description

Presenting a product

Listening 1 **1** Robert Saunders, the Sales Manager at Columbine Games, talks about two new products. Listen to his presentation. Which products does he talk about? How much do they cost?

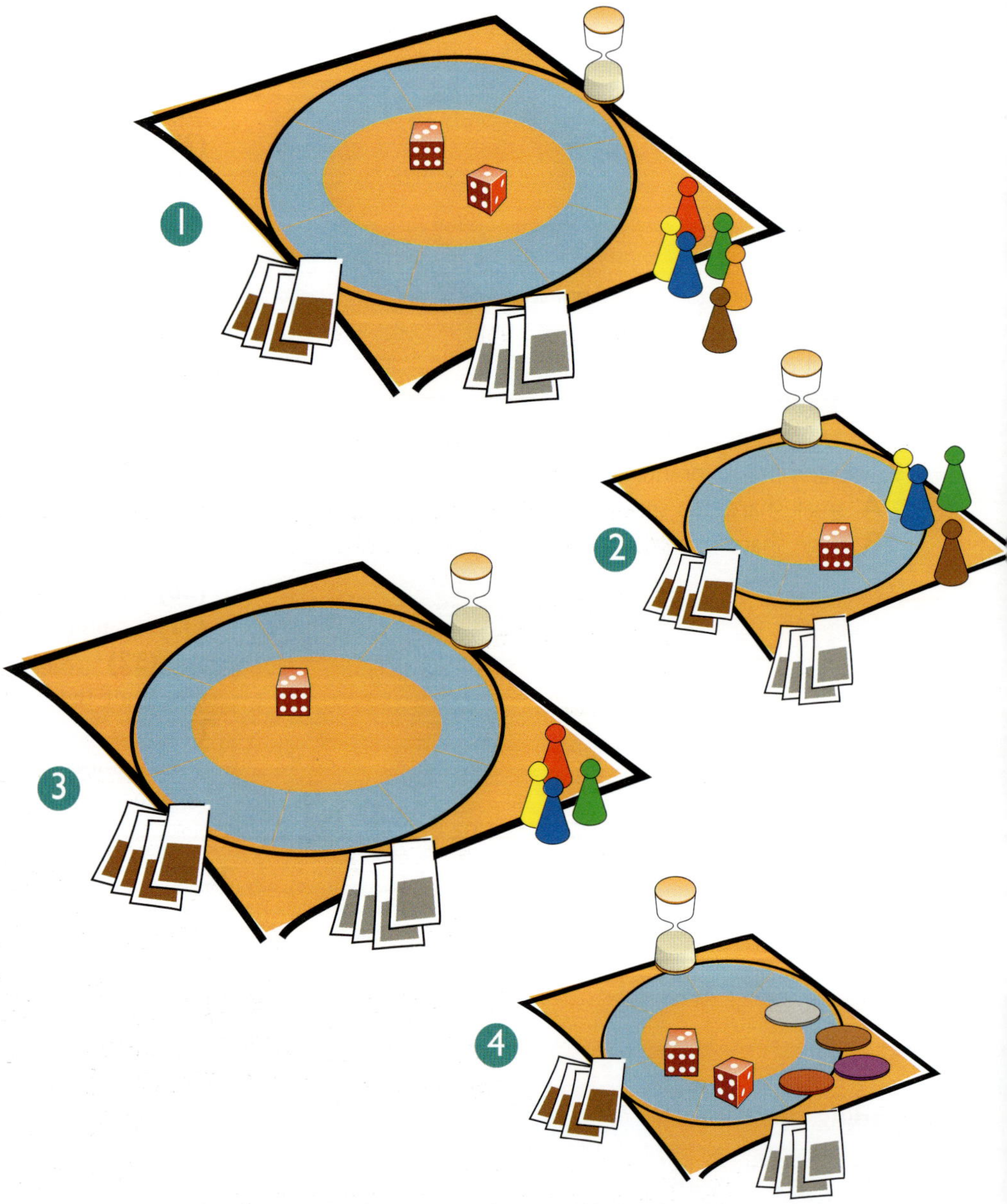

2 Listen to the presentation again. The speakers refer to the following things. What are they talking about?

1 General knowledge
2 Size, weight and cost
3 Wood
4 23 x 23 cm
5 300 grammes
6 £10.99

Grammar ❸ Write questions for the answers in Exercise 2.

1 What type of game is Mindtwist?

2 ______________________________

3 ______________________________

4 ______________________________

5 ______________________________

6 ______________________________

Speaking ❹ Work in pairs. Describe a board game that you like.

Describing a product

Listening 2 ❶ Robert Saunders talks to Sophie Powell, a retailer, about some of Columbine's products. Which games is Sophie interested in?

- Mindtwist
- Mindtwist Travel
- Collect

❷ Listen again. Answer the questions below.

1 Why is Sophie interested in board games?
2 What is special about Mindtwist?
3 How many travel size general knowledge games does Sophie stock?
4 What does Sophie not like about some of Columbine's board games?
5 Why is Sophie not interested in Collect?
6 What does Sophie think about the price of Mindtwist Travel?
7 How can Sophie get a discount on Mindtwist?

Don't forget!

Comparison

- The comparative is formed by adding **-er** to short words and **more/less** to longer words.
  *This game is small**er than** the other games on the market.*
  *Mindtwist is **more** interesting **than** the other games.*
- We use **as ... as** with two things that are the same and also with negatives.
  *Collect is **as** new **as** Mindtwist.*
  *It isn't **as** big **as** the other game.*
- The superlative of short words is formed with **-est**. With longer words we add **the most/the least**.

  *These games are **the** lat**est** in Columbine's range.*
  *This is **the least** interesting of the games.*

! *good - **better** - **the best***
*bad - **worse** - **the worst***

3 Correct the information about Columbine games in the sentences below.

1 Sophie is selling ~~fewer~~ more board games than before.

2 Mindtwist Travel is ~~heavier than~~ not as heavy as the standard game.

3 The instructions on Columbine games have become more difficult than before.

4 Collect is the biggest of the products that Robert shows Sophie.

5 Sophie's customers will be more interested in Collect than Mindtwist.

6 Mindtwist Travel costs the same as the standard version.

Speaking **4 Work in pairs. Think of something you have both bought. Make a list of the points you considered when you bought it. Discuss the importance of the points and put them in order. Then prepare to report back to the rest of the group.**

Product name ....

Points considered	Me	My partner
price		

1 Complete the groups of words below. Then use one word from each group to form a question.

1 weight / heavy / light

How heavy is the travel version of the game?

2 length / long / ....

____

3 cost / expensive / ....

____

4 .... / big / small

____

5 difficulty / difficult / ....

____

2 Look at the catalogue information comparing three display panels and complete the sentences below.

Portable Folding Display Panels

Product name	Number of panels	Weight	Dimensions	Price
Standard	4 panels	10 kilos	1.8 x 1.2m	£498.00
Super	6 panels	15 kilos	1.8 x 1.6m	£545.00
Extra	8 panels	17 kilos	1.8 x 2.4m	£660.00

1 The Extra has more panels than the Super.

2 The Extra is 2 kilos ________________

3 The Extra is more ________________

4 The Super is not as ________________

5 The Standard is the least ________________

6 The Standard is the ________________

3 Write about a product you have recently bought.

- Where was it made?
- What is it made of?
- Why did you buy it instead of a similar product?

4 **Exam practice**

- Read the text below about a fax machine.
- Choose the correct word from **A**, **B** or **C** to fill each gap.

Lomax KR 700 Plain Paper Fax/Digital Answerphone

The answer to your all your communication problems! The KR 700 is the latest addition to our extensive **(1)** ..... of fax machines. It is a **(2)** ..... advanced version of the KR 600 with an answerphone facility and **(3)** ..... other special features. One of these special features means that you **(4)** ..... perform one operation while the machine is **(5)** ..... another one. There are several dialling techniques **(6)** ..... allow you to send faxes easily, quickly and cheaply. It takes **(7)** ..... fifteen seconds to fax an A4 page. **(8)** ....., the laser printing **(9)** ..... you high quality pictures. The answerphone **(10)** ..... fourteen minutes' recording time, which is a bonus for any business. **(11)** ..... it is such a flexible machine, it is compact. It will fit into the **(12)** ..... space in the office or at home.

1	**A** variety	**B** range	**C** spread
2	**A** most	**B** more	**C** much
3	**A** many	**B** any	**C** every
4	**A** can	**B** must	**C** should
5	**A** perform	**B** performing	**C** performed
6	**A** which	**B** what	**C** who
7	**A** all	**B** less	**C** just
8	**A** Extra	**B** Addition	**C** Furthermore
9	**A** provides	**B** gives	**C** makes
10	**A** has	**B** have	**C** having
11	**A** However	**B** Although	**C** Also
12	**A** small	**B** smaller	**C** smallest

Unit 7b

Product development

Product testing

Speaking **1** How much do you know about the development of drugs in the pharmaceutical industry in the USA? Work in pairs and do the quiz below.

1 How many years of testing are there before a drug reaches the market?
A 6 B 12 C 18

2 About how much does it cost to develop a new drug in the USA?
A $160 million B $260 million C $360 million

3 What percentage of drugs tested on humans reaches the market?
A 20 B 40 C 60

4 How many stages of testing on humans are there in the USA?
A 3 B 4 C 9

5 How many people, on average, take part in testing drugs?
A 1,000 - 5,000 B 5,000 - 10,000 C 10,000 - 15,000

6 How long do the authorities take to approve a New Drug Application?
A 6 months B 2.5 years C 5 years

7 How much will be spent on drug development in five years' time?
A About $4 bn B About $12 bn C About $25 bn

Reading **2** **Read the article below to find the answers to the quiz.**

Drug development in the USA

The development of new drugs is essential if we are to stop the spread of diseases. However, it takes an average of twelve years to develop a drug and it costs a company about $359 million. Only five out of every 5,000 drugs that start the testing process are tested on humans. Only one in five of those actually reaches the market.

There are four stages of testing a new drug. First of all, a company carries out tests for about two and a half years in the laboratory and on animals. This is to show how the drug works against a particular disease and to show its level of safety. Then testing on humans can begin.

The first stage of human testing tests the safety of the drug on fewer than one hundred healthy people and lasts about a year. After that, the drug is tested for about two years on

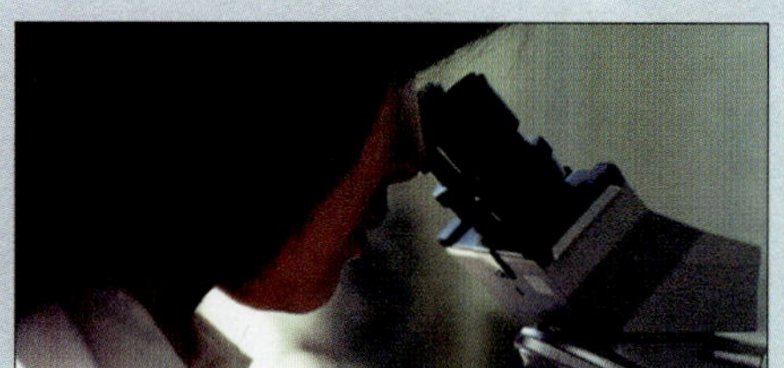

100 - 300 people who suffer from the disease to see how well the drug works. The final stage lasts about three years: the drug is usually tested on 1,000 - 3,000 patients in hospitals and clinics. While they are carrying out these tests, doctors monitor the patient closely and keep a record of the success of the drug and any side-effects.

23 *Science No*

Science Now, March 2001 *Issue no.*

When a company has completed the three stages of tests on humans, the company makes a New Drug Application to the authorities, which is often 1,000 pages or more. The authorities should take a maximum of six months to review a New Drug Application but they usually take longer; the average review time is 29.9 months.

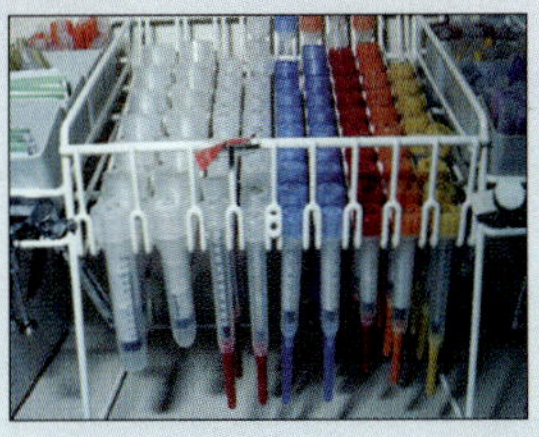

When the authorities have approved the New Drug Application, doctors can finally give it to their patients. The company still keeps a quality control record of the drug, including any side-effects.

Discovering and developing safe and successful new drugs is a long, difficult and expensive process. The research-based pharmaceutical industry is investing $12.6 billion in research and development this year and that investment will probably double in five years.

3 Read the article again and complete the table below.

	Laboratory	People		
		Stage 1	Stage 2	Stage 3
Test period:				
Tested on:				
Reason for testing:				

Vocabulary **4** Underline the sequencing words and phrases in the text.

Don't forget!

Sequencing

When we are describing a sequence or process, it is important to be clear about the order.

- We can talk about the stages involved:
  There are four stages of testing a new drug.
  The first/second/third/final stage is ...
- We can also use simple sequencing words:
  first/first of all *when*
  then/next/after that *while*
  finally

Writing **5** Work in pairs or groups. Your teacher will give you some cards describing drug development. Put the stages in order. Then write a description of the process.

Speaking **6** Work in pairs. Talk about the development of one of your company's products or services.

Marketing a product

Listening ❶ A medical journalist asks a marketing manager about a new drug for arthritis. Listen and answer the questions.

1 What is the drug called?
2 Who is the drug for?
3 Where will patients be able to get the drug?
4 What are the possible side effects?
5 How will patients get information about the drug?

❷ Listen again and note down any dates you hear. Then put the actions below into the correct order.

☐ give general information posters to doctors
☐ visit doctors to talk about the product
☐ launch the drug
☐ give information leaflets to patients
[1] send information packs to doctors (end of April)

Future arrangements and intentions

- We use **the present continuous** (often with a time phrase) to talk about arrangements in the future.
  *We**'re visiting** doctors at the beginning of May.*
  *When **are** you **launching** the new product?*
- We can use **going to** to talk about our intentions.
  *We **are going to work** closely with doctors.*
  *We **aren't going to** have any direct contact with patients.*

Speaking ❸ Work in pairs. Find out if your partner's company has plans for any of the following.

a new product launch	a new advertising campaign
new training courses	new projects

❹ Work in pairs. Your teacher will give you some cards. Ask your partner questions about his/her plans for the future.

1 Complete the text below with sequencing words.

The process for testing new drugs involves many stages. (1) First of all, they are tested in a laboratory and on animals. (2) ______________ the company applies to the authorities to start tests on people. There are three stages of testing on humans. The company completes the third stage of tests on humans and (3) ______________ it applies to the authorities for a licence to start using the drug. (4) ______________ the company has its licence, it supplies doctors and hospitals with the new drug. The company continues monitoring the drug (5) ______________ patients are using it.

2 Complete the conversation below about the launch of a new product. Put each verb into the correct form (present continuous or *going to*).

Philip Have you heard about the new product in our range?

Jane Yes. When (1 *you/launch*) are you launching it?

Philip On 11 September.

Jane How much advertising (2 *you/do*) ______________ before then?

Philip Oh, quite a lot. First, we (3 *start*) ______________ an advertising campaign on television on 10 September. Then we (4 *use*) ______________ newspaper advertisements the following week.

Jane (5 *you/use*) ______________ posters too?

Philip Yes, on the street and at stations.

3 Complete the sentences with the correct word.

1 Our company is ______________ a new product in spring.
A launching B bringing C giving

2 It ______________ several years to develop one of our products.
A lasts B needs C takes

3 I'm afraid that product isn't ______________ until next week.
A free B available C public

4 We'll have to ______________ sales of this new product for several months.
A monitor B look C see

5 What ______________ do you need?
A informers B information C informs

4 **Exam practice**

- Look at questions **1 - 5**.
- In each question, which phrase or sentence is correct?
- For each question, mark the correct letter **A, B or C.**

1

> While we are developing the product, we will write regular reports to ensure that you are informed of its progress.

A We're going to write reports before we develop the product.
B We're going to write reports at the same time as we develop the product.
C We're going to write reports after we develop the product.

2

> **MEMO**
> To: Peter
> From: Tom
> The publicity leaflets for the new model will not be back from the printers until Friday 11 July.

A We might have the leaflets before 11 July.
B We won't have the leaflets before 11 July.
C We are sure to have the leaflets before 11 July.

3

> **Launch schedule**
> 24/5 - Press conference.
> 31/5 - TV advertising starts. Distribute posters.
> 7/6 - Deliver leaflets. Radio advertising starts.
> 14/6 - Free competition starts on the radio.

How many written forms of publicity are there?
A two
B three
C four

4

> We are carrying out market research in the north and the Midlands from 22nd-26th.

A We have done the research in the north and the Midlands.
B We haven't done the research in the north and the Midlands yet.
C We have decided not to do research in the north and the Midlands.

5

> John
> Still waiting for approval from the authorities. Hope to get it next week so that we can finalise the launch date.
> Pete

A They have finalised a date for the launch.
B They hope to launch the product next week.
C They cannot yet finalise a date for the launch.

Business equipment

Office equipment

Vocabulary 1 Put the following words into the groups below.

computer	shredder	envelopes	eraser	fax machine
pencils	scissors	photocopier	printer	stapler

essential for you at work	necessary but you don't use every day	not important

Reading 2 Look quickly at the two advertisements for photocopiers.

- Which machine has more special features?
- Which advertisement includes a special offer?
  How long is the offer available for?

3 Read the advertisements again and look at the sentences below. Choose 'Right', 'Wrong' or 'Doesn't say' for each sentence.

1 The Agfa X220 has a lot of functions and is a convenient size.
A Right B Wrong C Doesn't say

2 Both copiers can make documents bigger and smaller.
A Right B Wrong C Doesn't say

3 Agfa will buy back the photocopier after three years.
A Right B Wrong C Doesn't say

4 The Xerox has a 5 year guarantee.
A Right B Wrong C Doesn't say

5 The copiers can be bought or rented.
A Right B Wrong C Doesn't say

6 The Xerox is a faster copier than the Agfa.
A Right B Wrong C Doesn't say

7 If the customer buys the Xerox, the printer costs only £198.
A Right B Wrong C Doesn't say

8 The Agfa can staple documents together.
A Right B Wrong C Doesn't say

Speaking

4 Work in pairs. The following people want to buy a photocopier immediately. Which of the two photocopiers should each person buy?

1 **James Clarkson** is a self-employed architect who works from home. He has one employee: a part-time secretary. He mainly needs to copy contracts before sending them to clients.

2 **Eleanor Lewis** is the Head of the Accounts Department at Pyramid, a large company. Her department keeps copies of invoices it receives for payment and also needs copies of a lot of the paperwork.

3 **David Hollingsworth** works as an account manager for Global Insurance. Although he sometimes works in the office, most of the time he visits clients or works from home. He does not have a photocopier at home at the moment but would like to be able to use one occasionally.

Reading

5 James Clarkson decides to get more information about the Xerox XC830 photocopier. Complete the request form below for him.

For further information about products featured in this catalogue, please complete the address panel and put a tick in the relevant boxes below.

Name: ______________________ Company name: Clarkson Design

Job title: ______________________ Tel: 01483 946211 Fax: 01483 946213

Address: Rose House, 94 Welham Park, GUILDFORD, Surrey GU6 2LK

1 ❑ Agfa X220 Copier	5 ❑ Canon Personal Copiers	9 ❑ Mitsubishi MT-30 Mobile Phone
2 ❑ Brit Vic Vending Machines	6 ❑ Hewlett Packard Laserjet 4000	10 ❑ Philips Speechmike
3 ❑ BT Video Conferencing System	7 ❑ Hewlett Packard Scanjet 6100C	11 ❑ Sharp Notevision Projector
4 ❑ Canon BJC-4200 & Powershot 350	8 ❑ Lotus Intranet Software	12 ❑ Xerox XC830

How many employees are there in your company? 1-25 ❑ 26-50 ❑ 51-100 ❑ 101-200 ❑ Over 200 ❑

Company activity:

❑ AGRICULTURE	❑ HOTELS AND CATERING
❑ BANKING/FINANCE/INSURANCE	❑ LEGAL/ACCOUNTING
❑ BUSINESS AND PROFESSIONAL SERVICES	❑ MANUFACTURING
❑ CENTRAL AND LOCAL GOVERNMENT	❑ REAL ESTATE
❑ CONSTRUCTION	❑ RESEARCH AND DEVELOPMENT
❑ EDUCATION AND TRAINING	❑ OTHER

Tick if you require this information for an immediate purchase ❑
Or for a purchase within 3-6 months ❑ 6-9 months ❑ 9-12 months ❑ 12+ months ❑

Giving instructions

Listening **1** The Accounts Department at Pyramid has bought a new shredder. The secretary, Anna, has a problem. She telephones Becky in the Purchasing Department. What is the problem? Listen to their conversation. What do they do about it?

2 Listen again and take notes. Then complete Anna's notice.

Instructions for use of shredder

How to use

- To switch on, press the green button.
- Put the paper in.
- To switch off, press the red button.

Possible problems	**What to do**
• The machine jams	
• The motor overheats	

Caution!

-
-

Call Customer Service on 01961 733 574 if there are any other problems.

Don't forget!

Giving instructions

- The easiest way to give instructions in English is to use the imperative.
  Switch on *the machine.*
- Sometimes you need to give negative instructions.
  Never insert *your fingers into the shredder.*
  Don't use *the machine without reading the instructions first.*

Speaking **3** Look at the Business Equipment Game on page 127. Your teacher will give you instructions.

4 Work in pairs. Student A: Choose one of the pictures below. Give instructions. Student B: What piece of equipment is it?

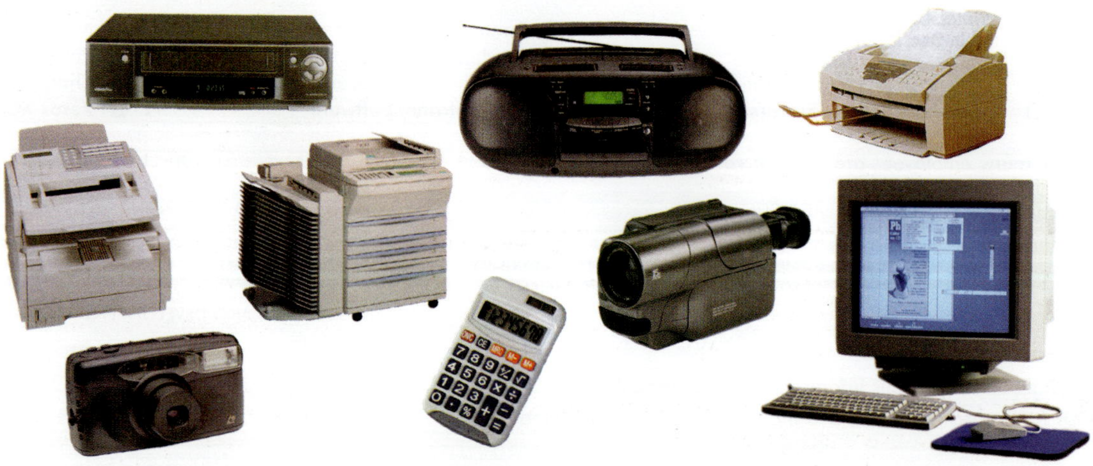

1 Put the following verbs into the groups below. You can use some verbs more than once.

dial	jam	enlarge	reduce	press	print
insert	shred	switch on	overheat	send	copy

Fax machine	Printer	Photocopier	Shredder
dial			

2 Complete the table below.

Noun	Verb
enlargement.......	enlarge
insertion	....
operation	....
....	reduce
copy	....
printer	....
removal	....

3 Read the problems below. What instructions would you give each person? Write your answers.

1 The pre-programmed number for our bank doesn't work.

Check the bank's fax number. Perhaps it's not correct.

2 The photocopier has run out of paper.

____

3 The cutter on the shredder has jammed.

____

4 Some paper is jammed in the photocopier.

____

5 The photocopier is overheating.

____

6 The stapler on the photocopier isn't working.

____

4 Write operating instructions for one of the pieces of equipment in Exercise 4 on page 55.

5 In each question, which piece of equipment does the sentence refer to? For each question, mark the correct letter **A**, **B** or **C**.

1 If your machine doesn't receive, contact the supplier.
A printer **B** shredder **C** fax machine

2 The cutter will jam if you insert too much paper.
A shredder **B** photocopier **C** printer

3 If you reduce the article, you can use A4.
A shredder **B** fax machine **C** photocopier

4 It's not sending because you've inserted the paper in the wrong place.
A photocopier **B** shredder **C** fax machine

5 It's a small machine but you can pre-programme up to 50 numbers.
A shredder **B** printer **C** fax machine

6 Remove the paper from the feeder and put it on the glass - it might work then.
A shredder **B** photocopier **C** printer

6 **Exam practice**

- **Look at the graph below. It shows the number of photocopies made by a company over eight months, and the proportions of recycled and new paper used.**
- **Which month does each sentence 1 - 5 describe?**
- **For each sentence mark the correct letter A - H.**
- **Do not use any letter more than once.**

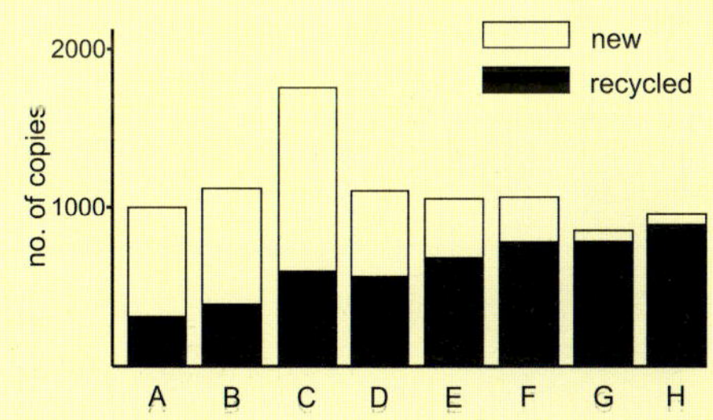

1 After a sharp rise in demand, the company was forced to use a larger proportion of new paper.

2 For the first time there was a higher proportion of recycled paper in use.

3 In this month a balance was achieved between the use of new and recycled paper.

4 This month saw the lowest number of copies made on recycled paper.

5 Whereas demand for recycled paper remained high, the overall number of copies made fell.

Correspondence

Sending a quotation

Reading **1** Alan Pickering works for Norwest Plant Hire. He is organising a training course for managers in his company. He writes to three companies to ask for quotations. Look at the replies and say who:

- has already organised courses for Norwest
- has not worked with Norwest before
- is a personal friend of Alan's.

19-APR-2001 16:26 FROM: ATC CONSULTING TO: NORWEST 01254882497 P.01/01

A T C
CONSULTING

ATC CONSULTING
12 King Street
LONDON
EC4N 1SP
Tel: 0207 234 968
Fax: 0207 234 999
E-mail: sales@atc.com

From: Julian Hughes Sales Co-ordinator
To: Alan Pickering Norwest Plant Hire
Date: 19 April
Pages: 2

Dear Alan
Many thanks for the enquiry about a one day Business Excellence Seminar.
Here's the information you requested and a quotation

Date:	14 May
Time:	10.00am - 4.00pm
Location:	ATC Consulting
No of people:	6
Price:	£525 per person

Prices include VAT, a small buffet style lunch and I've attached a copy of the seminar content.
Once again, thanks for the enquiry.

Best regards

Julian

SYNERGY
MANAGEMENT CONSULTANT
16 Pendall Way
Blackburn BB12 8HT
Tel: 01254 374973
Fax: 01254 374988

Mr Alan Pickering
Norwest Plant Hire
112 Milton Way
Poulton FY3 2PN
Lancs

17 April 200

Dear Mr Pickering
Re: Training course booking

Thank you for your enquiry of 16 April regarding ***Business Excellence*** *training courses. We are able to offer the following one-day seminars for the week commencing 14 May:*

Training:	***Business Excellence*** *Level 3*
Duration:	*1 day, 9.30am - 5pm*
Venue:	*Synergy Training Centre*
Delegates:	*Six*
Included:	*Training pack and seminar notes*
Cost per head:	*£549 (incl VAT)*
Available dates:	*14, 15, 16, 17 or 18 May*

Please find enclosed a copy of the seminar schedule. Should you have any further questions, please do not hesitate to contact me on 01254 374973 ext 204.

Yours sincerely

Rebecca Brooks

Rebecca Brooks
Seminar Sales
enc

>-----Original Message-----
>From: dwbowes@watson&ra
>Sent: 18 April 2001 11:07
>To: apickering@norwest.ac.uk
>Subject: Business Excellence Programme

>Alan

>Thanks for your call yesterday. Here's the quote you wanted for our Business Excellence programme:

>Date:	14 May
>Time:	09.30 - 16.30
>Place:	Here at Watson & Railton or in-company
>No. of people:	6
>Included:	Training pack & lunch
>Cost:	£499 (excl VAT) per person.

>If you have any questions, give me a call. I've attached a WORD file with the course schedule -
>hope you can open it OK.
>Best wishes

>Dave

❷ Answer the following questions.

1 Which is the longest seminar?
2 Which company's offer includes a training pack and food?
3 Which of the quotations is the cheapest?
4 Which company offers more than one possible date?
5 Which of the companies could do the seminar at Norwest?

❸ What differences are there between the fax, letter and e-mail?

Speaking ❹ Work in pairs. What percentage of letters, faxes and e-mails does your partner receive and write? Are any of them in English?

Letters of acceptance

Reading ❶ Alan decides to accept the Synergy offer and writes a letter of acceptance. Put the paragraphs of his letter into the correct order.

NORWEST
112 Milton Way
Poulton FY3 2PN
Lancashire
01254 882497

Rebecca Brooks
Synergy Management Consultants
16 Pendall Way
Blackburn
BB12 8HT

26 April 2001

Re: Your quotation of 17 April

Dear Ms Brooks

I am pleased to confirm the booking on the Business Excellence Level 3 seminar for six people on Tuesday 15 May.

I look forward to hearing from you in the near future.

As some of our managers are travelling from a distance, would it be possible to start the seminar at 10.00am instead of 9.30am as stated in your quotation? I would be grateful if you could send me information about the seminar and directions for travelling by car.

I am writing with reference to your quotation of 17 April regarding the one-day Business Excellence seminar at your premises in Blackburn.

❷ Match the functions with the paragraphs above. Underline the phrases that helped you.

making a request	making reference
giving the reason for writing	signalling the end of a letter

Vocabulary **3** Match the functions with the phrases.

1 Making reference	I am afraid that ...
2 Giving the reason for writing	With reference to your letter of ...
3 Giving good news	We would be grateful if you could ...
4 Giving bad news	I look forward to receiving your reply.
5 Making a request	I am pleased to ...
6 Enclosing something	I am writing to ...
7 Offering assistance	I enclose ...
8 Referring to future contact	If you require any further information, please do not hesitate to contact us.

Writing **4** Alan Pickering receives the invoice from Synergy after the training course. There are some items which he thinks are wrong. Use the invoice and his handwritten notes to write a reply to Synergy.

Before you write:

- plan the number of paragraphs you need
- make notes under the paragraph headings
- think of typical letter phrases that you can use.

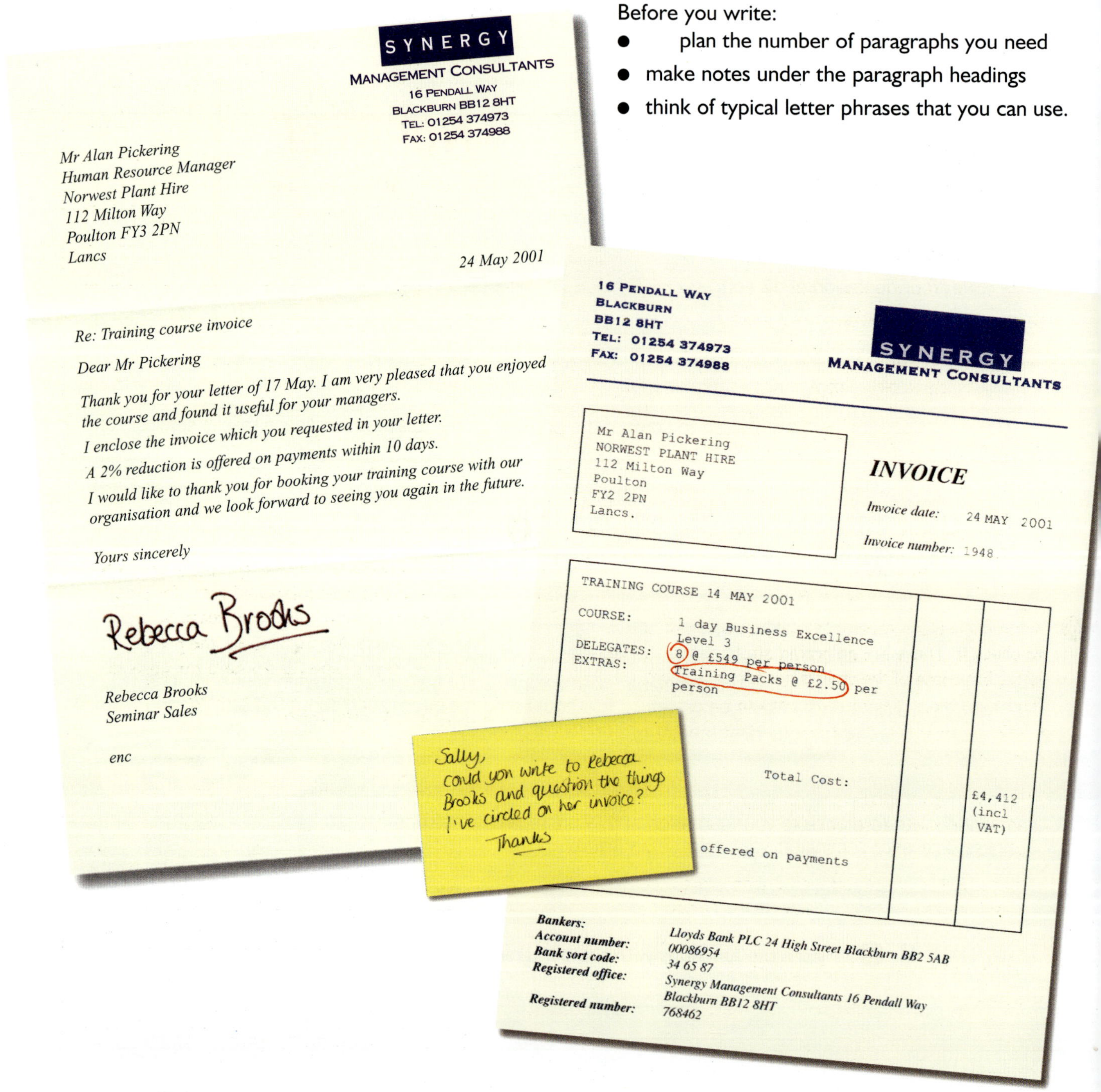
SYNERGY
MANAGEMENT CONSULTANTS
16 PENDALL WAY
BLACKBURN BB12 8HT
TEL: 01254 374973
FAX: 01254 374988

Mr Alan Pickering
Human Resource Manager
Norwest Plant Hire
112 Milton Way
Poulton FY3 2PN
Lancs

24 May 2001

Re: Training course invoice

Dear Mr Pickering

Thank you for your letter of 17 May. I am very pleased that you enjoyed the course and found it useful for your managers.

I enclose the invoice which you requested in your letter.

A 2% reduction is offered on payments within 10 days.

I would like to thank you for booking your training course with our organisation and we look forward to seeing you again in the future.

Yours sincerely

Rebecca Brooks

Rebecca Brooks
Seminar Sales

enc

16 PENDALL WAY
BLACKBURN
BB12 8HT
TEL: 01254 374973
FAX: 01254 374988

SYNERGY
MANAGEMENT CONSULTANTS

Mr Alan Pickering
NORWEST PLANT HIRE
112 Milton Way
Poulton
FY2 2PN
Lancs.

INVOICE

Invoice date: 24 MAY 2001
Invoice number: 1948

TRAINING COURSE 14 MAY 2001
COURSE: 1 day Business Excellence Level 3
DELEGATES: 8 @ £549 per person
EXTRAS: Training Packs @ £2.50 per person

Total Cost: £4,412 (incl VAT)

offered on payments

Bankers: Lloyds Bank PLC 24 High Street Blackburn BB2 5AB
Account number: 00086954
Bank sort code: 34 65 87
Registered office: Synergy Management Consultants 16 Pendall Way Blackburn BB12 8HT
Registered number: 768462

Sally,
Could you write to Rebecca Brooks and question the things I've circled on her invoice?
Thanks

1 What do the following abbreviations mean?

1 ASAP as soon as possible
2 enc ______
3 Dept ______
4 NB ______
5 re ______
6 wk ______
7 excl ______
8 incl ______
9 ext ______

2 Match the following opening and closing phrases.

1	Dear Ms Rees	Regards
2	Dear Paul	Yours truly
3	Dear Sir/Madam	Yours sincerely
4	Gentlemen	Yours faithfully

3 Are the following usually spoken (S) or written (W)?

1 A We got the goods yesterday.
B We received the goods yesterday.
2 A I want to ask about your new product.
B I would like to enquire about your new product.
3 A We're sorry that the order was late.
B We are afraid that the order was delayed.
4 A Could you please confirm the date?
B Let me know if the date is OK.
5 A If you require any further assistance, ...
B If you need any more help, ...
6 A I can't wait to see you.
B I look forward to seeing you.

4 A colleague has written a formal letter and asked you to check it. There are no grammatical mistakes in the letter but some of the style is not formal enough. Find and change the informal phrases.

> Dear Ms Daley
>
> I am writing because we want some information about your latest photocopiers. We are renting a photocopier from you but now we want to buy one.
>
> I'd be really happy if you sent us a brochure and some product literature. Please send us a price list as well.
>
> Thanks a lot. We can't wait to hear from you.
>
> Regards
>
> Marco Francone

5 **Exam practice**

Read the letter in Exercise 4 again.
- Write a reply to Marco Francone:
  * thanking him for his enquiry
  * enclosing a brochure and price list
  * telling him about a new special offer
  * asking him to contact you if he has any questions.
- Write **60 - 80 words**.

> Dear Mr Francone
>
> ______
>
> Yours sincerely

6 **Exam practice**

Simon Howe is leaving the company next week. You decide to have a farewell party for him.
- Write a notice to all your colleagues:
  * informing them about the party
  * saying when and where the party is
  * inviting them to the party.
- Write **30 - 40 words**.

Exam focus: Writing

The Writing Test

The Cambridge BEC Preliminary Writing Test has two questions.

Part	Input	Task
1	Instructions only	Write an e-mail, memo or note (30 - 40 words)
2	Memo, letter, notice or advertisement	Write a letter or memo (60 - 80 words)

Length: About 30 minutes of the Reading and Writing Test should be used for Writing.

How to succeed

Your ability to complete the task successfully is just as important as the accuracy of your grammar and vocabulary.

Task

- Successful task completion means following **all instructions**.
- Pay attention to the word limit. If you do not write enough words, you have probably not completed the task fully. If you write too many, you have probably included unnecessary information.
- Check whether the instructions tell you to use capital letters or not on the Answer Sheet.
- Even if you write a grammatically perfect answer, it may still get low marks if you do not include all the necessary information.

Language

- Task completion is so important that you can still get top marks even with small grammar and spelling mistakes.
- However, accuracy is important so use language that you feel confident about.
- Try not to repeat the same words. Show a range of vocabulary.
- Organise your ideas clearly
  - addition (*also, as well, furthermore etc.*)
  - contrast (*but, although, however etc.*)
  - sequence (*first of all, then, after that etc.*).
- Make sure the language is appropriate to the type of writing. (Short forms, e.g. *I'm*, are acceptable in notes but not in formal letters.)
- Check your writing when you have finished.

Memos and notes

1 Read the examination tips on the opposite page and look at the Part One task below. Underline the task and language errors. Then put them in order from best to worst.

Question 46

- You are attending a conference on 14-18 May in Budapest. You need to make your travel arrangements.
- Write a memo to Jessica Carston, your secretary:
  - * giving her the dates
  - * saying when you want to fly
  - * asking her to book a flight.
- Write **30 - 40 words**.

I have to go to a conference in Budapest. Could you book a flight for me please? I want to go on the 14th May and come back on the 18th. Thank you.

Candidate A

Candidate B

I am attending a conference on 14-18 May in Budapest. I need you to make travel arrangements. Please you book for me a flight.

I am very sorry to troubel you Jessica but you know that I am assisting a conference in Budapest and I am needing you to book me a fly in the morning early. Could you please to do it for me? I am very gratefull for your help.

Candidate C

Candidate D

Could you please book me a return flight for the conference in Budapest? I would like to arrive in Budapest before lunch 14th May and leeving 18th May after 6 pm. Thank you

2 Read these tips and do the exam question below.

1 Read all instructions **carefully**. Do you need to write a memo or a note?
2 Check you have completed all three parts of the task. Use the instructions as a checklist.
3 Check the length of your first draft and edit if necessary.
4 Think about ways of making notes shorter. Which words can you leave out?
5 Proof-read your answer before transferring it. Check grammar, vocabulary and style.

Question 46

- Your department has just received several large new orders. The company has decided to ask everyone in the department to work five extra hours per week.
- Write a memo to all staff in the department:
  - * explaining the situation
  - * saying when overtime will begin
  - * asking the staff to work overtime.
- Write **30 - 40 words**.

Letters and longer memos

1 Read the Part Two task and follow the instructions below.

Question 47

- Read this letter from Rebecca Yates, the Sales Manager at one of your suppliers.

12 July 2001

Mr Paul Wright
Purchasing Manager

Dear Mr Wright

As part of our customer service, we are pleased to enclose our latest brochure, showing our exciting new products and unbelievable prices.

We would like the opportunity to visit your company in order to inform you personally of the latest product developments and discuss ways of making our service even more suited to your needs.

If you would like to take advantage of a visit from a member of our sales team, could you please inform us of a suitable date and time? Could you also tell us which products would be of particular interest to you?

Yours sincerely

Rebecca Yates

Sales Manager

- Write a reply to Ms Yates:
  - * thanking her for the brochure
  - * accepting the offer of a visit from a salesperson
  - * suggesting a date and time for the visit
  - * saying which products you would be interested in.
- Write **60 - 80 words**.

1 Plan the structure of your answer. How many paragraphs will there be? What is their purpose?
2 Think of phrases and key vocabulary to put in the paragraphs.
3 Check that your plan fully completes all four parts of the task. Then write a first draft.
4 Check the first draft:
- *Does it fully complete the task?*
- *Is the information clearly organised?*
- *Is there any unnecessary information?*
- *How many words are there?*
5 Make changes to the first draft.
6 Check the final version:
- *Does it fully complete the task?*
- *Are the grammar, spelling, punctuation and style correct?*

Part One

- You have been waiting all morning for Mr Jablonski, an important client, to return a phone call. Now you have a meeting with a supplier.
- Leave a note for your colleague Louise White:
    * saying where you are
    * saying when you will be back
    * telling her what to say if Mr Jablonski calls.
- Write **30 - 40 words**.

Part Two

- Read this letter from a salesperson enquiring about the transport and accommodation arrangements for a conference you have organised.

> I am writing to confirm my attendance at this year's sales conference from 24th to 27th October.
>
> I will be arriving on 24th and would like to stay until the 28th so that I can do some sightseeing. Could you possibly reserve me an extra night in the same hotel? I would also be very grateful if you could recommend some places for me to visit in my free time.
>
> I look forward to hearing from you.

- Write a letter of reply:
    * agreeing to make the hotel booking
    * explaining that she will have to pay for the extra night
    * asking her for her flight details
    * suggesting places for her to visit.
- Write **60 - 80 words**.

Part One

- You are going to be out of the office.
- Write an e-mail to a customer:
    * reminding them that you are out of the office
    * saying when you will be back in the office
    * suggesting who should be contacted for urgent questions.
- Write **30 - 40 words**.

Part Two

- Your department needs a new photocopier and you have seen this advertisement in a magazine.

> **TX2000 OfficePro**
> Three machines in one!
>
> The new **TX2000 OfficePro** is all you need to print, copy or scan all your colour office documents. With the **OfficePro** you can print up to 4 high quality colour pages a minute, copy up to 3 near-photo quality A4 images a minute and scan full colour A4 documents.
>
> 
>
> Easy to use and compact, the new **OfficePro** is the ideal solution for the small office that needs to produce high quality documents.

- Write a memo to your boss:
    * mentioning the advertisement
    * describing some features of the TX2000
    * saying why the department should buy it
    * giving the price and delivery time.
- Write **60 - 80 words**.

Business hotels

Hotel facilities

Reading 1 Which of the three hotels should the following people stay at and why?

LONDON

Grosvenor Square *Royal London Hotel* ★★★★★

Centrally located, the elegant Royal London is in Mayfair, near shops, parks, theatres and other attractions. The hotel has express check-in, 204 standard rooms and 42 work rooms with desks and communication facilities. The hotel also has a large lounge, health club and well-equipped fitness centre.

Standard double room £265 per night

The Strand *St Steven's Hotel* ★★★

In the heart of theatreland, close to Covent Garden and only metres from Charing Cross, St Steven's is the ideal place for a London break. The hotel offers comfortable, well-equipped rooms and an efficient and friendly service. There is a restaurant, bar and free swimming pool access. The price includes a buffet breakfast.

Price per person per night £56
Midweek single supplement £56

Portman Square *Hyde Park Gardens Hotel* ★★★★

A quiet hotel a short walk from Oxford Street and West End theatres, the Hyde Park Gardens has the famous Maritime Restaurant, an informal dining room and a full fitness centre. It also offers a large buffet breakfast, afternoon tea in the lobby and a Sunday Jazz Brunch.

Price per person per night £97
All week single supplement £97

Marco and Francesca Bianchi
Marco is the Managing Director of a large Italian company. He has a meeting with an important supplier in London. His wife is coming to London with him.

Maurice Breton
Maurice is an advertising executive attending an international advertising conference in London. He wants to stay for just one night. He needs to e-mail a report back to his company before he leaves London.

Linda de Hamm
Linda has an interview on Friday for a job as a PA in London. She wants to stay for the weekend and do some shopping while she is in the city.

Speaking 2 Work in pairs. Which of the three hotels would your partner choose. Why?

The business traveller

Listening **1** Kevin Smith, the Deputy Manager of the Holiday Inn at Nelson Dock, talks about what is important for the business traveller. Before you listen, decide which five things below are most important. Then listen and compare your answers.

sauna	modem socket	bar	good room lighting
pool	secretarial service	fax	video conferencing
TV	quick check-in	room service	distance from airport

2 Listen again and choose the correct option to complete the sentences.

1 Many guests like to eat in their rooms
  A so they can watch TV while they eat.
  B because it is cheaper than the restaurant.
  C so they can do more work.

2 Good lighting means
  A low lighting so guests can relax.
  B bright desk lighting so guests can work.
  C bright lighting for the whole room.

3 The business centre at the hotel
  A is a self-service facility for copying and faxing.
  B organises the food during a conference.
  C recruits temporary secretaries during conferences.

4 The hotel provides
  A a free taxi service to the centre of London.
  B a cheap bus service to the centre of London.
  C a free bus service to the centre of London.

5 Corporate guests
  A do not usually exercise during their stay.
  B like to go swimming during their stay.
  C like to use the fitness room during their stay.

Grammar **3** Look at the tapescript. Find examples of verbs and adjectives followed by the infinitive. Write them below.

Verb + infinitive	Adjective + infinitive
want to	

Speaking **4** Work in pairs. Ask your partner about the best hotel he/she has stayed in. Would your partner recommend it to a business traveller? Why/Why not?

Asking the way

Listening **1** Montse Garcerón is staying at the Holiday Inn at Nelson Dock. She asks about travelling into central London. Listen and complete her notes.

Holiday Inn

Bus
Leaves every (1) ________ minutes between (2) ________ and nine in the morning. After that every (3) ________ minutes.
Takes: (4) ________ mins to Tower Hill Underground Station.
Costs: (5) ________.

River taxi
Leaves every (6) ________ mins during the rush hour. After that, runs to a timetable.
Takes: (7) ________ minutes.
Costs: (8) ________ each way.

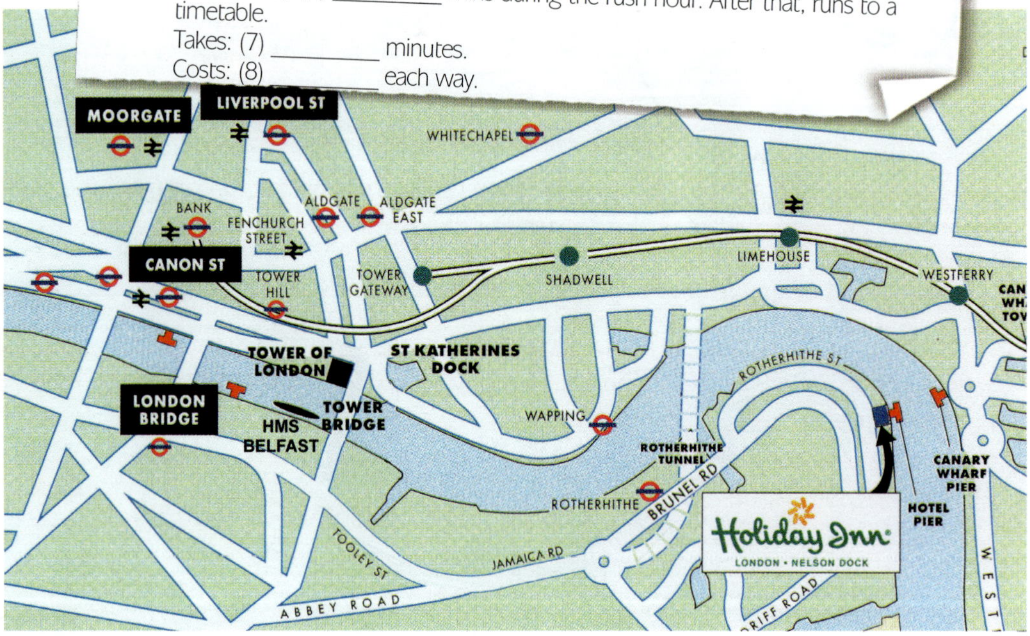

2 Listen again and draw the routes for the bus and the river taxi on the map.

Writing **3** You are the receptionist at the Holiday Inn, Nelson Dock. Write quick directions for the following guests.

- Mr Kiriakov wants to visit HMS Belfast. It is 9.30 am.
- Mrs Sanz wants to visit Canary Wharf Tower and then the Tower of London. It is 8.30 am.

Speaking **4** Work in pairs. Your teacher will give you some cards. Look at the map of London on page 133 and give your partner directions to the places on the cards. You both start from HMS Belfast. Use the words below.

Take the	first left/right.	Go	straight on ...	It's	next to ...
	bus to ...		past ...		near to ...
	train to ...		along ... Street.		opposite ...
Turn left/right at ...					on the left/right of ...

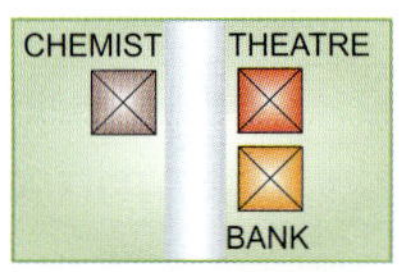

1 Complete the diagrams with adjectives from the advertisements on page 65.

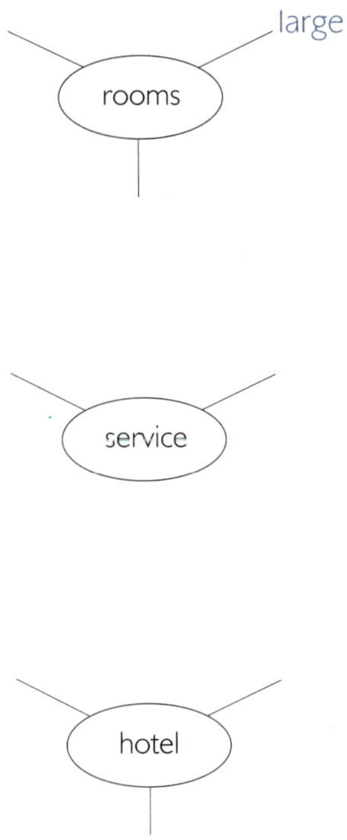

2 Match the words below.

1	room	supplement
2	modem	service
3	fitness	check-in
4	courtesy	socket
5	single	centre
6	express	club
7	rush	bus
8	health	hour

3 Complete the diagram with vocabulary from the unit.

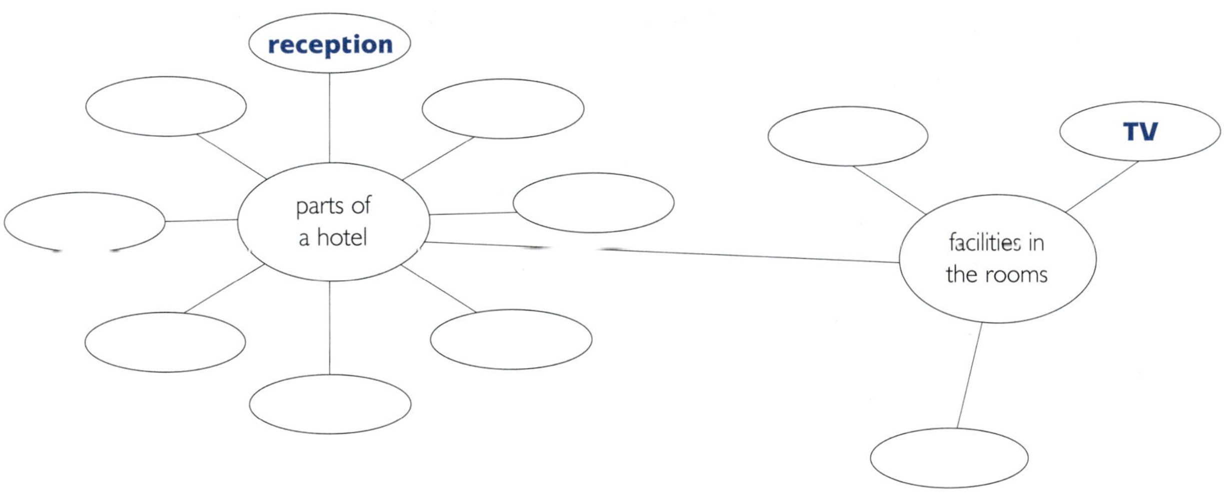

4 **Exam practice**

- You work for the Park Hotel in New York.
- Read this letter from a company enquiring about room vacancies.

KL Computers
95 Science Park Drive #02-03
The Curie
Singapore 118258

The Park Hotel
134 Central Park South
New York 10019
USA

18 June 2001

Dear Sir/Madam

I am writing to enquire about room vacancies for 9-11 July. We would need four double rooms, preferably with some kind of communication facilities for computers.

I would be very grateful if you could send me a quotation for the above rooms with information about the business facilities that the hotel offers.

Yours faithfully

Charles Chung

Charles Chung
Personal Assistant to Kim Lee

- Write a reply to Mr Chung:
  * confirming the availability of the rooms
  * confirming the dates
  * quoting the price
  * giving information about business facilities.
- Write **60 - 80 words**.

Commuting

Reducing traffic

Listening **1** Six people talk about the topics in the newspaper headlines below. Listen to the speakers and number the headlines.

ORT 23

Green tax could push up fuel prices by up to 60%

Leicester launches new pay-as-you-drive scheme

Government to tax parking at work

By Jane Suttie

Edinburgh reduces city centre traffic with pedestrian zones

New smart card to make buses and trains cheaper

Leeds city centre gets fast lane for people sharing cars

By Ian Robinson

ew bus lanes motorways 1

2 Listen again. Does each speaker agree or disagree with the particular transport scheme? Why?

	Agrees/disagrees	Reason
Speaker 1	Disagrees	Traffic will be twice as bad, more accidents, people will be stuck in traffic jams, late for work
Speaker 2		
Speaker 3		
Speaker 4		
Speaker 5		
Speaker 6		

Speaking ❸ Work in pairs. Look at the newspaper headlines on the opposite page. Which are the two best schemes? Why?

Transport policy

Reading ❶ Read the newspaper article about Government transport policy and complete the table.

THE GAZETTE MONDAY JUNE 23 2001

How much are we prepared to pay for our cars?

Bridget Connolly reports on the search for an effective *and* popular transport policy.

Everyone agrees that there are simply too many cars on the road but who will be the first to stop using theirs? Although everyone hates being stuck in traffic, no-one sees their car as part of the growing problem. However, with traffic growth of up to 84 per cent expected by 2031 and the ever-increasing cost of accidents and delays already at $160bn in Europe, there is a growing need to change our 'car culture' and develop alternative forms of transport as quickly as possible.

Changes in travel in Britain 1955-1995

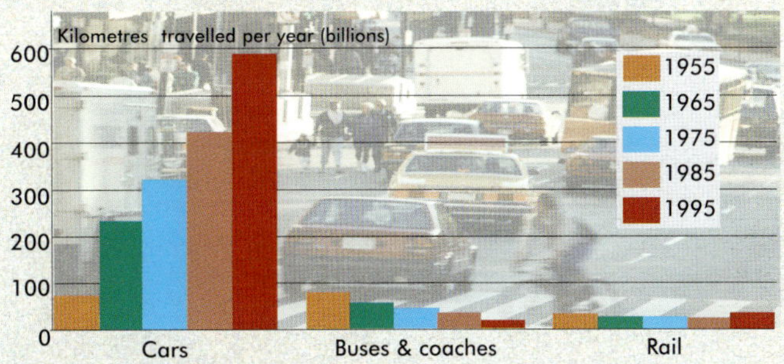

One answer is to make cars more expensive by increasing taxes on petrol. However, tax increases will affect the people who live in the country more than city drivers and do little to reduce inner city traffic. The Government is also looking at pay-as-you-drive schemes on motorways but this will push cars on to smaller 'free' roads, which will make the problem worse.

A successful transport policy is not just a question of making the car too expensive but of offering car drivers a real alternative. Many motorists dislike driving to work but say public transport services are too slow, offer poor quality and are far too expensive. If new transport policies are to succeed, public transport needs to be quick, reliable and affordable.

Transport planners are also developing ways of managing the existing road network more efficiently. New technology such as smart cards and electronic monitoring of roads will lead to a more efficient use of transport systems. However, technology will not reduce the number of cars on the road or solve the real problem of how to persuade car drivers to leave their beloved car at home more often.

Transport schemes	Effects
Increase tax on petrol	

❷ **Are the sentences below 'Right' or 'Wrong'? If there is not enough information to answer, choose 'Doesn't say'.**

1 Cars are the only form of transport that has grown since 1985.
A Right B Wrong C Doesn't say

2 Delays and accidents will cost Europe $160bn in 2031.
A Right B Wrong C Doesn't say

3 The Government is going to double the tax on petrol.
A Right B Wrong C Doesn't say

4 Pay-as-you-drive schemes will reduce the amount of traffic on motorways.
A Right B Wrong C Doesn't say

5 The Government is planning to build more roads in the future.
A Right B Wrong C Doesn't say

6 The use of new technology will reduce the amount of traffic.
A Right B Wrong C Doesn't say

Don't forget!

Making predictions

We can use both **going to** and **will** to make predictions about the future.

- We make spoken predictions with **going to** or **'ll**.
  Petrol prices ***aren't going to make*** *any difference.*
  *The traffic'****ll be*** *twice as bad.*
- **Will** is used in newspaper articles, formal letters and formal speeches.
  The Government ***will increase*** *tax on petrol next year.*
  The meeting ***will take place*** *on Tuesday 2 May.*

Speaking ❸ **Work in pairs. How will transport change in your country in the future? Think about the following issues.**

the use of company cars	the cost of public transport	the cost of driving
the quality of public transport	the use of alternative transport	

❹ **Look at the Commuter Game on page 128. Your teacher will give you instructions on how to play the game.**

1 Complete the crossword.

Across

1 Someone who travels into a city or town to work.
4 The opposite of early.
6 Put your car in a place where it can stay.
7 All cars and buses on the roads.
8 In Britain you drive in the left one.
9 Money you have to give to the Government.

Down

2 A fast road with three lanes in each direction.
3 The long piece of hard ground you drive on.
5 Something that happens when one car hits another.
6 Fuel for cars.

2 Complete the following sentences by adding the word *traffic* or *transport* in the correct place.

traffic
1 Every set of lights was on red this morning.
2 Public is very good in the city where I live.
3 The Government's new policy won't change anything.
4 Sorry I'm late. I was stuck in for hours.
5 There's always a jam on the motorway in the morning.
6 City centre was reduced by the park-and-ride scheme.
7 There isn't any alternative where I live.
8 With growth of over 2% a year, we need more roads.

3 Write about transport in your city. What are the problems? How is the Government dealing with these problems?

4 **Exam practice**

- Look at the newspaper headlines in questions **1 - 5**.
- In each question, which phrase or sentence is correct?
- For each question, mark the correct letter **A**, **B** or **C**.

1 **Motorway technology improves flow of rush hour traffic**

A There are fewer accidents during rush hour.
B There is less traffic during rush hour.
C There are fewer traffic jams during rush hour.

2 **Delays expected on commuter train services**

A People travelling to work by train may be late.
B There are problems with high speed trains.
C Due to problems, all trains will be late.

3 **Public transport fares to increase**

A There will be more bus and train services.
B It will be more expensive to travel by bus and train.
C Customer service will improve on buses and trains.

4 **Punctuality improves on bus services**

A The quality of service is improving on buses.
B More buses are now running on time.
C Buses are becoming cheaper to use.

5 **Pedestrian zones reduce city centre pollution**

A Traffic reductions have improved city centre air quality.
B Larger roads have reduced city centre traffic jams.
C Cycle areas have improved the flow of city centre traffic.

Arranging a conference

An enquiry

Vocabulary **1** Work in pairs. Your teacher will give you some cards about organising a conference. Put them in order.

Listening 1 **2** Daniel Black calls Rachel Day at Europa Events to discuss a conference. Listen to their conversation. Are the following sentences true or false?

1 Daniel is calling to confirm arrangements for a conference.
2 The company has made a final decision on the location.
3 The company wants to have the conference in autumn.
4 The delegates will have two nights at the hotel.
5 Rachel is going to ring Daniel back with a proposal.

3 Listen again and complete the form below.

Briefing Form

europa events LTD

Company name ____________

Contact name Daniel Black

Company address Westbourne Business Park
Brighton

Postcode ____________

Telephone number ____________

Number of delegates ____________

Location ____________

Budget ____________

Date ____________

Duration ____________

Room requirements ____________

Europa Events LTD, 112 Market Road, LONDON, SW4 8HN

Speaking **4** Work in pairs. What do you think Rachel Day's job involves?

Reading **5** Read the information below about conference packages. Which hotel:

- offers easy access to Prague city centre?
- is suitable for smaller conferences with fewer than 30 people?
- is suitable for a company which requires several different rooms for workshops?
- is in a quiet location?
- has its conference facilities in a separate building?
- offers the best facilities for business people?
- does not charge extra for the use of projectors, videos, etc?

europa events LTD

The Plaza, PRAGUE (Min. 40 delegates)

Situated in the heart of Prague, the Plaza is convenient for business travellers from all over Europe. The hotel itself provides the best accommodation and first class facilities for the business traveller. The whole of the fourth floor is dedicated to conference facilities: there are two large conference rooms and four smaller seminar rooms, a business centre, a rest area and a small restaurant.

Grand Hotel Vltava, PRAGUE (Max. 45 delegates)

This historic building in a peaceful setting overlooking the river provides the perfect venue for your conference. In their free time, delegates can enjoy the sights of Prague, many of which are within walking distance. For your convenience we offer a range of conference packages, which we can, of course, extend to meet your requirements.

Karoliny Conference Centre, PRAGUE (Min. 20 delegates)

This 60 bedroom hotel is located 30 minutes from the airport by car and just 20 minutes from the centre of Prague by train. We have a well-equipped conference centre next to the hotel itself and the bedrooms have communication facilities for the business user.

We are pleased to quote as follows:

	PLAZA	GRAND HOTEL	KAROLINY
Single room inc breakfast	£90	£107	£150
Conference room (per day)	£310	£345 (smaller, max 20: £240)	£760
Seminar room (per day)	£180 (smaller, max 10: £130)	£190	£200
Technical equipment (per day)	£200	£340	Included in price
Lunch per person	£15+	£16+	£18.50+
Dinner per person	£20+	£21+	£25+

Speaking **6** Work in pairs. Which hotel would be cheapest for Daniel Black's conference? Would you choose this hotel for him?

Confirming arrangements

Listening 2 ❶ Rachel telephones Daniel to check some details about the conference. Listen to their conversation and take notes.

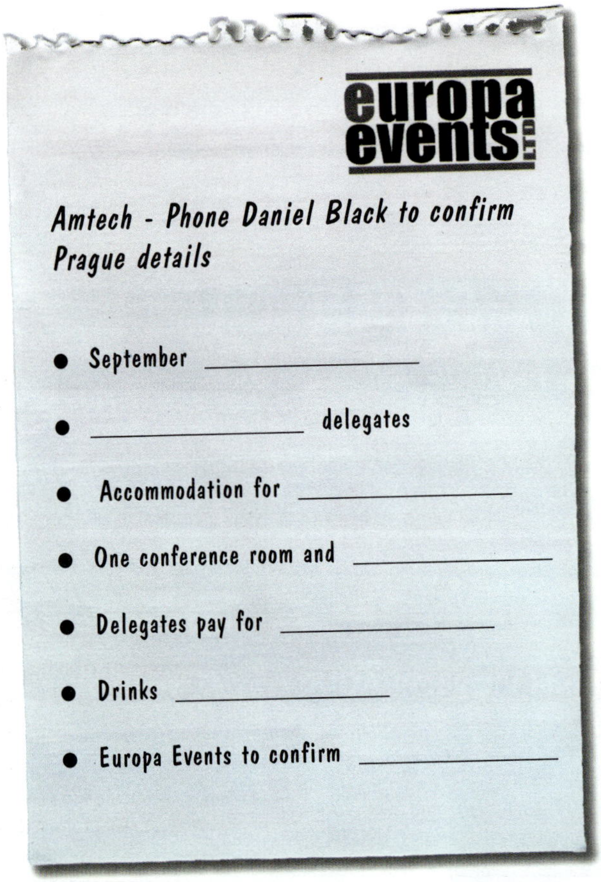

europa events LTD

Amtech - Phone Daniel Black to confirm Prague details

- September ____________
- ____________ delegates
- Accommodation for ____________
- One conference room and ____________
- Delegates pay for ____________
- Drinks ____________
- Europa Events to confirm ____________

Checking and confirming

- We often have to check information on the telephone.
  I'd like to check some details.
  So, … Is that correct?
  Sorry, did you say …?
- We often confirm arrangements with a letter or fax.
  I am writing to confirm …
  We are happy to confirm …

Speaking ❷ Work in pairs. Student A: Look at the Activity sheet on page 126. Student B: Look at the Activity sheet on page 130.

Writing ❸ Work in pairs. Write Rachel's letter to Daniel to confirm the conference booking. Enclose the programme from Exercise 2. Plan the letter before you begin to write.

- What information do you need to include?
- How many paragraphs do you need?
- What information will you write in each paragraph?
- What phrases will you use in each paragraph?

1 Match each verb with a noun.

1 arrange	a quotation
2 decide on	a conference
3 ask for	delegates
4 make	a budget
5 invite	details
6 finalise	a proposal

2 Complete the sentences with the correct form of the words below.

quote require locate arrange propose confirm

1 When I have all the details of your requirements, I'll make a ______________ in writing.

2 The conference is in a quiet ______________.

3 Rachel Day is ______________ a conference for us in October.

4 Please let me know if any delegates have any special food ______________, for example, if they are vegetarians.

5 They have given us a ______________ of £50,000 for the organisation of our sales conference.

6 I'll send you a letter of ______________ next week.

3 You are a conference organiser. A client wants to organise a conference. Write questions to ask the client about the following.

1 delegates How many delegates will there be?

2 location ______________

3 budget ______________

4 time of year ______________

5 duration ______________

6 rooms ______________

4 Look back through the unit (including the tapescripts). How many words connected with *conference* can you find? Now write words which go **before** and **after** *conference*.

....to arrange....		.........room.........
....		....
....	**(a) conference**	....
		....
		....
		....

5 You are Rachel Day. Make your letter to Daniel Black more concise. Write only the essential information. Write 60 - 80 words.

6 **Exam practice**

- You are Daniel Black. You have organised a marketing conference for your company at the Karoliny Conference Centre, Prague.
- Write a memo to the delegates:
  - * saying where the conference will be
  - * saying when the conference will be
  - * asking everyone to confirm if they can attend.
- Write **30 - 40 words**.

MEMO

From: Daniel Black

To: Marketing Personnel

____

At a conference

Welcome to the conference

Listening 1 **1** Frank Stanford, the Sales Director of Vitesse Sportswear, makes the opening speech at the company's Annual Sales Conference. Listen and complete the programme.

Vitesse Annual Sales Conference 2001

Saturday 16 June

10.00	Arrival
10.15	Opening speech
10.30	**(1)** ______________
12.30	Lunch
14.00	**(2)** ______________
15.30	Coffee
16.00	Guest speaker:
	(3) ______________
	(Allman & Partners)
(4) ____	Sessions end
19.00	**(5)** ______________
20.00	Dinner

Sunday 17 June

(6) ____	Workshop: **(7)** ______________
10.30	Coffee
11.00	**(8)** ______________
12.00	Farewell lunch

2 Listen again and answer the questions.

1 How many annual sales conferences has the company already had?
2 How many days do Vitesse conferences normally last?
3 Why are all the delegates together at the first session?
4 What is the guest speaker going to talk about?
5 How far away is the restaurant?
6 Where is Jodie Cox based?

Grammar **3** Read the tapescript and underline the verb forms that follow *as soon as*, *after*, *when*, *until* and *before*. Then complete the information on the opposite page.

Don't forget!

Time clauses

- When we express time in the future, **before**, **after**, **when**, **as soon as** and **until** are followed by the ______________ or ______________ .
  *We'll start the session **as soon as** he **arrives**.*
  *We can go for lunch **after** she**'s finished** her presentation.*

Speaking **4** Work in pairs. Your teacher will give you some cards. Use the information on the cards, the agenda and the words below to form complete sentences.

before	after	when	as soon as	until

5 Work in pairs. A company is organising a weekend conference in your city. The delegates are arriving at 6pm on Friday and leaving at 8pm on Sunday. Four hours of sightseeing is on the programme. What would you show them and when would be the best time?

The conference report

Reading **1** Two weeks after the conference Vitesse produces a report summarising the conference sessions. Match the extracts from the report with the sessions on the programme.

A **An extremely useful presentation that gave us all something to think about. I'm sure everyone will benefit from the helpful tips for dealing with customer calls. We are planning a training pack to improve the way the group deals with incoming calls.**

B **A highly productive workshop session that resulted in some intelligent ideas for promoting the company's latest product. The launch will mean that we all have an exciting and busy twelve months ahead of us.**

C **As always, it was interesting to see how the whole company has performed over the last twelve months. All the presentations were brief, professional and extremely well-prepared. The positive figures were certainly a great start to the conference.**

D **This workshop session gave people the opportunity to discuss the company's sales objectives and strategies. This was a hard but rewarding session with serious and occasionally heated discussion on a range of issues.**

❷ Answer the questions.

1 What is Vitesse going to do as a result of the guest speaker's session?
2 In which session did the speakers make short presentations?
3 How has the company performed over the last twelve months?
4 What did the delegates find difficult to agree on?

Vocabulary ❸ Read the extracts from the report again and underline all the adjectives describing the sessions. What are the opposites of the adjectives?

Listening2 ❹ All the Vitesse delegates have to fill in a feedback form. Listen to Jodie Cox talk to a colleague about the conference and fill in the form for her.

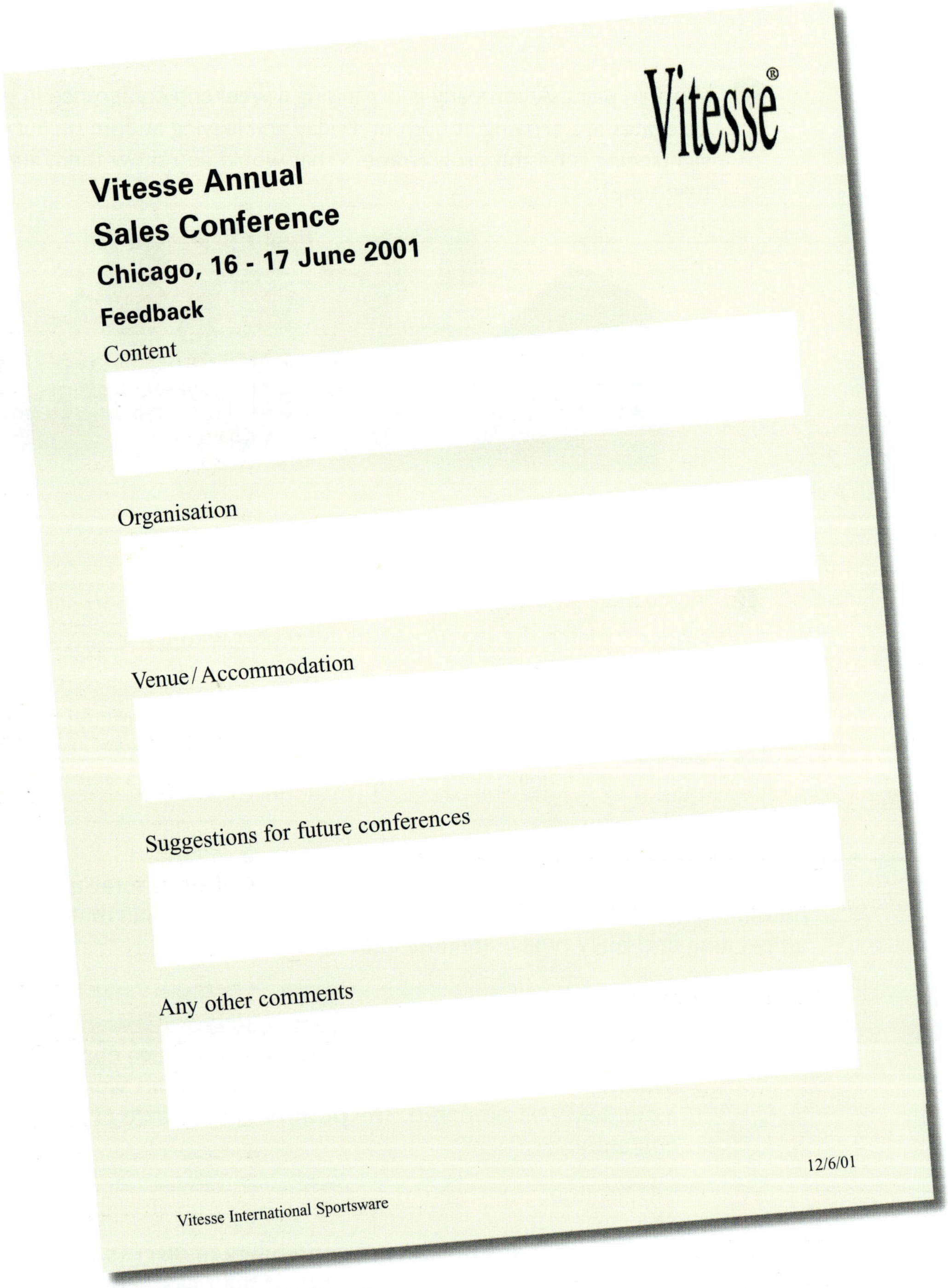

Vitesse®

Vitesse Annual Sales Conference
Chicago, 16 - 17 June 2001

Feedback

Content

Organisation

Venue / Accommodation

Suggestions for future conferences

Any other comments

12/6/01

Vitesse International Sportsware

Speaking ❺ Work in pairs. What makes a good conference?

1 Complete the following sentences in your own words.

1 We'll send everyone a memo as soon as ...
we make the final arrangements.
2 We can't book the rooms until ...
______
3 I'll give you the programme before ...
______
4 The conference will finish after ...
______
5 We'll start the session as soon as ...
______
6 I'll copy the report for you when ...
______

2 Look at the adjectives below. Write the opposite adjective next to it.

1 helpful ......unhelpful.....
2 well-prepared ....
3 positive ....
4 useful ....
5 productive ....
6 exciting ....
7 rewarding ....

3 Write the opposites of the sentences below.

1 She sent me a *long* conference report.
She sent me a short conference report.
2 The conference was *hard* to organise.
______
3 She gave a *long* sales presentation.
______
4 Some of the sessions were too *long*.
______
5 The hotel beds were very *hard*.
______
6 The journey to the restaurant was *long*.
______
7 The speaker was *hard* to understand.
______

4 **Exam practice**

- Look at questions **1 - 5**.
- In each question, which sentence is correct?
- For each question, mark the correct letter **A**, **B** or **C**.

1 **Due to circumstances beyond our control, the conference will be postponed.**

A The conference will take place as planned.
B The conference will not take place.
C The conference will take place at a later date.

2 **Delegates are asked to check out by 10.30 a.m.**

The delegates should leave their rooms
A before half past ten.
B at ten thirty.
C earlier than half past eleven.

3 **Could all speakers please produce summaries of the sessions they gave.**

The speakers should write
A full details of what is in their session.
B a brief report about their session.
C a proposal for their session.

4 **WORKSHOPS**

Improving margins	**Wagner suite**
Selling on the telephone	**Schumann suite**
Marketing new products	**Bach suite**

The workshop on increasing profits will be in the
A Wagner suite.
B Schumann suite.
C Bach suite.

5 **Mr Sylvester is used to giving presentations to large audiences.**

Mr Sylvester
A doesn't give presentations to large groups any more.
B often gave presentations to large groups in the past.
C often gives presentations to large groups.

Exam focus: Listening

The Listening Test

The Cambridge BEC Preliminary Listening Test has four parts.

Part	Input	Task
1	Short conversations	Multiple-choice
2	Short telephone conversation or monologue	Gap-filling (numbers and one spelling)
3	Monologue	Gap-filling (words and one date)
4	A longer conversation or monologue (3-4 mins)	Multiple-choice

Length: A total of 12 minutes of listening material played twice, plus 10 minutes at the end to transfer answers to the Answer Sheet.

Before listening

❶ It is important that you use your time well even **before** you listen. Here are some tips.

- Always read the instructions very carefully before you listen.
- Check the type of answer you need to give. Is it a letter, numbers or words?
- Check the number of words you should write for each answer.
- You will always be given time to read through the questions before you listen. Use this time well. Try to predict words you might hear and what the answer might be.

❷ Work in pairs. Look at the Listening Test below. Predict words that you might hear in the recordings.

1 Which bar chart shows the sales of Solex Ltd?

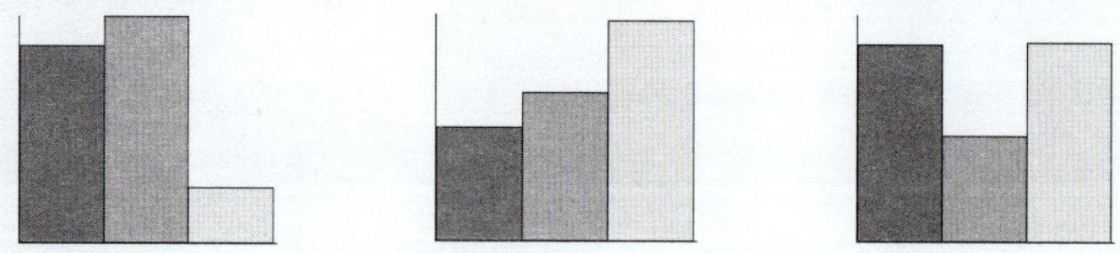

A B C

2 Which sign are the speakers talking about?

A	B	C
LIFT OUT OF ORDER	CANTEEN CLOSED DUE TO STAFF ILLNESS	QUIET PLEASE EXAM IN PROGRESS

While listening

You will hear every part of the Listening Test twice.

First listening
Try to get an idea of the general context and answer as many of the questions as possible. However, do not worry if you do not understand every word. Also, do not worry if you do not know all the answers yet. The second listening will give you a second chance.

Second listening
Do not stop listening if you think you know the answer: with multiple-choice questions the recordings often include words from the incorrect options. Listen for negatives and words such as *but* or *instead of*.

After listening

1 In order to obtain a high mark, you need to check carefully. Here are some tips.

- Make sure that you give only **one** answer for each question.
- Make sure that you answer **every** question.
- Check your answers after transferring them on to the Answer Sheet.

Find the candidates' mistakes on the question papers below.

Questions 16 - 22

- Look at the notes below.
- Some information is missing.
- You will hear part of a presentation by a Human Resources manager.
- For each question, fill in the missing information in the numbered space using one or two words.

Department: **(16)** ....

Vacancy: **(17)** New department Secret...

Questions 23 - 30

- Listen to two managers discussing the price of a product.
- For each question **23 - 30**, mark the correct letter **A, B** or **C**.
- You will hear the conversation twice.

23 The managers want to raise the price because

(A) materials have become more expensive.
B the product is selling very well.
(C) of a pay rise for the workers.

Exam practice

Part One

Listening tips

1 Read the instructions carefully.
2 Read the information before you listen.
3 Listen to the end of each extract before you choose your answer.
4 Use the second listening to check your answers.
5 Transfer your answers carefully to the Answer Sheet.

Questions 1 - 8

- For questions **1 - 8**, you will hear eight short recordings.
- For each question, mark one letter **A**, **B** or **C**.
- You will hear each recording twice.

1 What is Maria's job title?
A Sales Executive
B Marketing Manager
C Managing Director

2 Where are they going to take the visitors?

A	B	C
The Italian Experience	The Thai House	The Potato House

3 What was the final decision about the meeting?
A It will take place as arranged.
B It will take place at a later date.
C It will not take place.

4 Which part of the job offer was George unhappy about?
A The amount of pay.
B The number of hours.
C The number of holidays.

5 Which graph is the Head of Department talking about?

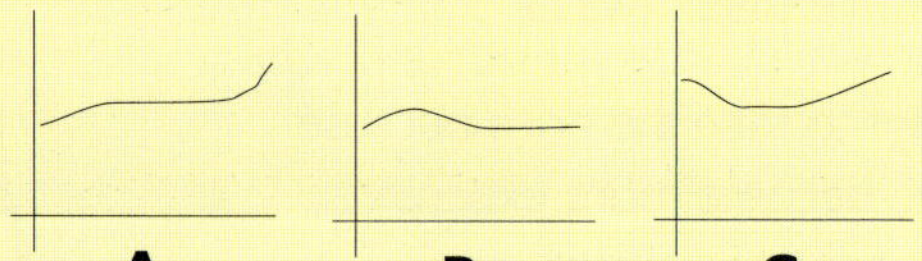

A **B** **C**

6 When are the visitors arriving?
A Ten o'clock.
B Half past ten.
C Eleven o'clock.

7 Which photocopier do they decide to buy?
A The X40.
B The BT100.
C The RX200.

8 Which part of the factory does Alan want to change?
A The packing hall.
B The warehouse.
C The production line.

Part Two

Listening tips

1 Read the instructions carefully.
2 Read the information before you listen.
3 Use the second listening to check your answers.
4 Transfer your answers carefully to the Answer Sheet.

Questions 9 - 15

- Look at the notes below.
- Some information is missing.
- You will hear two people discussing an invoice.
- For each question, fill in the missing information in the numbered space using a word, numbers or letters.
- You will hear the conversation twice.

SHARPENERS - the stationers!

Invoice number: **(9)** ....

Invoice date: **(10)** .... February 2002

Photocopy paper: **(11)** .... boxes @ £9.94

V.A.T. @ **(12)** .... %

Total to pay: **(13)** £ ....

To reach us by: 17th March 2002

Contact name: **(14)** Marjorie ....

Telephone no.: **(15)** 01623 ....

Part Three

Listening tips

1 Read the instructions carefully.
2 Read the information before you listen.
3 Think what kind of information the answer might be: a name, address, number etc.
4 Use the second listening to check your answers.
5 Transfer your answers carefully to the Answer Sheet.

Questions 16 - 22

- Look at the notes.
- Some information is missing.
- You will hear a woman talking to some journalists about a new product range.
- For each question, fill in the missing information in the numbered space using one or two words.
- You will hear the recording twice.

JollyGood Skincare

Head Office:	**(16)**	
Core market:	**(17)**	
New range:	**(18)**	***cosmetics***
Target market:	**(19)**	***women***
Selling point:	**(20)**	
Launch date:	**(21)**	
Advertising slogan:	**(22)**	

Part Four

Listening tips

1 Read the instructions and questions carefully.
2 Do not worry if you miss the answer first time.
3 Use the second listening to check your answers.
4 Transfer your answers carefully to the Answer Sheet.

Questions 23 - 30

- Listen to a Head of Department talking to an employee about her performance.
- For each question **23** - **30**, mark the correct letter **A**, **B** or **C**.
- You will hear the conversation twice.

23 Sharon started working for the company
A some time last year.
B one year ago.
C over a year ago.

24 Sharon found out about the vacancy from
A a friend.
B a newspaper.
C an internal memo.

25 Sharon does not enjoy
A answering the telephone.
B typing invoices.
C preparing price lists.

26 The biggest problem with the computer is that
A she doesn't know the program very well.
B it regularly stops working.
C the monitor is too small.

27 Sharon would like the company to buy
A new software.
B new computers.
C new monitors.

28 When dealing with complaints, she would like to
A take more responsibility.
B pass the customer on to her boss.
C give the customers money back.

29 Sharon's boss thinks that some customers
A often receive faulty orders.
B often make mistakes.
C are not always honest.

30 Sharon's main aim for next year is to
A get to know the customers a lot better.
B make fewer mistakes.
C learn more about the products.

Production

Bread production

Listening 1 **1** Brian Benfield, Production Manager at Gossens, a UK food group, explains how baguettes are produced. Before you listen, put the following stages of the process into the correct order.

☐ cool the baguettes	☐ box the baguettes	☐ mix the dough
☐ wrap the baguettes	☐ form the baguettes	☐ bake the baguettes
☐ weigh the ingredients (flour, yeast and water)		

Now listen and check your answers.

2 Look at the floorplan below. Listen again and write the correct numbers next to the following:

☐ circuit	☐ first prover	☐ baguette former	[1] mixers
☐ divider	☐ second prover	☐ oven	☐ cooler

Floorplan of the bakery

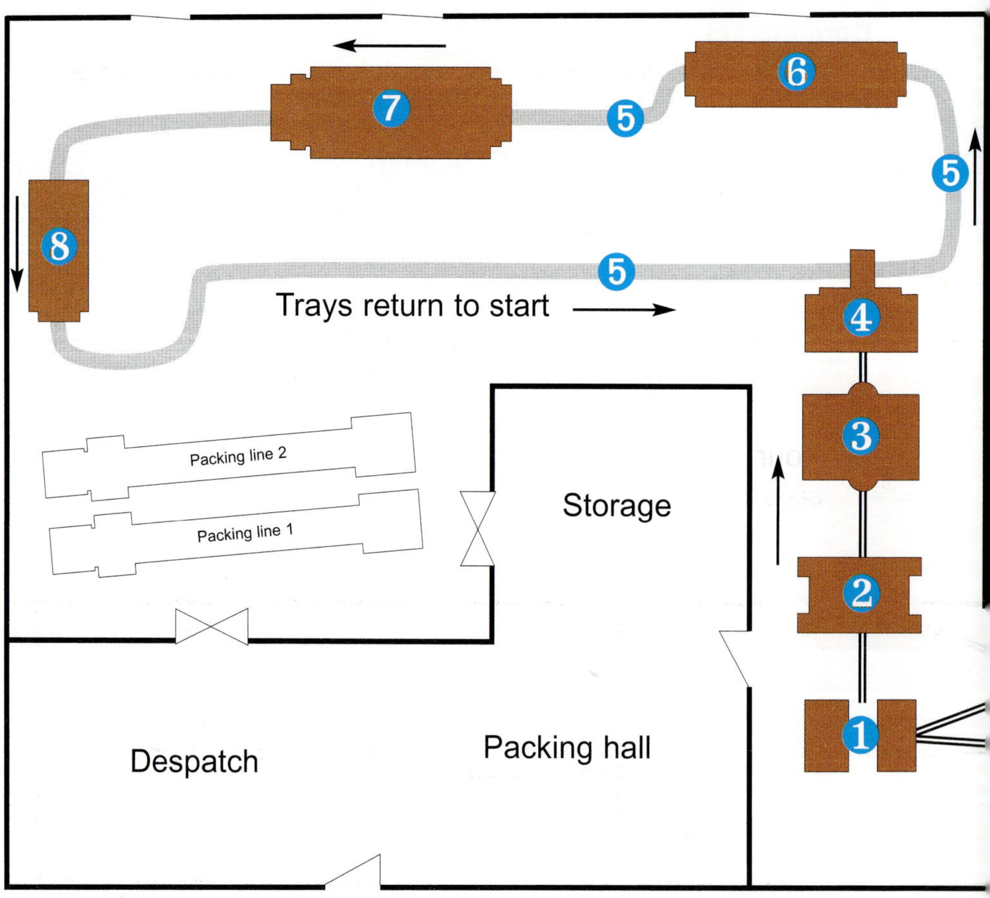

Speaking **3** What happens at each of the machines on the production line?

❹ Complete the information below.

The Passive

The passive is formed with the verb ________________
(in the correct tense) and the ________________ of the verb.

The ingredients ***are weighed****.*
The company ***was set up*** *in 1982.*

Vocabulary

❺ Which verbs can be used with each noun? Tick (✔) the correct boxes.

	weigh	mix	bake	cool	wrap	box	despatch
ingredients	✔						
dough							
baguettes							
boxes							

Now think of another noun to go with each verb.

weigh ....
mix ....
bake ....
cool ....
wrap ....
box ....
despatch ....

Speaking

❻ Work in pairs. Think of three processes. How many of the verbs below can you use to describe each process?

check	cool	cut	despatch	heat
mix	press	weigh	wrap	collect

Sending a parcel

First the object ***is wrapped****. Then the parcel* ***is weighed****. It is taken to the post office or* ***collected*** *by a courier. Then the parcel* ***is despatched****.*

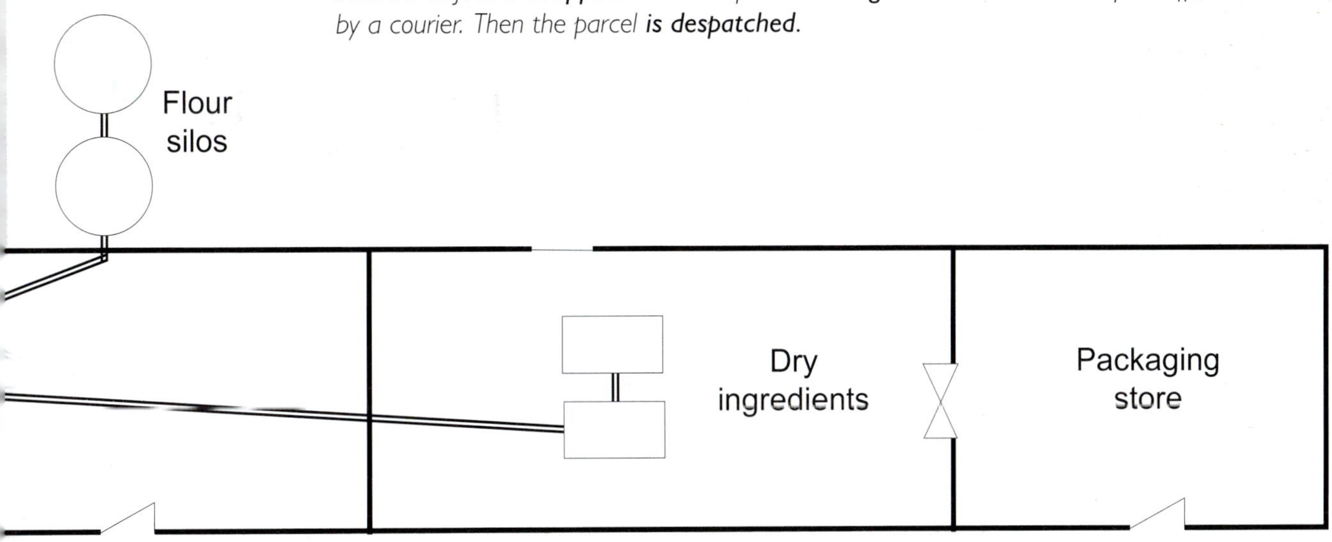

Production problems

Listening 2 **1** Brian Benfield talks about production problems at the bakery. Before you listen, decide which of the following would cause problems most often. Then listen and compare your answers.

- human problems
- electronic problems
- mechanical problems

2 Listen again and complete the sentences.

1 The computer stops the whole process ______________________.
2 If the computer gets the mix wrong, ______________________.
3 If a mixerman forgets the yeast and additives, ______________________.
4 When an old tray loses its shape, ______________________.
5 We can lose up to an hour and a half of production ______________________.

Don't forget!

When or *if*?

- **When** is used when we expect something to happen.
  The trays pass through a sensor ***when*** *they enter the oven.*
- **If** is used when we are unsure if something will happen.
  We can lose an hour and a half ***if*** *we have a really bad day.*

Grammar **3** Match the following sentence halves and complete the sentences with *when* or *if*.

The trays pass a sensor when they enter or exit any machine.

1 The trays pass a sensor	they get jammed in them.
2 The baguettes do not rise	they enter or exit any machine.
3 The line produces 6,000 baguettes an hour	the oven temperature is too high.
4 The baguettes are taken off the trays	the dough does not prove first.
5 Old trays can damage machines	everything runs properly.
6 The baguettes burn	they have left the cooler.

Speaking **4** Work in pairs. What goes wrong at your partner's place of work? What does he/she do when things go wrong?

1 Rewrite the following sentences using the passive.

1 We weigh the ingredients.
The ingredients are weighed.

2 The system feeds the ingredients into the mixers.

____

3 A machine drops the baguettes onto a tray.

____

4 Ovens bake the baguettes for ten minutes.

____

5 A blower blows cool air over the baguettes.

____

6 Packing machines pack the baguettes in boxes.

____

2 Look at the flow chart below. Write a short text describing the start-up process for the baguette production line. Add any words which are necessary (articles, sequencers etc.).

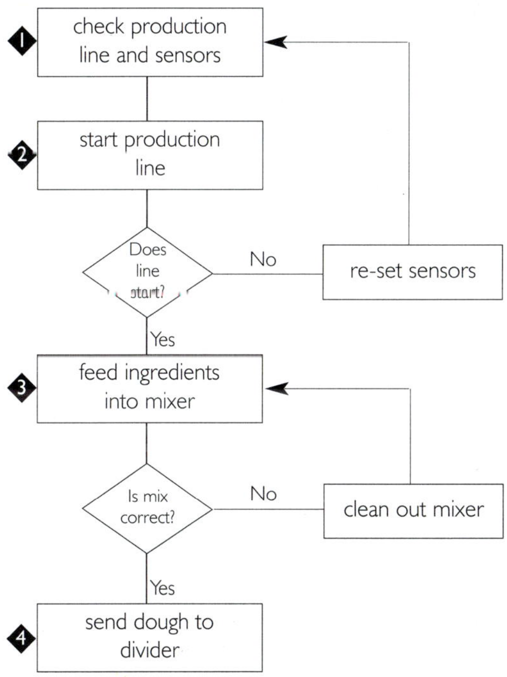

3 Complete the diagram with vocabulary from the tapescript for Listening 1 on page 140.

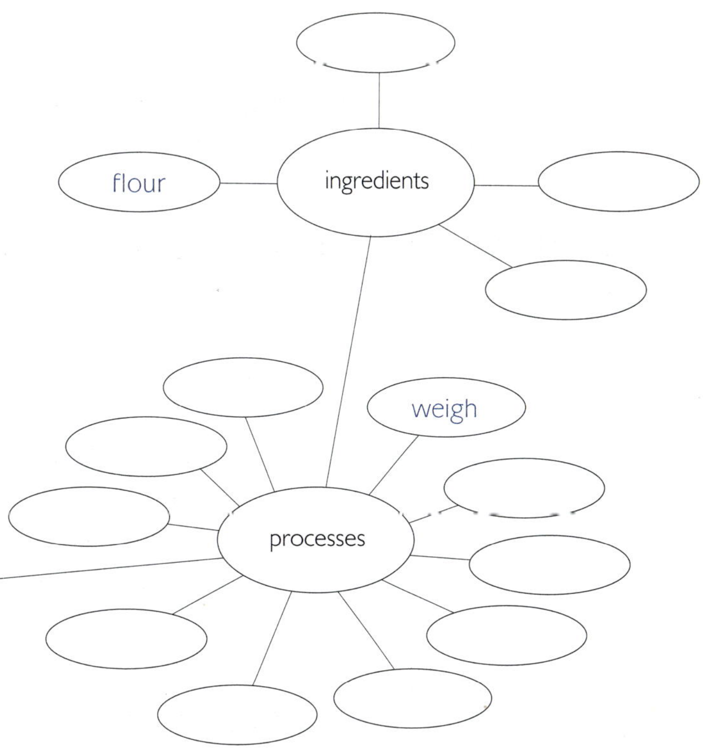

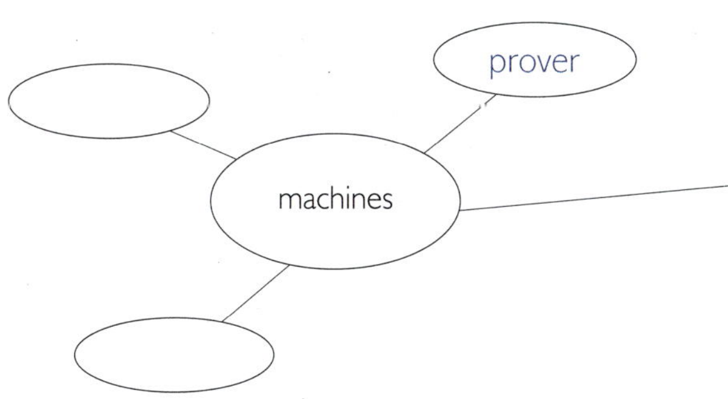

4 **Exam practice**

- You are the Production Manager at a factory.
- You notice that some packing machines are not set correctly for some new packaging.
- Write a memo to all packing machine operators:
  - * explaining the problem
  - * saying which machines are having problems
  - * asking them to check the machine settings.
- Write **30 - 40 words**.

MEMO

To: All packing machine operators
From: Production Manager

____

Unit 13b

Quality control

Monitoring quality

Speaking **1** What does the job of a quality control (QC) manager at a snacks factory involve? Use the verbs below.

check monitor inspect sample reject

Listening 1 **2** Pauline Carr is Head of Quality Control at Coopers, a UK snack producer. She talks about monitoring quality. Listen and complete the table below.

Quality Control at Coopers

Inspection points

1 Suppliers	2 Goods in	3 __________	4 Finished goods
• QC processes	• quantities	• cooking oil	• __________
• __________	• __________	• flavouring	• packet seal
	• __________	• __________	• __________
		• crispness	

3 Listen again and answer the questions.

1 Why is hygiene very important for the supplier?
2 Why is it important to check transport packaging?
3 What happens if the snacks are too oily?
4 How do they check the taste of the snacks?

Speaking **4** Work in pairs. What QC processes are there at your partner's place of work?

Improving quality

Listening 2 **1** Pauline is in a meeting with Jack Simmons, the Production Director, and Keith Taylor, the Operations Manager. Read the memo below. Then listen to their discussion and answer the questions.

1 What is the problem?
2 What causes it?
3 Which proposals do Keith and Pauline each support?
4 What action does Jack decide to take?

Coopers Quality Snacks Coopers

Internal Memorandum

To: Pauline Carr
cc: Keith Taylor
From: Jack Simmons
Date: 8 March 2001

Re: QC Meeting 9 March 2001

Our reject levels have risen by over 5% in three weeks. Chemical analysis shows that fat levels are above the acceptable maximum.

Here are some ideas for dealing with the problem. Please be prepared to discuss them at the meeting.

1 Increase the sampling rate
2 Change the cooker temperature sensors
3 Change the cooking oil more often

2 Listen again and choose the best option to complete the sentences.

1 The samples do not pick up the high fat levels because
A the cooker does not work properly.
B the oil temperature changes too quickly.
C the factory is running at full capacity.

2 Pauline does not want to increase the sampling rate because she
A thinks the rate is already good enough.
B has not got enough staff in her department.
C does not think it will make a difference.

3 Keith does not want to change the sensors because
A the sensors are very expensive.
B it would mean losing production.
C he has already changed them.

4 The temperature sensors do not work properly
A when the cooker oil gets dirty.
B if samples are not taken regularly.
C because the cookers are old.

5 Keith does not want to change the oil more often because
A it will be expensive and cut production.
B he thinks changing sensors is a better idea.
C he does not think it will make a difference.

Grammar 3 Look at the tapescript on page 140. Underline examples of the present simple. What are the different uses of the present simple in the conversation?

Don't forget!

Conditional (real possibility)

- We can use the following conditional forms to talk about the possible results of an action:

  If + present simple, will
  going to + infinitive
  might

- We can use **will / going to** when we are sure of the result.
- We can use **might** when we are not sure of the result.

4 You are discussing changes to the place where you work. Here are some of your colleagues' suggestions. Your thoughts are in brackets. Write responses using conditional sentences.

1 "I think we should buy new machinery." (Very expensive!)

If we buy new machinery, it'll be expensive.

2 "We need to spend more on training." (Possibly improve quality)

____

3 "We have to work more overtime." (Problems with the workforce!)

____

4 "Why don't we increase the workforce?" (Spend too much time training new people)

____

5 "Let's increase our QC activities." (Possibly reduce reject levels)

____

6 "We can only offer workers a 2% pay rise." (Never accept it!)

____

Speaking 5 You are the directors of a small soft drinks producer. You are going to hear descriptions of different problems at your company and possible solutions. Discuss the problems and decide what action to take. Use some of the words below.

Let's ...	Why don't we ...?	We should ...

1 Match the words. Then use them to complete the sentences below.

1	quality	life
2	inspection	control
3	shelf	analysis
4	finished	in
5	goods	goods
6	chemical	points

1 All ______________ are stored in a warehouse ready for despatch.
2 There are five main ______________ in our quality control programme.
3 The ______________ department is next to the production hall.
4 The ______________ of our ingredients is about two weeks. After that we throw them away.
5 We check all ______________ when they arrive at our warehouse.
6 The ______________ is carried out in a laboratory in the QC department.

2 Match the words with their opposites. Then complete the text with the correct form of the words. Do not use any word more than once.

1	demand	fall
2	goods in	increase
3	rise	accept
4	reject	supply
5	reduce	finished goods

The problems started about 6 months ago. We were already at full capacity when (1) ______________ suddenly went up by 30%. We only had one warehouse so both (2) ______________ and (3) ______________ were in the same place. There was no way we could (4) ______________ our storage space so we worked very closely with our (5) ______________, who delivered the ingredients just when we needed them and not before. On the production side, both workers and machinery had to work overtime and our quality levels began to (6) ______________. We soon noticed a (7) ______________ in our (8) ______________ levels and we had to throw away more and more finished goods. But we couldn't really do anything about it without (9) ______________ capacity so we just had to (10) ______________ the situation.

3 Complete the following sentences with the correct form of the verb in brackets.

1 We (*need*) _'ll need_ to increase capacity if we (*get*) _get_ any more orders.
2 Even if we (*change*) ______________ the sensors, it (*not/make*) ______________ any difference.
3 If it (*not/make*) ______________ any difference, we (*talk*) ______________ about it again next week.
4 If demand (*increase*) ______________, we (*have to*) ______________ increase overtime.
5 What (*happen*) ______________ if we (*keep*) ______________ the oil in the cooker longer?
6 We (*have to*) ______________ spend more on training if we (*want*) ______________ to improve quality.
7 If the goods (*not/arrive*) ______________ soon, we (*look*) ______________ for a new supplier.
8 The QC department (*not/be*) ______________ happy if we (*increase*) ______________ the sampling rate.

4 **Exam practice**

- **Look at the notice below. It shows the different divisions of a manufacturing company.**
- **For questions 1 - 5, decide where each person should go.**
- **For each question, mark the correct letter A - H.**
- **Do not use any letter more than once.**

A Production line
B Warehouse
C Despatch
D Research & development
E Quality control
F Packing line
G Canteen
H Washrooms

1 Sam needs to get changed and freshen up after her shift.
2 Vince wants to research how the goods are currently manufactured.
3 Kate needs to take sample products for inspection.
4 John needs to check the quality of the storage facilities.
5 Ian wants to see what happens to the goods after they have been packed.

Direct service providers

The call centre

Speaking **1** Call centres are a rapidly growing business sector in the UK. Why do you think companies are investing so much money in them?

Listening 1 **2** George Watt, the National Sales Manager at Direct Line, talks about call centres. Listen and complete the journalist's notes.

Notes: Direct Line

No. of call centres: (1) ____________

Total staff: (2) ____________

Advantages

Lower (3) ____________ for the company and lower (4) ____________ for the client.

When customers call, they get an immediate (5) ____________.

Products

- Insurance lines: motor, (6) ____________, travel and life.
- Financial services: mortgages, personal (7) ____________, savings and (8) ____________.
- Vehicle breakdown service.

Future

Will become harder to (9) ____________.

Staff might (10) ____________.

❸ Listen again and choose the correct option to complete the sentence or answer the question.

1 Direct Line's costs are lower because the company does not have to
   A pay as many claims as competitors.
   B rent shops or pay commission.
   C pay for advertising.

2 Operatives can deal with a call quickly because
   A they are good at making decisions.
   B the company employs a lot of staff.
   C of the technology.

3 Call centre technology means that operatives
   A need a lot of special training.
   B have a lot of responsibility.
   C can deal with almost every call.

4 In future, direct service providers will have to
   A reduce the size of their call centres.
   B make job offers more attractive.
   C cut wages to keep prices down.

40,000

Direct Line's motor telesales operators handle around 40,000 incoming calls a day.

Vocabulary

❹ Match the words with the meanings.

1 broker	money you pay for insurance
2 premium	person who buys and sells things, e.g. insurance, for other people
3 claim	money paid to a salesperson for every sale he/she makes
4 policy	loan to buy a house
5 mortgage	request for money to be paid by an insurer
6 commission	insurance contract

Future possibility and probability

- We can express possibility in different ways.
  Call centre staff ***will possibly*** *work from home.*
  Companies ***could/might*** *find it hard to compete in the future.*
- We can also talk about probability in different ways.
  Companies ***will probably*** *have difficulty finding staff.*
  Prices ***are likely to*** *fall in the next few years.*

Speaking

❺ Work in pairs. Are the following situations possible in your country?

1 Companies will provide more of their services by telephone.
2 The price of insurance will fall because of cheap competition.
3 Fewer insurance companies will use agents in the future.
4 Call centres will use video-phones for face-to-face contact.

Working in a call centre

Listening 2 **1** **Work in pairs. George Watt talks about working conditions in a call centre. Before you listen, decide whether the following statements are true or false. Then listen and check your answers.**

1 The computer system monitors the workers every minute of their shift.
2 Call centre operatives can earn productivity bonuses for selling a lot of policies.
3 Operatives normally work a lot more hours than office workers.
4 Operatives work the same hours every month.
5 The call centre is open from 9am until 5pm on weekdays.
6 Call centres employ a lot of young people and women.
7 The company tries to make working in the call centre more interesting.

Reading **2** **Which of the following people would be interested in working in a call centre? Why?**

Zoe Connolly, 22
I've just finished university and I'm looking for a job. I've got a degree in business studies but I'm not really sure what I want to do. I'd like to take some time off and travel around the world but I don't have any money.

Steven Gregory, 32
I'm unemployed at the moment. I've worked in sales a lot and I'd like to continue in that area. I really enjoy working with people and visiting customers. Sales is always interesting because you know you can always sell more, so you never relax.

Helen Taylor, 26
I worked as a secretary after leaving school but I stopped work last year to start a family. My daughter is now nearly six months old and I would like to go back to work. My husband works in an office from 9 to 5.

Speaking **3** **Work in pairs. More and more organisations are offering their services and products directly over the telephone and on the Internet. What changes could this make to our daily lives?**

1 Look back through the unit (including the tapescripts). How many words connected with *insurance* can you find? Now write words which go **before** the word *insurance* and words which go **after**.

......motor......		......broker......
....		....
....	**insurance**	....
....		....

2 Which is the odd one out?

1	contract	policy	agreement	memorandum
2	cost	claim	premium	price
3	premium	location	price	commission
4	instant	immediate	exciting	fast
5	life	loan	motor	house
6	volume	total	quality	number
7	loan	mortgage	provider	pension

3 Complete the sentences with the words below.

supervisor	loan	premium
policy	monitor	broker
claim	commission	enquiry

1 I changed my car insurance because the ______________ was lower.

2 I bought the car with a ______________ from the bank.

3 We know a ______________ who advises us on insurance.

4 As an insurance salesman he earns ______________ on everything he sells.

5 A new customer phoned me to make an ______________.

6 The system lets us ______________ what the operatives are doing at any time.

7 My car has just been stolen so I need to make a ______________.

8 Her house insurance ______________ ran out last month.

9 A ______________ makes decisions if operatives have to deal with large or unusual risks.

4 **Exam practice**

- Read the newspaper article below about call centres.
- Choose the correct word from **A**, **B** or **C** below.
- For each question, mark the correct letter **A**, **B** or **C**.

New call centre creates 2000 jobs in north-east

More good news. Barclays Bank is setting up a call centre in Sunderland **(1)** ..... of the growth of its telephone banking service. This is a welcome decision for the north-east, **(2)** ..... companies considered less attractive **(3)** ..... regions such as London and Scotland in **(4)** ..... list of the best locations for call centres. Opening early next year, the centre **(5)** ..... expected to employ 2,000 people over the next three years.

Barclaycall, the telephone banking service, **(6)** ..... introduced in 1994 and has **(7)** ..... than 600,000 customers. The service has 650 employees in Coventry and **(8)** ..... 200 at a centre in Manchester. Barclaycall is **(9)** ..... 25,000 new customers every month and the bank expects one million customers **(10)** ..... the next two years. One director said: "Opening another call centre shows **(11)** ..... popular our telephone banking service is **(12)** ..... our customers. Barclays will continue to invest to satisfy their needs."

1	**A** because	**B** despite	**C** due
2	**A** where	**B** what	**C** which
3	**A** that	**B** than	**C** as
4	**A** there	**B** their	**C** its
5	**A** are	**B** be	**C** is
6	**A** was	**B** were	**C** have
7	**A** more	**B** many	**C** much
8	**A** extra	**B** different	**C** another
9	**A** attractive	**B** attracted	**C** attracting
10	**A** at	**B** over	**C** on
11	**A** why	**B** very	**C** how
12	**A** with	**B** between	**C** through

The banking sector

The banking revolution

Reading 1 Read the article and match the headings with the paragraphs.

New banking products	Warnings of redundancies
The future of banking	Reasons for reducing costs

Stormy times for Europe's banks

In spite of all the recent mergers and cost-cutting in the European banking sector, experts are warning that thousands of jobs are still at risk. UK banks could cut up to 20,000 jobs over the next two years as they try to compete with supermarkets and direct providers. Switzerland and Germany, with their over-crowded retail banking markets, could see even greater job losses.

The need to reduce non-IT costs is becoming increasingly important as Europe's banks invest heavily in electronic banking and meet the costs of dealing with the millennium bug and European economic and monetary union (Emu) all at the same time. The domestic branch networks will suffer most, with several European banks planning to close up to 15 per cent of their smaller branches.

The staff reductions are made possible by the development of electronic banking services such as telephone banking, smart cards and PC banking. Alan Higgins, Manager of Direct Financial Services at Carlisle NSB, a UK bank, is hoping that home banking technology will put the company ahead of its competitors. "We are testing a product called HomeBank with 2,000 of our customers who have a 24-hour direct modem connection."

The banks have to find a way of cutting staff and using technology without affecting the quality of service. "We have to take the bank to the customer" says Alan Higgins. "I do a lot of my day-to-day banking on a Sunday." However, in spite of the warnings about jobs, recent figures suggest that banks will continue to make record profits.

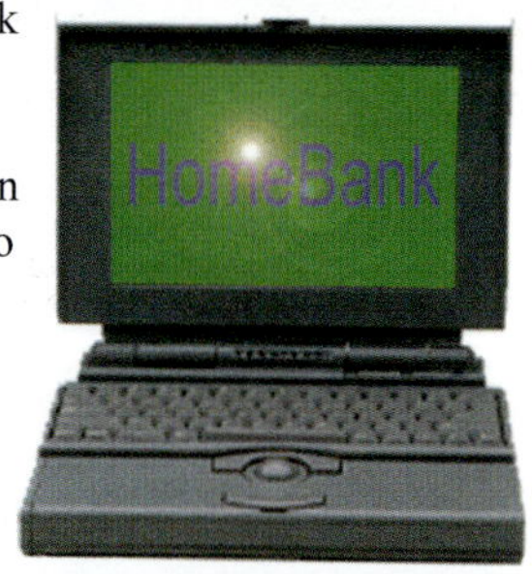

	France	Germany	Italy	Netherlands	Spain	Sweden	Switzerland	UK
Number of banks	627	3,730	1,004	128	315	107	395	591
Bank branches per million inhabitants	445	600	397	317	893	460	1,066	339
Average pre-tax return on capital 1996	9.6%	13.7%	8.8%	14.5%	17.1%	31.8%	5.0%	28.1%

Writing ❷ Take notes from the text under the following headings.

The banks' plans	Reasons for cutting costs	Banking services
Cut jobs		

❸ Choose the correct option to complete the sentences or answer the questions.

1 Over 20,000 jobs could be cut by
 A supermarkets and direct providers.
 B banks in the United Kingdom.
 C Swiss and German banks.

2 The banks have to cut staff costs
 A so they can finance IT investment.
 B in order to expand the branch network.
 C because they are losing money.

3 How does HomeBank work?
 A Customers telephone the bank during office hours.
 B The bank answers telephone calls 24 hours-a-day.
 C Customers do their banking on a home computer.

4 How are the banks performing?
 A They are making more money than ever before.
 B Increased competition means they are making less money.
 C The cost of IT investment has reduced profits.

Grammar ❹ Find words ending in *-ing* in the article. Write them in the groups below.

-ing as a noun	*-ing* after prepositions	*-ing* in the present continuous
cost-cutting		

Preposition + *-ing*

- Prepositions are usually followed by **-ing** or a noun.
  *Banks have to meet the costs **of** dealing with the euro.*
  *Banks are investing **in** new **technology**.*

Vocabulary **5** Complete the table with the correct verb or noun.

Verb	Noun	Verb	Noun
merge	merger	compete	....
....	increase	invest	....
reduce	....	....	closure
....	cut	....	development

Speaking **6** Work in pairs. What changes are taking place in your partner's sector?

Home banking

Listening 1 **1** John Barnard enquires about telephone banking. He has noted down some questions. Listen and take notes to answer his questions.

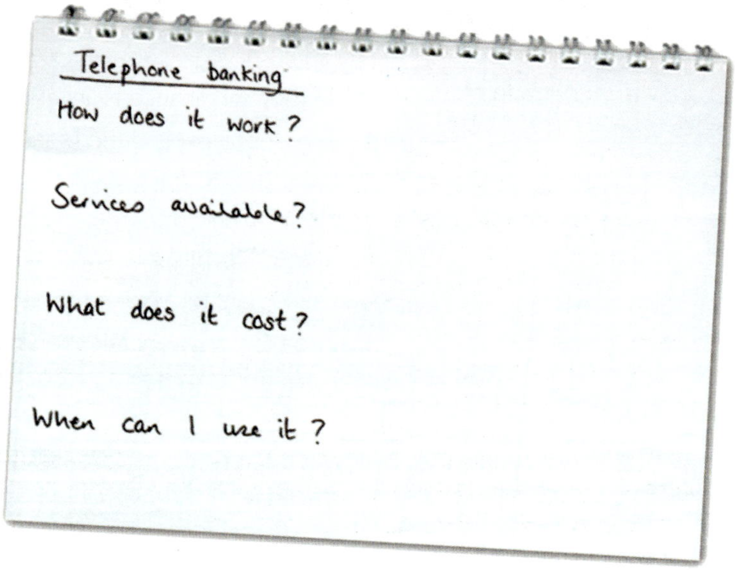

Listening 2 **2** John applies for the telephone banking service. Listen and complete the form.

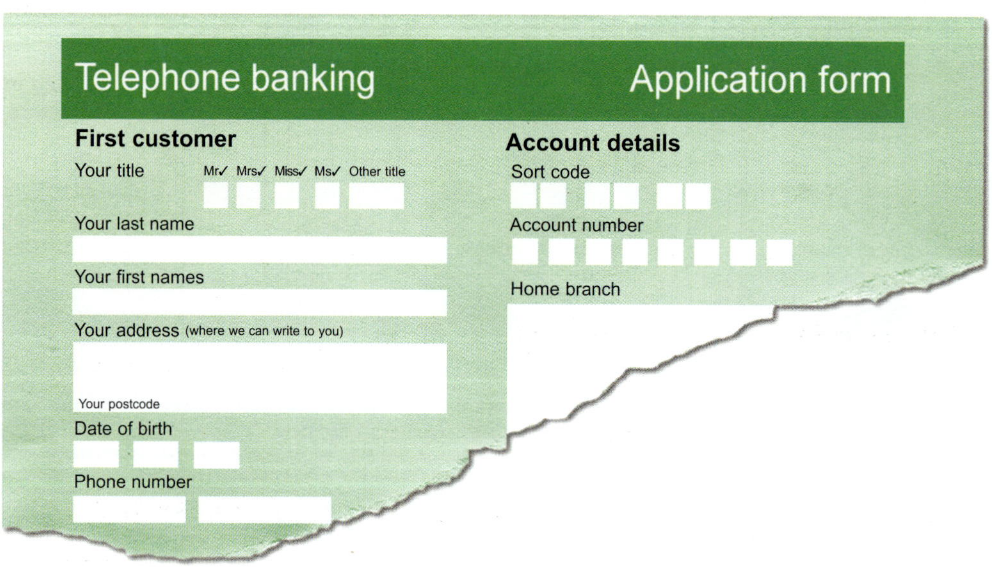

Telephone banking — **Application form**

First customer

Your title — Mr✓ Mrs✓ Miss✓ Ms✓ Other title

Your last name

Your first names

Your address (where we can write to you)

Your postcode

Date of birth

Phone number

Account details

Sort code

Account number

Home branch

Speaking **3** Work in pairs. What home banking services does your partner's bank offer? Does your partner use any of them? What other services would he/she like?

1 Complete the crossword.

Across
1 A print-out with information about your account.
4 A local office of a bank.
6 Abbreviation for European Monetary Union.
7 To make something smaller.
10 A plastic card with a computer chip on it.
11 The banks are still making a lot of it.
12 Abbreviation for information technology.

Down
2 Where you keep your money at the bank.
3 A joining together of two companies.
5 An area of economic activity.
8 A type of bank account.
9 The people who work for an organisation.
11 You need one for computer banking.

2 Match the verbs and nouns.

1 check	bills
2 transfer	a balance
3 pay	a form
4 order	a PIN number
5 sign	a statement
6 follow	money
7 key in	instructions

3 Match the words below to make phrases from the unit.

1 compete	in	a service
2 deal	with	a form
3 invest	down	another company
4 pay	in	some details
5 fill	for	problems
6 note	with	new technology

4 **Exam practice**

- Read the fax and note below.
- Complete the note to Jane Little.
- Write a word, phrase or number in spaces **1 - 5**.

To: Lisa Jones
Island Clothing Co.
From: Andy Smith
HomeBank Customer Services
Carlisle NSB
Date: 22 February 2001
Pages: 1

Hello Lisa

Here's the information you needed about using your computer for PC banking. Using your PC shouldn't be a problem as you can even use the software on old computers.

Anyway, what you need is an IBM compatible PC with a 386SX processor or higher. We recommend you use a computer with at least 4MB of RAM. You'll also need Windows software, version 3.0 or higher.

Finally, you'll need a fast modem. I hope that answers all your questions. If you need any more help, give me a call.

All the best

Andy

Peter

Jane in Accounts wants to know whether her computer is OK for PC banking. Here's a fax I received from the bank. Could you send her a note with the information she needs?

Thanks

Lisa

To: Jane Little
(1) ______________ Dept.
From: Peter Hargreaves

(2) ______________ contacted us with the information you wanted about PC banking.
Here are the requirements:

Processor **(3)** ______________
RAM **(4)** ______________
Software **(5)** ______________

Exam focus: Speaking

The Speaking Test

The Cambridge BEC Preliminary Speaking Test always takes place with two or three candidates and two examiners.

Part	Format	Input	Task
1	Examiner talks to both candidates	Examiner asks questions	Speaking about yourself Expressing preferences
2	Candidate talks to candidate	Written prompt	Giving a one-minute talk
3	Candidates discuss a topic together	Written prompt or visual prompt	Completing a collaborative task

Length: A total of 12 minutes.

How to succeed

During the Speaking Test one examiner will ask questions and give instructions. The second examiner in the Speaking Test does not speak to the candidates but is also there to assess your English. Here are some simple tips to remember in the test.

Interactive communication

- Listen carefully to all instructions and respond appropriately. Perfect grammar is useless if you do not answer the question you are asked.
- Ask the examiner to repeat any instructions you are not sure about.
- Give full answers, not just one or two words.
- Keep to and complete the task. Do not talk about other things.
- Good communication means helping the other candidate by asking questions, checking understanding and giving very clear information.
- Work **together** with the other candidate to complete the task in Part Two. Remember to speak to the other candidate and not the examiner.

Organisation of ideas

Show that you can organise your ideas. They can be organised in many ways, such as:

- sequence (*first of all, then, after that etc.*)
- importance (*I think the most important thing is …*)
- contrast (*but, although etc.*).

Grammar and vocabulary

- Do not try to use complicated words and structures. It is better to use simple words well than difficult ones badly.

Pronunciation

- Speak clearly and at a natural speed.
- Relax and think before you speak. It is better to pause before a sentence than in the middle of it.

Personal information

1 After introducing him/herself, the examiner will check that the information on the entry form is correct. He/she will then ask both candidates a few general questions. Write three questions for each of the topics below.

family	transport
free time	places to live

Now work in pairs. Ask and answer questions about the topics.

Speaking **2** Work in pairs. Your teacher will give you some cards with possible Cambridge BEC Preliminary conversation topics on them. Take a card and ask your partner about the topic on it. Then take another card and find a different partner.

Listening **3** Listen to Caroline and Cénéric doing Part One of a Speaking Test. Read the exam tips again and listen to the test. What do they do wrong?

4 Now listen to the same candidates doing Part One of the test again. Is it better this time? In what way?

Short talk

Speaking **1** The examiner will ask each candidate to talk about a given topic. Look at the following topic. Think of two things to say about each point.

What is important when ...?

Choosing which airline to fly with

- Price
- Safety record
- Customer service

2 Now look at the tips for Part Two of the Speaking Test below.

- Give an opinion about all the main points in the question.
- Use words such as *and*, *but*, *as well*, *because*, *so*.
- Think of a question to ask the other candidate.

Work in pairs. Discuss how you could improve your answer.

Listening **3** Listen to Cénéric doing Part Two of the Speaking Test. What does he do wrong?

4 Now listen to Caroline doing Part Two of the Speaking Test. What is the difference? Think of a question to ask her.

Speaking **5** Work in pairs. Look at the Activity sheet on page 131. Take it in turns to pick a topic and give a short talk. Remember to ask each other questions.

Collaborative task

Speaking **1** In Part Three of the Speaking Test the examiner will ask you and the other candidate to discuss a situation and try to reach a decision.

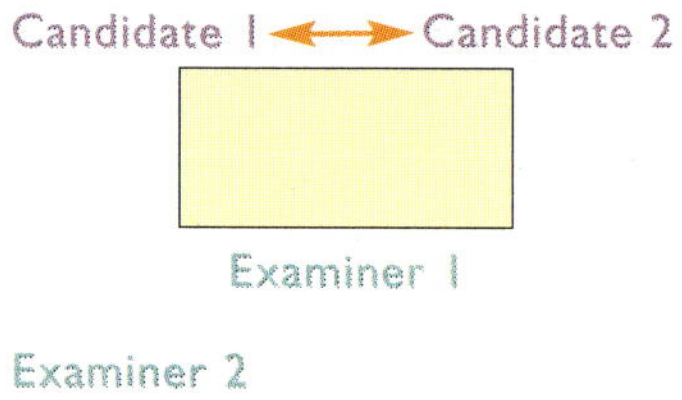

Look at the tips for Part Three of the Speaking Test below.

- Listen to the examiner very carefully.
- Ask the examiner to explain if you do not fully understand.
- Ask your partner what they think and react to their ideas.
- If you do not agree, say why and give a reason.

2 Work in pairs. Your teacher will read you a scenario. Look at the prompt below. Discuss the situation together to complete the task.

Listening **3** Now listen to Caroline and Cénéric complete Part Three of the Speaking Test. What do they do wrong?

4 Now listen to the same candidates do Part Three again. What are the differences between the way they do the two tests?

Speaking **5** Work in pairs. Look at the Activity sheet on page 132. Use the information to practise Part Three of the Cambridge BEC Preliminary Speaking Test.

Exam practice: Reading

Questions 1 - 5

- Read the memo and the information about office laser printers.
- Complete the form below.
- Write each word, phrase or number in **CAPITAL LETTERS**.

Close & Sons

Memo

To: Tim Nicholls
From: Rachel West
Date: 10 December 2001

New Colour Laser Printer

We'll have to order the new printer today or it won't be delivered before Christmas. Could you look at these 3 printers and choose one? We need a printer that is fast but not the most expensive. Could you place the order for me this morning and leave me a copy of the order form?

Thanks

	560Pro	Tek200	Pro-jet
Width	50cm	40cm	62cm
Depth	53cm	50cm	49cm
Height	40cm	33cm	37cm
Pages per min.	3	6	4-5
Memory	12MB	24MB	20MB
Price	£2995	£3495	£3900

ORDER FORM

Company name: **(1)** ....

Contact person: **(2)** ....

Date of order: **(3)** ....

Product: **(4)** ....

Price: **(5)** ....

Exam practice: Writing

Part One

- You have decided to work at home tomorrow.
- Write a note for your colleague:
  - * saying you won't be in the office tomorrow
  - * explaining why you are going to work from home
  - * giving your home telephone number.
- Write **30 - 40 words**.

Part Two

- You are visiting a trade fair in Barcelona with your boss. You have seen this hotel in a brochure.

Hotel Gaudí

Rambla de Catalunya 38, Barcelona

The Gaudí is situated in the heart of Barcelona city centre with its exciting nightlife. The hotel has 120 rooms including 42 business rooms specifically designed for the business traveller and fully-equipped with communication facilities.

The hotel enjoys direct bus and train connections to the airport (35 mins) and exhibition centre (25 mins). Other facilities include express check-in and check-out, 24-hour room service, two bars, restaurant, fitness room and full business centre.

- Write a memo to your boss:
  - * mentioning the hotel in the brochure
  - * describing some of the facilities listed
  - * saying why you think you both should stay there
  - * asking him which dates you should book.
- Write **60 - 80 words**.

Delivery services

Parcel carriers

Speaking 1 Work in pairs. Complete the information about UPS (United Parcel Service) with the figures below.

326,000	22 billion	3.04 billion
157,000	500	12 million

1 Its turnover is more than ________ dollars a year.
2 Each year UPS delivers ________ parcels and documents.
3 The company owns ________ vehicles (cars, vans, trailers etc.).
4 UPS also owns over ________ aircraft.
5 UPS delivers ________ parcels and documents daily.
6 The company employs about ________ people worldwide.

Reading 2 Now read the first part of the UPS brochure and check your answers.

Welcome to UPS

UPS is the world's largest package distribution company with an annual revenue of $22.5bn. Our customers understand our commitment to quality service and trust us to deliver over 12 million of their parcels and documents to over 200 countries every day. This means our 157,000 vehicles and over 500 aircraft deliver more than three billion parcels annually. The UPS Worldwide Guarantee ensures documents and packages arrive on time, every time. Because you can rely on us, your business partners can rely on you. Whichever UPS service you choose, our 326,000 employees guarantee its quality and reliability will be the same.

UPS Express Plus
This is UPS's fastest service for your most urgent documents and packages. It guarantees delivery by 8.30 am next day to hundreds of cities across Europe and the USA. The service also includes automatic confirmation of delivery by phone as soon as your shipment is delivered.

UPS Express
This is the ideal service for most of your urgent deliveries. It guarantees delivery by 10.30 am the next business day to over 200 countries. Full electronic tracking means confirmation of delivery is available within minutes in many cases.

UPS Expedited
UPS Expedited offers quality, reliability and scheduled delivery for your less urgent shipments. The service guarantees door-to-door deliveries within 48 hours. Full electronic tracking means confirmation of delivery is available within minutes in many cases.

UPS Standard
The UPS Standard service offers the benefits of UPS's quality,

Reading 3 Match the phrases below with one of the features of the UPS services.

1 Only UPS Express Plus guarantees ...
2 All three services provide ...
3 With UPS Expedited you can arrange ...
4 Both UPS Express Plus and Express guarantee ...

A same day delivery
B next day delivery
C delivery to only EU countries
D next day delivery by 8.30am
E confirmation of delivery
F worldwide next day delivery by 10.30am
G delivery on a particular day

Vocabulary 4 Read through the brochure again and find examples of the following.

- words and phrases that are repeated several times
- words and phrases written to impress the reader

Don't forget!

Prepositions of time

- **By/until**. **By** refers to a point in time. **Until** refers to a period of time.
  *I can do it **by** 10 o'clock. (I can finish it sometime before 10 o'clock.)*
  *We'll wait **until** 10 o'clock. (We'll wait for the period between now and 10 o'clock.)*
- **Within** refers to a period of time. It can always be replaced by **in**.
  *We can deliver the package **within** two days.*
- **In/on time**. You arrange to meet a colleague at 1 o'clock.
  *Don't worry, she'll arrive **in time**. (She'll arrive before 1 o'clock.)*
  *Don't worry, she'll arrive **on time**. (She'll arrive at exactly 1 o'clock.)*

5 Match the following sentence halves.

1 Don't worry, an Expedited parcel will arrive in	3.30.
2 An Express parcel will get there within	two days.
3 To arrive tomorrow, the package needs to leave by	on time.
4 I'll stay here until	in time.
5 It arrived at 8.30, which was exactly	24 hours.
6 We sent it by UPS Express, so it should arrive	UPS collects the parcel.

Speaking 6 Work in pairs. Which three of the following features do you think are the most important for a parcel delivery service?

next day delivery	reliability	global network
confirmation of delivery	low prices	high quality of service

Sending a parcel

Reading **1** Your company wants to send three packages to different countries. How much will each item cost?

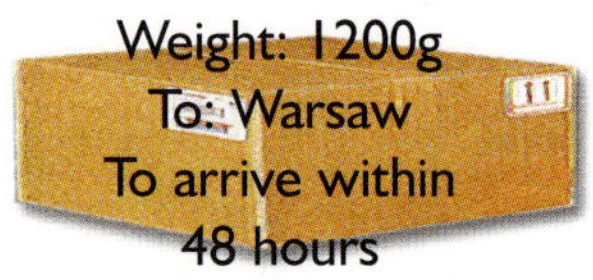

How to use the guide

All shipping charges are based on three considerations: the service selected, the weight of the shipment and the zone number for the destination. To find the correct rate for your shipment, follow these three steps:

1 Select your service
UPS offers a choice of Express, Expedited or Standard. Refer to the zone chart to see which services are available.

2 Select the zone
Locate the destination country and find its zone number.

3 Find the rate
Turn to the rate chart and match the shipment rate with the correct zone number.

zone chart

Destination	Express	Expedited
Finland EU	4	
Poland	5	
United States *For areas below* New Jersey: 07000 - 07999, 08500 - 08999; New York: 10000 - 11999	6	2
Other destinations	7	3

...kage shipments

Express Packages

Weight	zone 4 £	zone 5 £	zone 6 £	zone 7 £	zone 8 £
0.5 kg	27.70	33.50	28.50	34.00	37.50
1.0 kg	31.90	36.80	31.00	37.00	42.00
1.5 kg	34.50	39.40	33.00	40.00	46.50
2.0 kg	37.10	42.00	35.00	43.00	49.10
2.5 kg	39.70	44.60	37.00	46.00	51.70
3.0 kg	42.30	47.20	38.80	48.30	54.30

Expedited Packages

Weight	zone 1 £	zone 2 £	zone 3 £	zone 4 £	zone 5 £
1.0 kg	35.80	27.40	34.25	37.80	37.80
2.0 kg	40.80	31.20	38.75	43.40	43.40
3.0 kg	45.80	34.60	43.25	48.90	48.90
4.0 kg	50.00	38.00	47.75	54.30	54.30
5.0 kg	54.20	41.40	52.25	59.70	59.70
6.0 kg	57.20	43.00	55.05	63.70	64.10

Speaking **2** Work in pairs. What kind of parcel delivery service does your partner's company use? Why?

3 What other ways are there to send documents and parcels abroad? What are the advantages and disadvantages of each method?

4 Work in pairs. Your teacher will give you two sets of cards showing items and destinations. Take one from each set and decide the best way to send the item to that destination.

1 Complete the sentences with the prepositions.

in	on	by	until	within

1 We sent it by Express Plus so it should arrive __by__ 8.30 tomorrow morning.

2 We chose UPS Expedited in order to guarantee delivery ________ 24 hours.

3 She's very punctual. She always arrives exactly ________ time.

4 If you e-mail it, it'll get there ________ minutes.

5 We can't send it ________ we've weighed it.

6 If you want delivery ________ a particular day, you can send it Expedited for scheduled delivery.

7 It needs to arrive ________ tomorrow so we'll have to send it Express.

8 Please wait ________ I inform you that I have received the package.

2 Complete the sentences with the words below.

destinations	urgent
charge	weight
documents	packages
vehicles	rate

1 UPS will deliver both your ____________ and parcels.

2 If you have the zone and the weight, you can work out the delivery ______________.

3 Most UPS delivery ______________ are vans.

4 You can send really ______________ parcels to arrive before 8.30am the following day.

5 There is a standard postal ______________ for EU countries.

6 They deliver to ______________ in almost every country.

7 It is more expensive to send heavy ____________ by post than by parcel delivery services.

8 The cost of the service depends on the ______________ of the package and the speed of the service.

3 Exam practice

- Look at questions **1 - 5**.
- In each question, which phrase or sentence is correct?
- For each question, mark the correct letter **A**, **B** or **C**.

1

> **For additional charges, please refer to page 10.**

You should turn to page 10

A to see about possible discounts.
B to find out about extra costs.
C for information about the product.

2

> **Guaranteed delivery within 48 hours.**

The parcel will arrive

A in less than two days from now.
B in exactly two days' time.
C in at least two days' time.

3

> **Export documentation may be required for non-EU destinations.**

Packages sent outside the EU

A must be documents only.
B will need special documents.
C might need special documents.

4

> **Payment to be made by cash on delivery.**

The invoice has to be paid

A after the shipment arrives.
B before the shipment arrives.
C when the shipment arrives.

5

> **Transport papers must include an approximate value of the shipment.**

The transport documents have to show

A how much the shipment is worth.
B the delivery charges for the shipment.
C a list of what is in the shipment.

Unit 16b

Trading

An import agent

Listening ❶ Raupack Ltd is a small company based near London. Listen to Wolfgang Rauch, the Managing Director, and complete the factfile.

FACTFILE

Company Raupack Ltd

Activities Agent for German packing machine manufacturers.

Services
- Provides UK sales network.
- (1) ________________ documents, specifications and (2) ________________ lists.
- Deals with customer enquiries and (3) ________________.
- Arranges (4) ________________ ________________.

Founded In (5) ________________.

Customers Major companies include SmithKline Beecham, Boots and (6) ________________.

❷ Listen again and choose the best phrase to complete the sentence.

1 Wolfgang Rauch left his job in 1982 because
   A he did not like the company.
   B he saw a good business opportunity.
   C the company had financial problems.

2 Raupack expanded because
   A its suppliers built very good machines.
   B the whole market grew very quickly.
   C its prices were very low.

3 Raupack became known for the
   A fair prices of its products.
   B quality of its products and service.
   C skill of its sales people.

4 Raupack's suppliers will have to develop
   A their machines and customer support services.
   B reliable and low priced machines.
   C technically advanced and reliable machines.

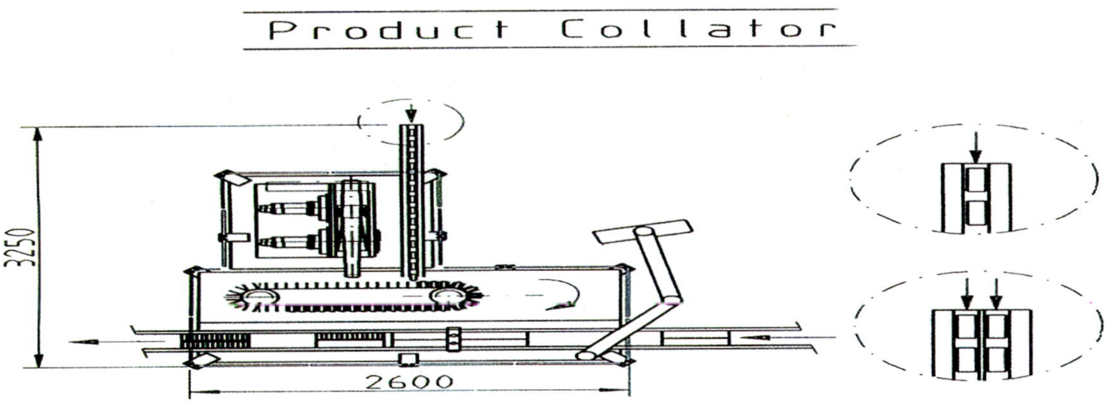

Speaking 3 Work in pairs. Your teacher will give you some cards describing how a customer orders parts through Raupack. Read the cards and put the process into the correct order.

1 Now decide which of the faxes or letters is
- an enquiry
- a quotation
- confirmation
- an invoice

2 Which of the faxes or letters would be
- in English?
- in German?

Grammar 4 Look at the tapescript on page 143. Underline examples of the following tenses. How does Mr Rauch use them?

1 Present simple — company activities (e.g. *we translate their documents*)
   opinions (e.g. *I think*)

2 Past simple ____________________

3 Present perfect ____________________

4 Present continuous ____________________

Speaking 5 Work in pairs. Ask your partner questions and write a factfile for his/her company.

Ordering parts

Reading ❶ A customer has received a quotation from Raupack. Read the letter and Jenny's note and choose the best phrase to complete the sentences.

RAUPACK LTD

11 CASTLE STREET
GUILDFORD
SURREY
GU1 6KG

Tel: (01483) 564700
Fax: (01483) 564710
e-mail: sales@raupack.com

Fax no: 32725

Date: 09.04.01
To: Eversham Dairy Products
FAO: Jennifer Tanner

Dear Ms Tanner

Re: Parts Quotation for SM300/Machine type 3000.002.93

Thank you for your enquiry. We are pleased to quote as follows:

Qty	Description	Parts No	Unit Price
100	Tension spring	RZ-0531 9907.15	
10	Starting disc	3000.010.19	
4	Grooved bearing	6007-2RS1 9908	
1	Level switch	WF02	

Could you write back to Raupack and order these spares? Could you also ask how much the extra costs will be and how long they'll take to get here. Thanks.
Jenny

The above prices are quoted in euros and are ex works in Germany. These prices do not include packing, transport, insurance and VAT. Our standard terms and conditions apply.

The parts would be ready for despatch from Germany approximately six weeks after receipt of the order.

Kind regards

Gisela Mason

Gisela Mason
RAUPACK LTD

1 The customer would like to
A buy some spare parts for a machine.
B buy a new packing machine.
C enquire about a new machine.

2 The letter is in reply to a
A confirmation of an order.
B request for information.
C letter of complaint.

3 The customer has to pay
A no extra costs.
B only import tax.
C all extra costs.

4 The order could
A leave the factory in about six weeks.
B be delivered in about six weeks.
C leave the factory immediately.

Speaking ❷ Work in pairs. Find five things your partner's company orders. Does it order them by telephone, fax, e-mail or letter? Which type of communication is best? Why?

Writing ❸ Work in pairs. Read the note again and write a reply to Raupack. Write 50 - 60 words. Plan your letter carefully with your partner before you write it.

1 Look at the tapescript on page 142. Find the nouns that go with the verbs below.

1 deal with — ...customers... / .... / ....

2 translate — .... / .... / ....

3 provide — .... / .... / ....

2 Match the sentence halves about the history of Raupack.

1 Mr Rauch began by ... G

2 The company's smaller suppliers wanted ...

3 So Mr Rauch set up ...

4 His suppliers were very good at ...

5 Moreover, his company developed a name for ...

6 Raupack is now looking for new staff ...

7 In the future, suppliers will have to develop the machines technically without ...

8 And Raupack will have to continue ...

A the quality of its products and service.

B developing technically advanced machines.

C someone to sell only their machines.

D to provide the best possible service.

E to help the company grow.

F losing any of their reliability.

G working in sales for an international company.

H his own company.

3 Re-arrange the words to make phrases from a written quotation.

1 you / enquiry / thank / your / for

____

2 pleased / to / follows / we / quote / are / as

____

3 apply / our / conditions / terms / standard / and

____

4 in / is / price / quoted / euros / the

____

5 does / price / include / the / not / VAT

____

6 hearing / forward / from / look / we / to / you

____

4 **Exam practice**

- Look at the checklist below. It shows the documents **A - H** which are needed to export machinery.
- For questions **1 - 5**, decide which documents **A - H** the people are talking about.
- For each question, mark the correct letter **A - H**.
- Do not use any letter more than once.

A Shipping papers
B Drawings
C Invoice
D Specifications
E Handbook
F Parts list
G Registration form
H Guarantee

1 2% discount if payment is within ten days.

2 The customer fills it in and returns it in order to go on our customer mailing list

3 If they aren't correct, the machine won't get through customs.

4 It's translated so the engineers know how to operate the machine properly.

5 We normally mark on it the spares that we think the customer should always keep in stock.

Recruiting staff

Recruitment methods

Speaking **1** Work in pairs. How many different ways can a company recruit applicants to fill a job vacancy?

Reading **2** Read the magazine article about recruiting staff and complete the diagram on the opposite page.

profile

The right person for the right job

Finding the right job applicant to fill a vacancy is never easy. ***Julie Bain*** *looks at the pros and cons of different recruitment methods.*

Recruiting the right candidate to fill a vacancy can be a difficult and costly task. Appointing the wrong person could be an expensive mistake which could cause personnel problems for the whole department. And, as every HR Manager knows, it is much more difficult to get rid of someone than it is to employ them.

The HR Manager's first decision is whether to recruit internal applicants or advertise the vacancy outside the company. Internal applicants are easy to recruit by memo, e-mail or newsletter. Furthermore, they are easy to assess and know the company well. However, they rarely bring fresh ideas to a position. Moreover, a rejected internal candidate might become unhappy and leave the company.

Recruiting outside the company means either advertising the vacancy directly or using an employment agency. If the company decides to advertise the vacancy directly, it has to decide where to place the advertisement. Traditionally this has meant newspapers and professional journals but now the Internet is also very popular. The decision normally depends on the vacancy. Companies advertise blue-collar or clerical jobs in local newspapers and senior management positions in national papers or professional journals, while the Internet is one of the best ways of advertising IT vacancies or recruiting abroad. However, with the Internet there is a risk of receiving unsuitable applications from all over the world.

An agency can be either a commercial business or a government employment centre. A company often uses a government agency to recruit blue-collar workers but normally prefers a commercial agency for its white-collar staff. However, a commercial agency could be very expensive and the applicants are less likely to stay with the company for a long time.

3 What are the advantages and disadvantages of each recruitment method?

4 Look at the following extracts from the article and answer the questions.

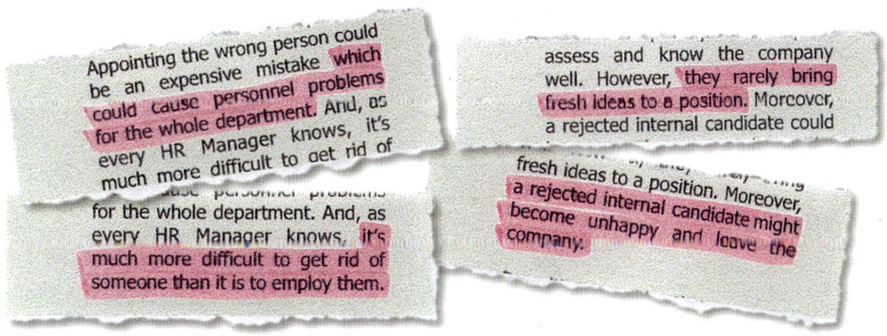

Appointing the wrong person could be an expensive mistake which could cause personnel problems for the whole department. And, as every HR Manager knows, it's much more difficult to get rid of

for the whole department. And, as every HR Manager knows, it's much more difficult to get rid of someone than it is to employ them.

assess and know the company well. However, they rarely bring fresh ideas to a position. Moreover, a rejected internal candidate could

fresh ideas to a position. Moreover, a rejected internal candidate might become unhappy and leave the company.

1 How could the wrong candidate cause problems for the whole department?
2 Why is it difficult to get rid of someone?
3 Why don't internal applicants have fresh ideas?
4 Why might an unsuccessful candidate leave the company?

Don't forget!

Hypothetical situations

- We can use **would** to talk about the expected results of a hypothetical situation.
  *A large company **would** advertise in a national newspaper.*
- We can use **could**/**might** to talk about the possible results of a hypothetical situation.
  *Appointing the wrong person **could**/**might** be an expensive mistake.*

Speaking 5 Work in pairs. How would you advertise the following vacancies?

finance director	graphic designer	marketing manager
bilingual secretary	truck driver	computer programmer

Advertising a vacancy

Reading ❶ Read the two advertisements below and answer the questions.

1 Where would the advertisements appear?
2 How is the information organised in the two advertisements?
3 What extra information does the newspaper advertisement include?
4 Which advertisement tries to "sell" the position more? How?

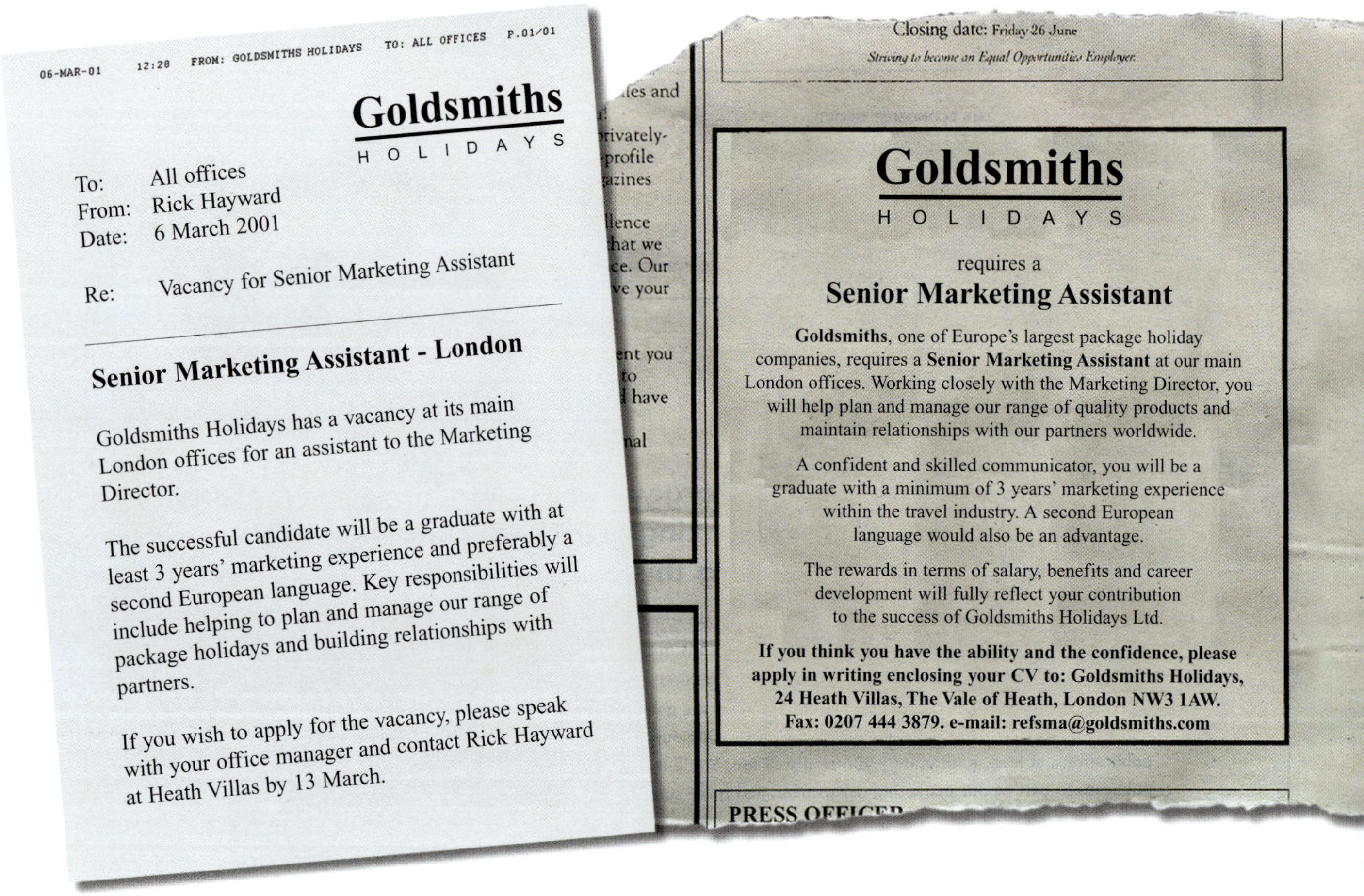

06-MAR-01 12:28 FROM: GOLDSMITHS HOLIDAYS TO: ALL OFFICES P.01/01

Goldsmiths
HOLIDAYS

To: All offices
From: Rick Hayward
Date: 6 March 2001

Re: Vacancy for Senior Marketing Assistant

Senior Marketing Assistant - London

Goldsmiths Holidays has a vacancy at its main London offices for an assistant to the Marketing Director.

The successful candidate will be a graduate with at least 3 years' marketing experience and preferably a second European language. Key responsibilities will include helping to plan and manage our range of package holidays and building relationships with partners.

If you wish to apply for the vacancy, please speak with your office manager and contact Rick Hayward at Heath Villas by 13 March.

Closing date: Friday 26 June
Striving to become an Equal Opportunities Employer.

Goldsmiths
HOLIDAYS

requires a
Senior Marketing Assistant

Goldsmiths, one of Europe's largest package holiday companies, requires a **Senior Marketing Assistant** at our main London offices. Working closely with the Marketing Director, you will help plan and manage our range of quality products and maintain relationships with our partners worldwide.

A confident and skilled communicator, you will be a graduate with a minimum of 3 years' marketing experience within the travel industry. A second European language would also be an advantage.

The rewards in terms of salary, benefits and career development will fully reflect your contribution to the success of Goldsmiths Holidays Ltd.

If you think you have the ability and the confidence, please apply in writing enclosing your CV to: Goldsmiths Holidays, 24 Heath Villas, The Vale of Heath, London NW3 1AW. Fax: 0207 444 3879. e-mail: refsma@goldsmiths.com

Listening ❷ Two HR managers discuss the vacancy at Goldsmiths. Listen to the conversation. Which advertisement do they decide to place first? Why?

❸ Listen again. What are the disadvantages of each type of advertisement?

Grammar ❹ Look at the tapescript on page 142. Underline all the verbs in the past simple. How many of them refer to the past? What do the others refer to? Now complete the information below.

Don't forget!

Hypothetical conditionals

- We can use the following conditional forms to talk about the results of an action which we do not expect to happen.

If + ______________ tense, ______________ + infinitive
(would / ______________ / ______________)

Speaking ❺ Work in pairs. How would your partner recruit people for his/her own job?

1 Choose the best word to complete the sentences.

1 We had over 30 *applicants/assistants* for the vacancy we advertised in the local paper.
2 I had to fill in *a CV/an application form* and return it to the Personnel Department.
3 We *appointed/filled* someone to the position over two weeks ago.
4 We advertised the *employment/vacancy* on the Internet.
5 We need to *apply/recruit* ten more people before the summer.
6 I am going to interview the *candidates/appointments* tomorrow.

2 Look back through the unit and tapescript. Find three words to go with each of the following.

1 ....
.... a vacancy
....

2 ....
.... applicants
....

3 ....
recruit ....
....

4 ....
advertise ....
....

3 Complete the sentences below. Use your own words.

1 If I decided to change my job,
I'd look for a different type of work.

2 If you wanted to recruit more people to work in your department,
____

3 If I lost my job,
____

4 If I worked abroad,
____

5 Would you accept it if
____

4 **Exam practice**

- **Look at the graphs below. They show the passenger volumes for eight different airlines.**
- **Which airline does each sentence 1-5 describe?**
- **For each sentence, mark the correct letter A-H.**
- **Do not use any letter more than once.**

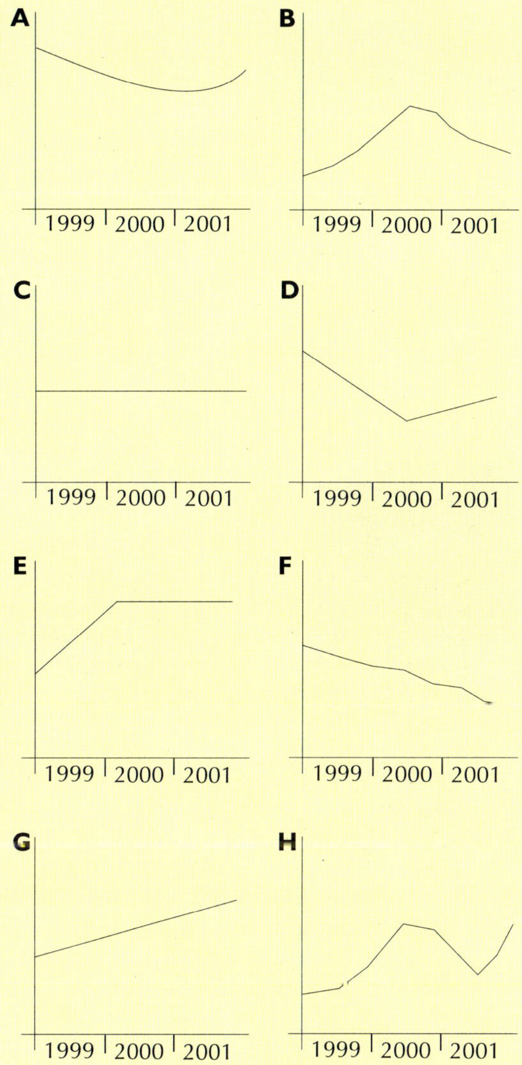

1 After a sharp fall in 2000, business recovered slightly the following year.

2 Passenger volumes showed strong growth in 1999 but levelled off in 2000.

3 The number of passengers decreased steadily throughout the three year period.

4 Passenger volumes peaked in 2000 and then fell steadily afterwards.

5 The number of passengers remained steady between 1999 and 2001.

Applying for a job

Application letters

Reading ❶ Almudena Ribera is a secretary in Madrid. She is looking for work in Britain and replies to the advertisement below. Read the advertisement and answer the questions.

1 What do the following abbreviations mean?
£16K   O/T   60wpm   langs
2 Is the position permanent or temporary?
3 What are the duties?
4 What skills are required for the job?
5 What personal qualities are looked for?

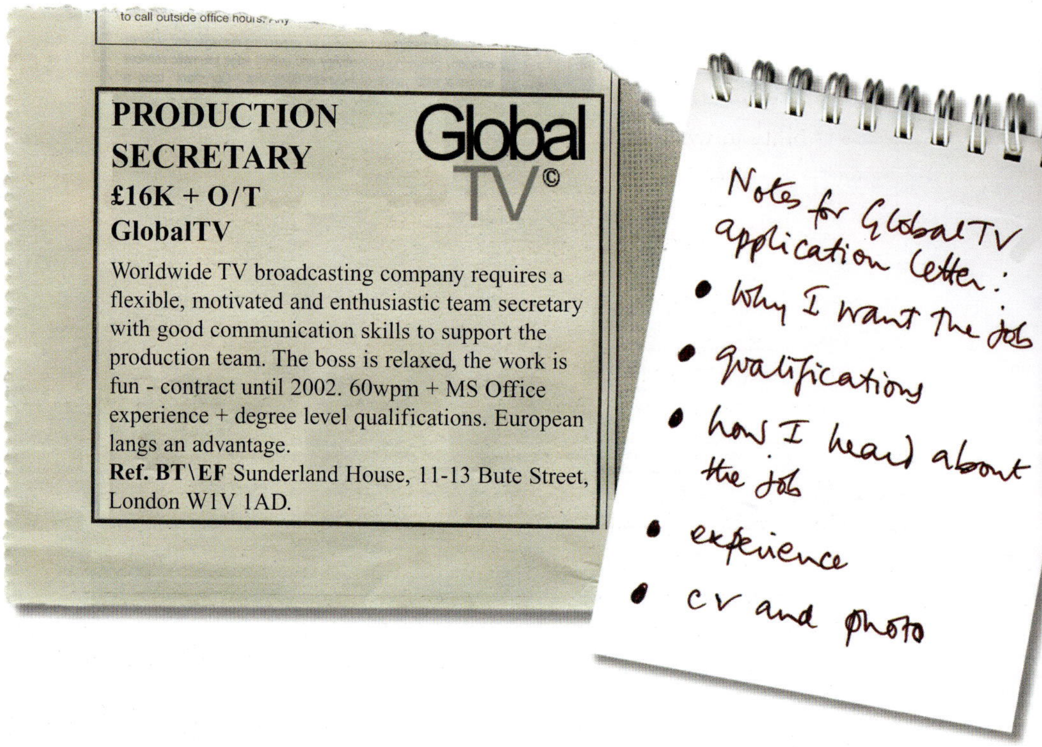

PRODUCTION SECRETARY
£16K + O/T
GlobalTV

Worldwide TV broadcasting company requires a flexible, motivated and enthusiastic team secretary with good communication skills to support the production team. The boss is relaxed, the work is fun - contract until 2002. 60wpm + MS Office experience + degree level qualifications. European langs an advantage.
Ref. BT\EF Sunderland House, 11-13 Bute Street, London W1V 1AD.

❷ Almudena begins to plan her application letter. Put her notes above into the correct order for the letter. How many paragraphs should there be?

❸ Match the phrases below with Almudena's notes.

1 I am writing with reference to your advertisement in the ...
2 I graduated from Madrid University with a degree in ...
3 Since 1996 I have been working as ...
4 I am very interested in the position because ...
5 Please find enclosed ...

Writing ❹ Work in pairs. Write Almudena's letter of application to GlobalTV. Decide what information you should include. Use the phrases above and the information in the curriculum vitae (CV) on the opposite page.

Attending an interview

Listening ❶ Almudena attends an interview at GlobalTV. Before you listen, read the HR Manager's notes about Almudena's CV. Change his notes on the CV into polite questions. Then listen and compare your questions with his.

CURRICULUM VITAE
ALMUDENA

Duncan
Thanks for agreeing to do the interview for me on Tuesday. Here's the candidate's CV – I've marked a few things you should ask her about. And don't forget to take notes!
Thanks

Personal details

Name: **Almudena Ribera**
Address: c/ Lozano n°24 1°B 28019 MA
Telephone: 00 34 91 6342918
Date of birth: 10.02.1973
Marital status: Single
Nationality: Spanish

Key skills

- Ability to work to deadlines.
- Experience of dealing with clients in different countries. – *Which countries?*
- Good written and spoken knowledge of English and Italian. – *What about French?*
- Good keyboard skills and knowledge of current software packages.

Work experience

Wpm?

1996 - present
Ediciones Gómez S.A., Madrid
Currently working as a bilingual secretary for Ediciones Gómez, a Madrid-based publisher. Duties include dealing with international partners both on the phone and in writing, sending invoices, making arrangements for visitors and general office duties.

1994 1996 – *Why did she leave?*
Informática S.A., Madrid
Which software?
Support Secretary for the Training Director. Used various software packages. Assisted the Director in the organisation of training courses for software designers and presentations to IT managers. Responsibilities also included dealing with correspondence and general office duties.

What kind? With computers?

Summer work 1992 -1994
Instituto Calderón de la Barca, Madrid
Teaching Spanish as a foreign language. Duties included planning and teaching Spanish lessons to adults. I also organised cultural trips to museums and exhibitions.

Qualifications

1991 - 1994
Complutense University, Madrid
Graduated with an honours degree in Modern European Languages, specialising in English and Italian. The degree also included French language studies, English commercial correspondence and IT skills.

- 1 -

❷ Now listen again and write down Almudena's answers to the questions.

Grammar **3** Look at the direct and indirect forms of the question below. What are the grammatical differences?

- Which programs do you use?
- Could you tell me which programs you use?

- Can you leave your present job immediately?
- Could you tell me if you can leave your present job immediately?

Speaking **4** Work in pairs. Imagine your partner is applying for a job at GlobalTV. Complete the application form with your partner's details.

Please write clearly in BLOCK CAPITALS.

Global TV©

Position applied for:

Title:

Full name:

Nationality:

Marital status:

Date of birth:

Address:

Phone number:

e-mail:

Current employment:

Higher education:

Professional qualifications:

Computer skills:

Language skills:

Interests:

Signature: *Date:*

5 Work in pairs. Look at the interview questions below. How would you answer them?

What don't you like about your current position?

Where does your employer think you are today?

What are your professional objectives?

What are your weaknesses?

Now look at the text **Attending interviews** on the opposite page. It contains a recruitment consultant's advice on how to answer these questions. Do you agree?

1 Rewrite the following as indirect questions.

1 Where is the interview room?

Could you tell me where the interview room is?

2 Where do you work at the moment?

____

3 Does the position include a pension?

____

4 How did you hear about the vacancy?

____

5 Is there any training?

____

6 What is your present salary?

____

2 Complete the diagram with vocabulary from the unit.

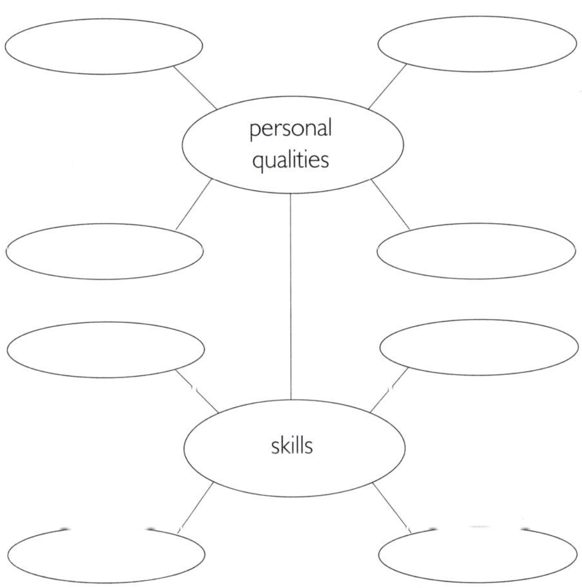

3 Re-arrange the following words to make phrases from a letter of application.

1 Please / copy / my / CV / a / find / enclosed / of

____

2 I / because / position / am / in / the / interested / very

____

3 Since / as / been / have / 1996 / I / working

____

4 I / reference / am / advertisement / writing / with / to / your

____

4 **Exam practice**

- Read the text below which advises candidates how to answer difficult interview questions.
- Are the sentences below 'Right' or 'Wrong'?
- If there is not enough information to answer 'Right' or 'Wrong', choose 'Doesn't say'.
- For each question, mark the correct letter **A**, **B** or **C**.

Attending interviews

Good interviewers prepare their questions carefully in advance according to the candidate's application and CV. So candidates need to prepare just as carefully. Here are some useful tips on answering interview questions.

1 What don't you like about your current position?
No job is perfect; there's always something we don't like. Be honest but don't give a list of complaints. The important thing is to talk positively about how you deal with problems at work.
2 Where does your employer think you are today?
Be honest. If you lie to your current employer, you'll lie to your next employer. Don't phone in sick on the day of the interview. Take a day's holiday but don't say why.
3 What are your professional objectives?
Think about these before the interview. Your objectives should be relevant to the job you have applied for and achievable. If the new job can't offer you everything you want, the interviewer will think that you probably won't stay with the company very long.
4 What are your weaknesses?
Be honest: no-one is perfect. Think about this before the interview and choose your answer carefully. Talk about how you deal with a weakness; this is far more important than the weakness itself.

1 Interviewers ask every candidate the same questions.
A Right **B** Wrong **C** Doesn't say

2 You shouldn't mention problems with your current job.
A Right **B** Wrong **C** Doesn't say

3 You should arrange to have a day off for the interview.
A Right **B** Wrong **C** Doesn't say

4 You should give your personal objectives.
A Right **B** Wrong **C** Doesn't say

5 Your objectives should suit the position you apply for.
A Right **B** Wrong **C** Doesn't say

6 You should practise your answers at home.
A Right **B** Wrong **C** Doesn't say

7 You shouldn't discuss things you aren't good at.
A Right **B** Wrong **C** Doesn't say

Exam practice

Reading and Writing Test

Reading

Questions 1 - 5

- Look at questions **1 - 5**.
- In each question, which phrase or sentence is correct?
- For each question, mark the correct letter **A**, **B** or **C**.

1

The Supplies Department will provide overalls.

The company provides
A an overcoat.
B a uniform.
C a suit.

2

Mrs Rothe called - she's unavailable for the meeting tomorrow.

Mrs Rothe will
A be late for the meeting tomorrow.
B take part in the meeting tomorrow.
C not be at the meeting tomorrow.

3

8.7.01 Mike called yesterday to say he's flying to Turkey tomorrow.

Mike is flying to Turkey on
A 7 July.
B 8 July.
C 9 July.

4

European sales have recovered this year.

Compared to last year, European sales have
A improved.
B remained steady.
C decreased.

5

Thank you for your enquiry of 18 February.

The company received a letter asking for
A a delivery date.
B information.
C an order.

Questions 6 - 10

- Look at the graphs **A - H** below. They show how eight different companies recruited staff over a four-year period.
- Which company does each sentence **6 - 10** describe?
- For each question, mark the correct letter.
- Do not use any letter more than once.

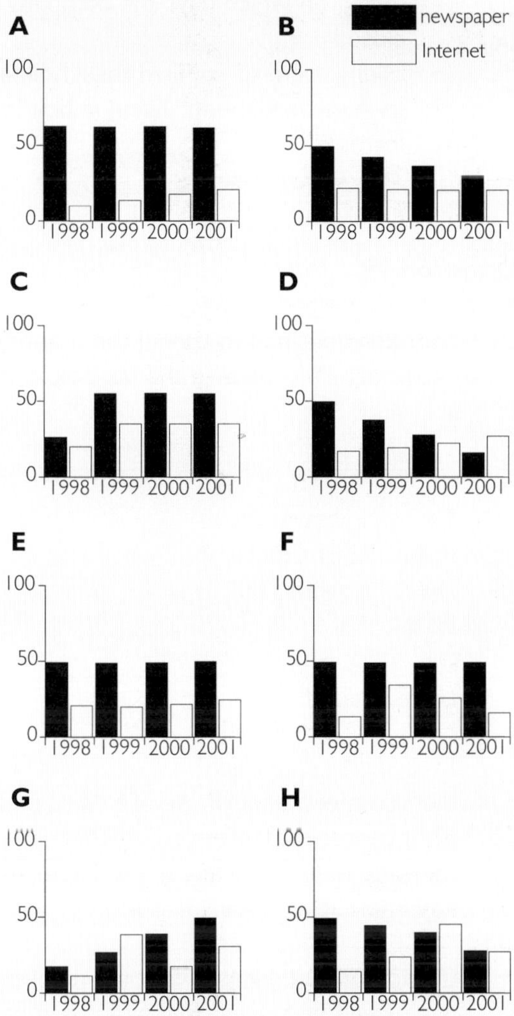

6 While recruitment through newspapers fell, the number of employees recruited via the Internet rose steadily throughout the period.

7 Recruitment through national newspapers remained constant, whereas after an increase in 1999 Internet recruitment fell steadily.

8 The number of staff recruited through both methods levelled off after a sharp rise.

9 Internet recruitment peaked in 2000, while newspaper recruitment fell steadily from 1999 to 2001.

10 While the rate of Internet recruitment fluctuated over the four-year period, there was a steady rise in recruitment through newspapers over the same period.

Questions 11 - 22

- Read the newspaper article below about a new alliance in the packaging industry.
- Choose the correct word from **A**, **B** or **C** below.

Packaging alliance

This week sees more changes in the packaging world. DD Holdings, the UK group, has **(11)** ..... an alliance with three other European packaging companies. The company hopes the alliance will help **(12)** ..... members to win more orders from multinational pharmaceutical groups.

There is a **(13)** ..... trend in the pharmaceutical industry for large multinationals to use pan-European suppliers. **(14)** ..... has presented problems particularly for small and medium-sized companies **(15)** ..... produce in just one country.

DD Holdings, based in Yorkshire, is teaming up **(16)** ..... partners in France, Germany and Spain to form an alliance called Pharmapak. **(17)** ..... the partners will continue to work **(18)** ..... separate companies, they will share **(19)** ..... of their sales and marketing resources. The deal **(20)** ..... customers with the opportunity to negotiate Europe-wide contracts.

DD is the **(21)** ..... of the four companies, with 15 production facilities throughout Europe and **(22)** ..... annual turnover of about £120m.

11	**A** announced	**B** advised	**C** alerted
12	**A** our	**B** its	**C** their
13	**A** grown	**B** growth	**C** growing
14	**A** These	**B** This	**C** That
15	**A** which	**B** what	**C** who
16	**A** with	**B** to	**C** in
17	**A** However	**B** Despite	**C** Although
18	**A** as	**B** than	**C** that
19	**A** some	**B** any	**C** lot
20	**A** provided	**B** provides	**C** provide
21	**A** largest	**B** larger	**C** large
22	**A** some	**B** a	**C** an

Questions 23 - 27

- Read the memo and the information about office laser printers.
- Complete the form below.
- Write each word, phrase or number in **CAPITAL LETTERS**.

Memo

To: Jane Little
From: Howard Morgan
Date: Thursday 2 July

Epcom visit on Friday

Could you book some theatre tickets for tomorrow for the five Epcom visitors and me? We'll be in a meeting all day until about 4.30 and then we'll have an early dinner together at the hotel. Could you phone the ticket agency and find a play or something that starts after half past seven? Use the company VISA card to pay for the tickets.

<u>**What's on: Theatre**</u>
Hamlet at the Barbican.
Performances start at 19.15. Tickets £8.50 - £44
West Side Story at the Playhouse. Show starts at 19.00. Tickets £7 - £55
Buddy Holly at the Palace Theatre.
Performances at 15.30 and 20.00. Tickets £8 - £60

BOOKING

Name of show: **(23)** ....

Venue: **(24)** ....

Date: **(25)** ....

Time: **(26)** ....

No. of tickets: **(27)** ....

Writing

Question 28

- It is the beginning of December and you have been asked to find out how many days' holiday staff in your department intend to take over Christmas.
- Write a memo to all staff in the department:
  - * saying on which days the company is closed
  - * asking them to confirm their holidays
  - * giving a deadline for filling in holiday forms.
- Write **30 - 40 words**.

Question 29

- You had arranged to meet Christine Hendrikson but had to cancel the meeting at short notice. You receive the fax below from her.

To: Fiona Andrews
From: Christine Hendrikson
Date: 8 April 2002
Pages: 1

Dear Fiona

I received a message this morning saying that our meeting on Friday 12 April had been cancelled. Unfortunately, the message didn't give any more details or any alternative dates.

Could you just confirm that the meeting has indeed been cancelled and possibly suggest another date?

Best regards

Christine

- Write a fax to Christine:
  - * apologising for cancelling the meeting
  - * giving a reason for the cancellation
  - * offering a new date and time
  - * asking her to confirm the new date and time.
- Write **60 - 80 words**.

Listening Test

Questions 30 - 37

- For questions **30 - 37**, you will hear eight short recordings.
- For each question, mark one letter **A**, **B** or **C**.
- You will hear each recording twice.

30 What does Alison order?

A Fish
B Steak
C Chicken

31 Which is the flight to Sydney?

A	B	C
LH4521	**LH4152**	**LH4125**

32 Which hotel does Graham's colleague recommend?

A The Orion
B The Grand Hotel
C The Plaza

33 Which machine are the people talking about?

A A fax machine
B A printer
C A photocopier

34 What happens to the phone call?

A The receptionist puts the caller through.
B The receptionist takes a message.
C The caller offers to ring back later.

35 How much does the retailer pay for each game?

A $7 a unit
B $8 a unit
C $9 a unit

36 How long will the order take to arrive?

A 3 days
B 4 days
C 5 days

37 What is wrong with the printer?

A It has run out of paper.
B The paper has jammed.
C It needs a new ink cartridge.

Questions 38 - 45

- Listen to the Manager talking to staff about the way they answer the telephone.
- For questions **38 - 45**, mark the correct letter **A**, **B** or **C** for the correct answer.
- You will hear the conversation twice.

38 The information was

A recorded by the company.
B given by the company's customers.
C collected by a consultancy.

39 The company's staff answer the phone

A very quickly.
B reasonably quickly.
C far too slowly.

40 The groups average friendliness score was

A six out of ten.
B seven point five out of ten.
C eight out of ten.

41 When dealing with enquiries, staff usually

A know who to pass the caller on to.
B can't answer the caller's questions.
C have to take a message.

42 When putting a call through, staff should always

A ask for the caller's name.
B play the hold music.
C ask the caller to wait.

43 Employees should answer the phone after

A two rings.
B three rings.
C four rings.

44 The company is most worried about how

A quickly staff answer the phone.
B efficiently staff deal with enquiries.
C friendly staff sound on the phone.

45 The handout has a list of

A pieces of good hold music.
B useful telephone phrases.
C extension numbers.

Student A
Unit 4a

❶ You have an appointment with Andrew Jones of Collingwood Pharmaceuticals on 14 May at half past two. Telephone him to:

- confirm the date
- change the time to 3 o'clock
- give the name of the colleague who is attending the meeting with you.

❷ You are a receptionist at Isis, a company based in Los Angeles. Someone calls to speak to Rosemary Burton. She is not in the office today. Offer to take a message.

Student A
Unit 5a

Describe the graph below to your partner.

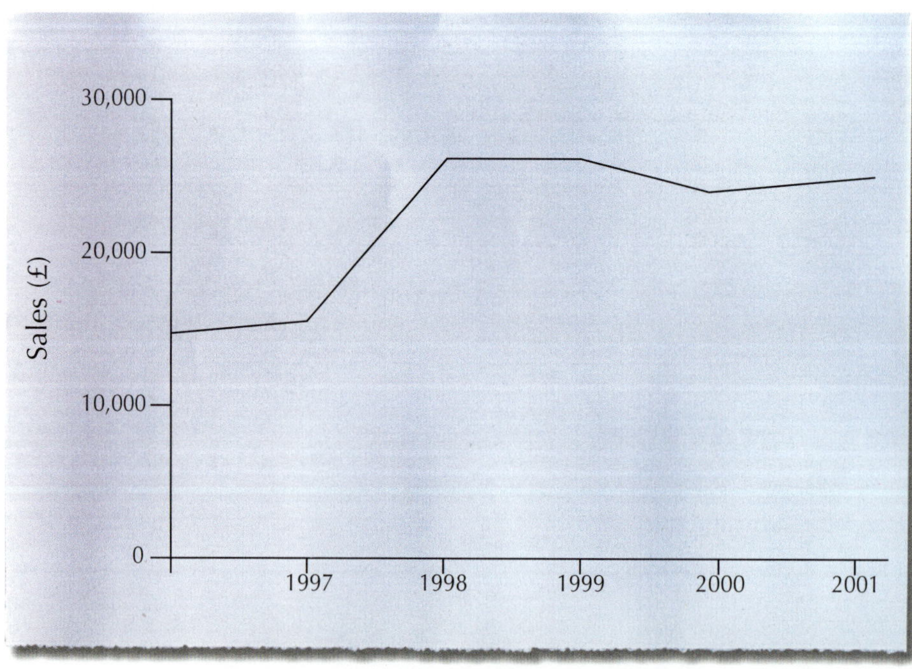

Student A Unit 5a

Draw the graph that your partner describes.

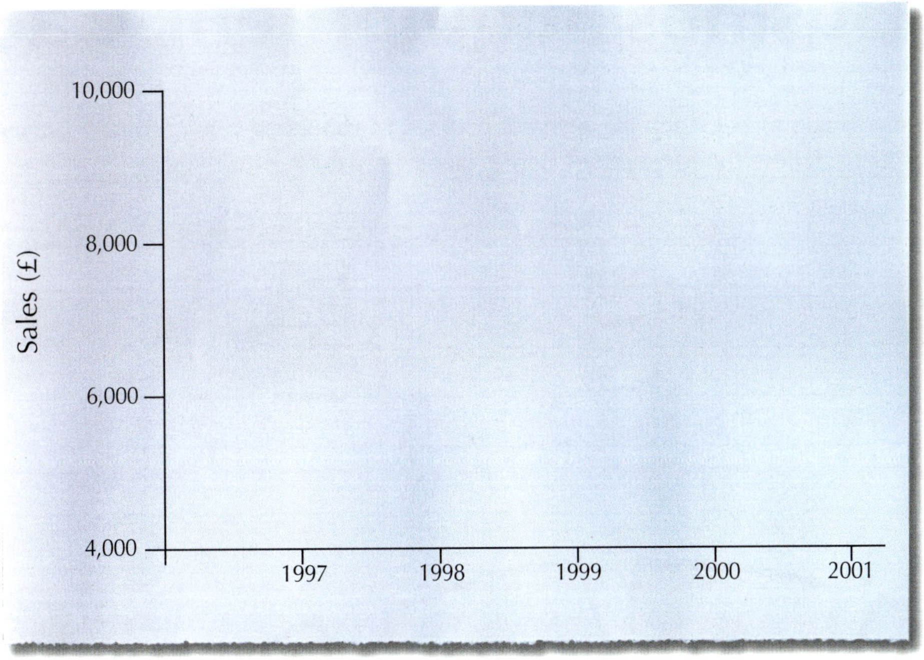

Student A Unit 11a

Ask your partner for the information to complete the conference programme below.

Amtech Marketing Conference 2001 Programme

Hotel
The Plaza
Drobárova 8
130 00 Praha 3
Czech Republic

Tel + 420 (2) 768 897 *Fax + 420 (2) 717 544 88*
E-mail: Plaza_Pra@compuserve.com

Friday 21 September

_____	Drinks reception (hotel bar)
19.30	Dinner at __________

Saturday 22 September

9.00	Opening session (Dvořák room)
11.00	Coffee
11.30	Plenary session
13.00	Buffet lunch
14.00	Workshops (Dvořák room and Smetana room)
_____	Coffee
16.30	Plenary session
18.00	End of session
_____	Dinner at a local restaurant

Sunday 23 September

9.30	__________ (Dvořák room and Smetana room)
11.00	Coffee
11.30	Plenary session
13.00	End of conference
13.15	__________
14.45	Departure from hotel

The Business Equipment Game

Play the game in a group of 2-4. Each player has a counter to represent one of these machines. When you land on a square, follow the instructions only if they refer to your machine.

Fax

Photocopier

Printer

Shredder

Toss two coins.

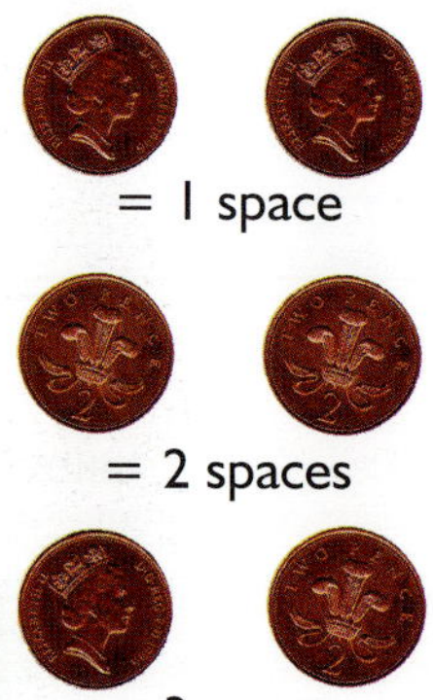
= 1 space

= 2 spaces

= 3 spaces

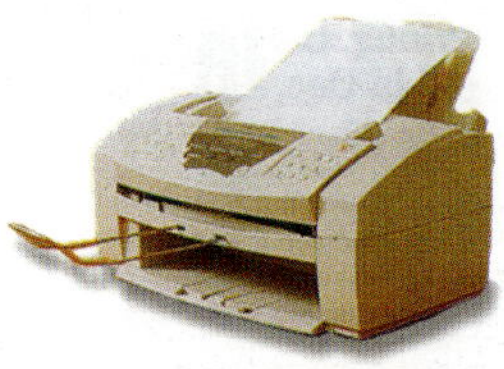

START

You programme the dialling codes. **+2**

The paper jams. **-1**

The machine has a new cutter. **+2**

The machine runs out of paper. **-1**

The machine shreds quickly. **+1**

The line connects easily. **+2**

Photos don't print clearly. **-2**

The cutter jams. **-1**

The stapler on the machine works. **+2**

The enlarger doesn't work properly. **-2**

You have to press the SEND button again. **-2**

The machine prints clearly. **+2**

Someone inserts stapled paper into the cutter. **-2**

The machine overheats. **-1**

The machine reduces documents. **+1**

FINISH

The Commuter Game

You have to get to work for a very important meeting at 9.00. When you land on a red or green traffic light, another player will pick up a card and tell you what to do or ask you a question. If you decide to break the law, toss a coin to see whether the police catch you. Heads: the police catch you and you return to the start. Tails: they don't and you continue as normal. If you land on amber, do nothing. The first person to arrive at work is the winner.

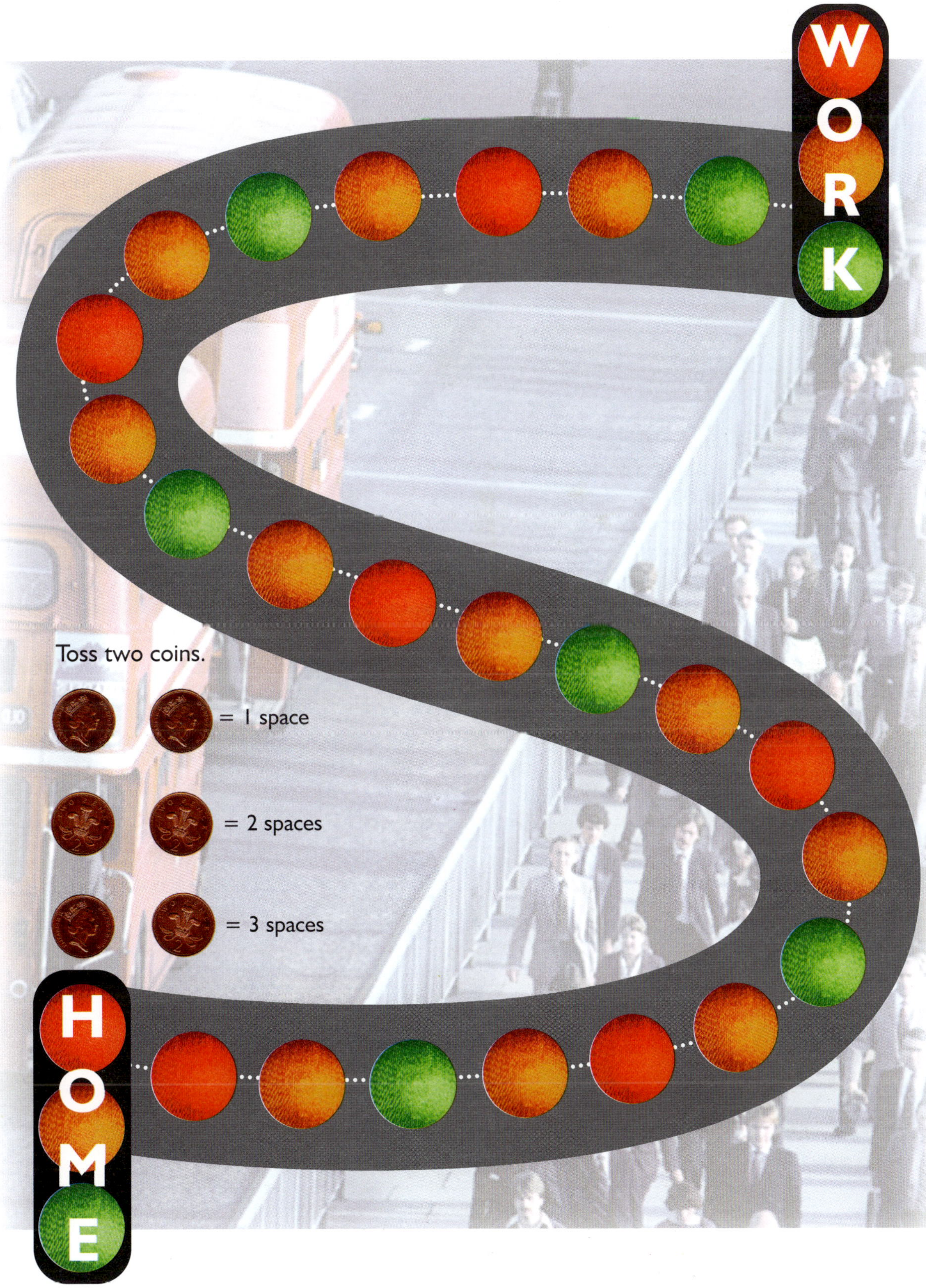

Student B
Unit 4a

1 You are a receptionist at Collingwood Pharmaceuticals. Someone calls to speak to Andrew Jones. He is in a meeting. Take a message.

Message for ....

From ....

Message ....

....

....

2 You are flying to Los Angeles to visit Rosemary Burton at a company called Isis. Telephone her to:

- say that your flight on Thursday 22 April lands at 10:00 not 14:30
- confirm the flight number: BA 348
- ask who will meet you at the airport.

Student B
Unit 5a

Draw the graph that your partner describes.

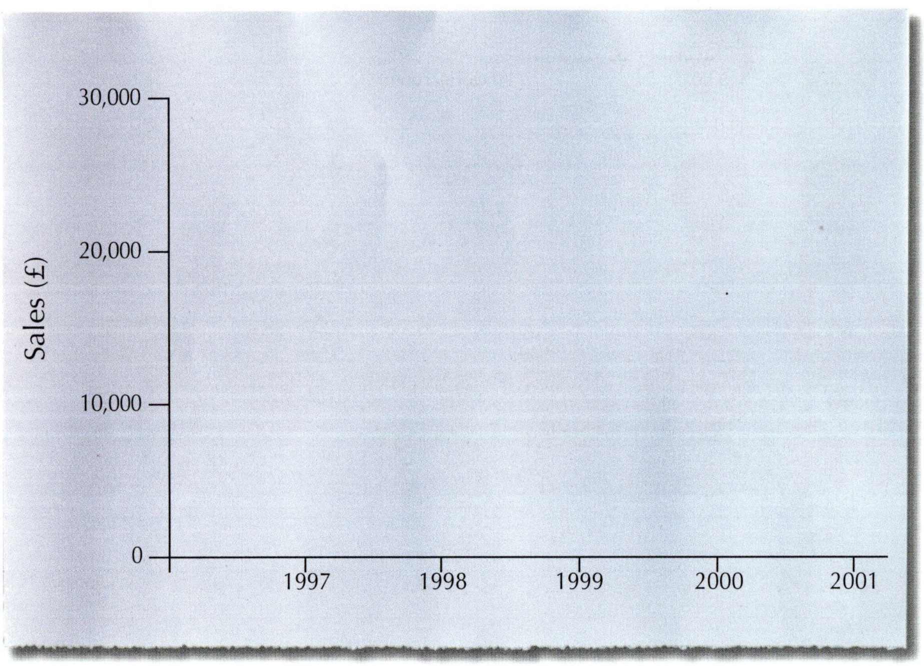

Student B
Unit 5a

Describe the graph below to your partner.

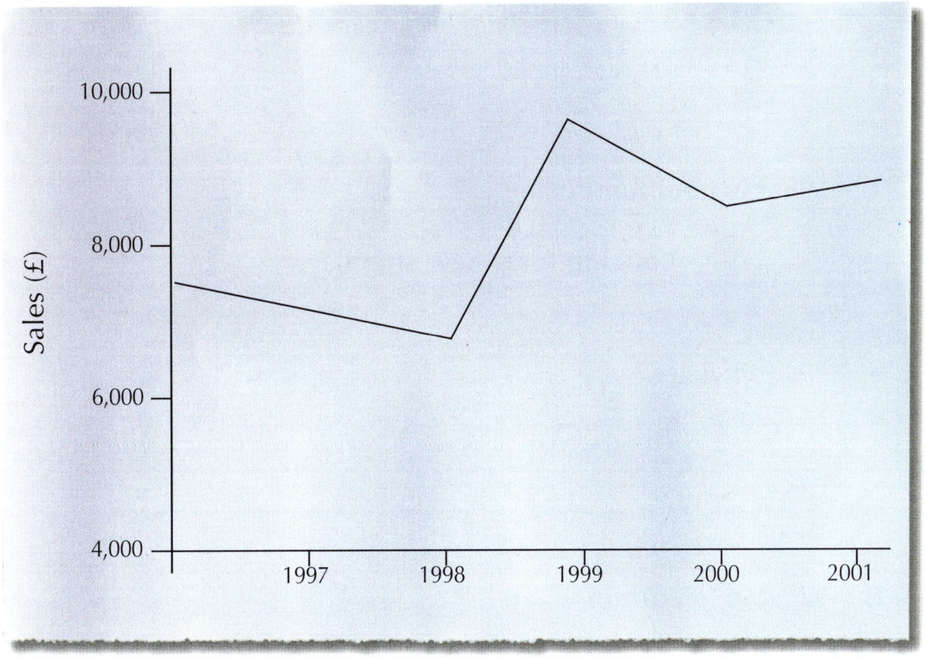

Student B
Unit 11a

Ask your partner for the information to complete the conference programme below.

Amtech Marketing Conference 2001 Programme

Amtech SOFTWARE

Hotel
The Plaza
Drobárova 0
130 00 Praha 3
Czech Republic

Tel + 420 (2) 768 897   Fax + 420 (2) 717 544 88
E-mail: Plaza_Pra@compuserve.com

Friday 21 September

18.30	Drinks reception (hotel bar)
19.30	Dinner at hotel

Saturday 22 September

9.00	__________ (Dvořák room)
11.00	Coffee
11.30	Plenary session
13.00	__________
_____	Workshops (Dvořák room and __________ room)
16.00	Coffee
16.30	Plenary session
18.00	End of session
19.30	Dinner at a local restaurant

Sunday 23 September

9.30	Workshops (Dvořák room and __________ room)
_____	Coffee
11.30	Plenary session
_____	End of conference
13.15	Lunch
14.45	Departure from hotel

Speaking Test Part Two

A What is important when ...?

Looking for a new supplier

- Quality
- Delivery times
- Discounts

B What is important when ...?

Arranging a conference

- Location
- Hotel facilities
- Number of delegates

A What is important when ...?

Recruiting staff

- Qualifications
- Experience
- Age

B What is important when ...?

Applying for a job

- Curriculum Vitae
- Interview
- Appearance

Speaking Test Part Three

1. English lessons

- Lesson times?
- Who pays?
- Location?
- Number of students?

2. New office

- Computer
- Desk chair
- Arm chair
- Printer
- Fax machine
- Radio
- Water cooler / drinks machine
- Ashtray

3. Choosing a hotel

- Price
- Location, near city centre / airport / exhibition centre
- Business facilities
- Leisure facilities
- Food

Map of London

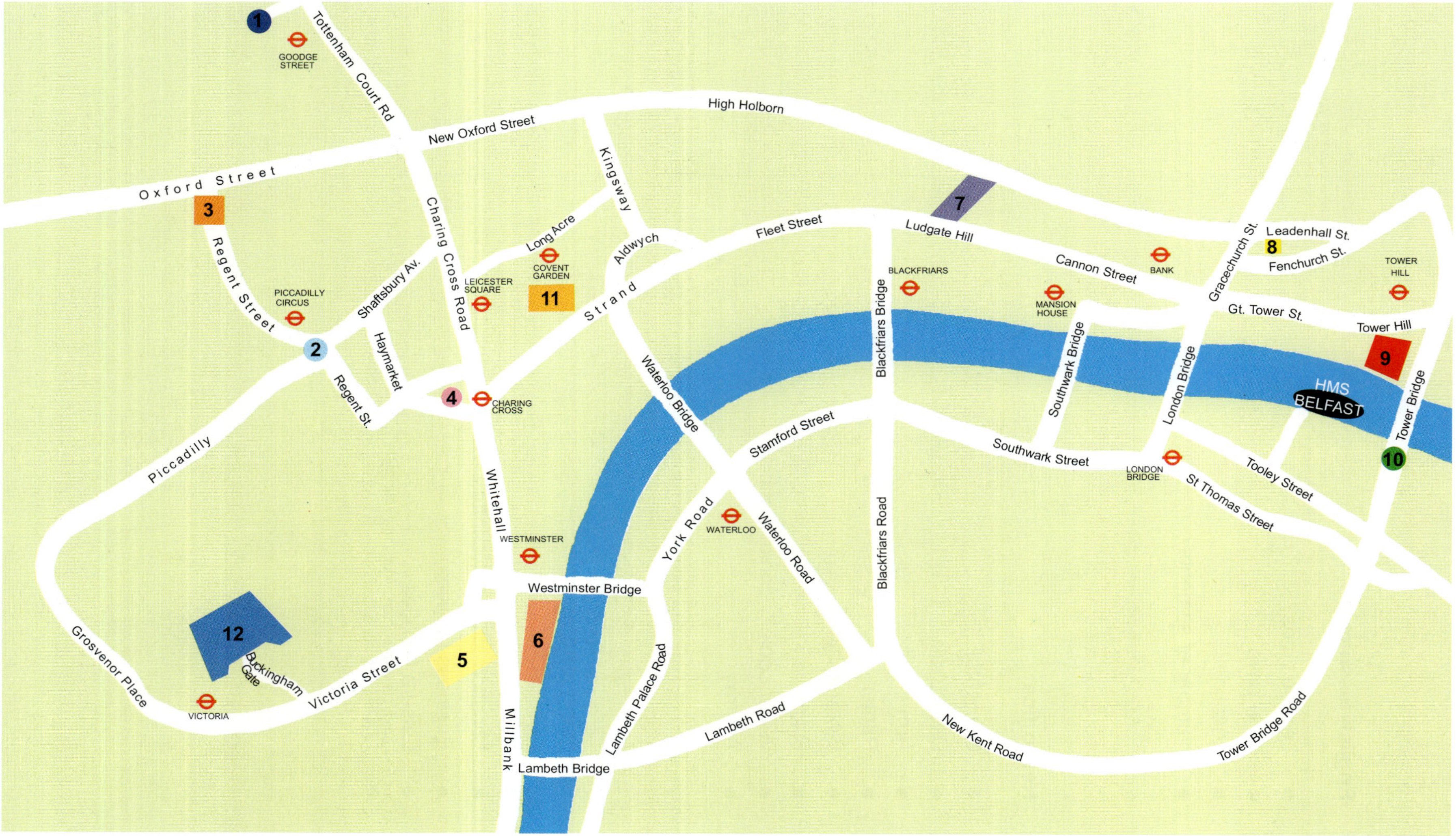

- 1 Telecom Tower
- 2 Piccadilly Circus
- 3 Regent Street
- 4 Nelson's Column
- 5 Westminster Abbey
- 6 The Houses of Parliament
- 7 St. Paul's Cathedral
- 8 Lloyd's Building
- 9 Tower of London
- 10 Tower Bridge
- 11 Covent Garden
- 12 Buckingham Palace

Tapescripts

Unit 1a: Job descriptions

Listening 1

Ri = Richard   K = Katy   Ro = Robin
H = Helen   T = Thomas   B = Beth

Conversation 1

Ri So, are you from London then - or just here for the meeting?
K No, I'm not from London, but my company has offices here.
Ri What kind of company is it?
K I work for an IT company. I'm a consultant.

Conversation 2

Ro Where do you work?
H I work for a large pharmaceutical company.
Ro And what do you do?
H I'm the head of the Marketing Department.

Conversation 3

K So what kind of products do you sell?
T Anything that helps people make money.
K How do you mean?
T Financial services. I sell investment products.

Conversation 4

T Tell me, does your consultancy work with big companies?
B No, we do the accounts for small and medium-sized companies.
T Ah, I see. Do you have clients in London?
B Some but not many. Most of our clients are in Reading.

Conversation 5

H So, you work in the food industry?
Ri Yes, I'm a factory manager.
H Oh, really? What do you make?
Ri We produce frozen food.

Conversation 6

B And what do you do?
Ro I'm a manager in Personnel.
B What kind of company do you work for?
Ro We make packaging for fresh food.

Listening 2

Helen Marsden

Hello, I'm Helen Marsden. I work as a marketing manager for a large pharmaceuticals company. My department produces vaccines against hepatitis and so on. We normally sell our vaccines directly to doctors so one of my jobs is to discuss our new products with doctors. Marketing managers don't always do this, but I do as I'm a qualified doctor. I'm also responsible for our publicity material so I have to deal with designers and printers. My area is central Europe, so I have to deal with the health authorities in those countries. That means my job involves a lot of travelling. And finally, when we produce a new vaccine, it's my job to organise a conference for the medical press so that they can ask us questions about it.

Robin Seaton

Hello, I'm Robin Seaton. I work for a company called Vacupack. I'm responsible for employing most of the people in the company. I write the job advertisements and then I have to choose which applicants I want to interview. Usually, I interview the applicants with the head of the department where the vacancy is. I then have to contact the applicants after the interview, both the successful and unsuccessful ones. Another duty is dealing with employees' problems. Of course many of them are work-related, but people do sometimes come to discuss personal problems with me. My job also involves informing employees if the management isn't satisfied with their work, which isn't a pleasant part of the job.

Unit 4a: Telephoning

Listening 1

Cl = Clare   Ca = Caller

Call 1

Cl Good morning, Baker and Kerr. Can I help you?
Ca Could you put me through to Elaine Pearson, please?
Cl Who's calling, please?
Ca Lewis Taylor of SRT.
Cl One moment please, Mr Taylor ... Hello, Mr Taylor. I'm afraid the line's busy. Can I take a message?
Ca No, it's all right, thank you. I'll call back in about ten minutes.
Cl OK. Thank you for calling.

Call 2

Cl Good morning, Baker and Kerr. Can I help you?
Ca Yes, please. Could I have extension 184, please?
Cl Who's calling, please?
Ca Jack Symes.
Cl Thank you. I'll put you through.
Ca Thank you.

Call 3

Cl Good morning, Baker and Kerr. Can I help you?
Ca Can I speak to William Grogan, please?
Cl I'm afraid he's in a meeting. Can I take a message?
Ca Do you know when he'll be free?
Cl He should be available after lunch.
Ca Right, I'll call back then. Thanks.

Call 4

Cl Good morning, Baker and Kerr. Can I help you?
Ca Jasmine Singh, please.
Cl I'm afraid she's interviewing all day. Can I take a message?
Ca Yes, my name's Mary Banks, from Walkers. She called me earlier. I'm returning her call.
Cl Mary Banks, from Walkers. Right. I'll tell her you called back.
Ca OK. Thanks.

Call 5

Cl Good morning, Baker and Kerr. Can I help you?
Ca Hi Clare. It's Fiona. Is Keith available?
Cl I'm afraid the line's busy, Fiona.
Ca It's OK. I'll hold.
Cl Fiona?
Ca Yes.
Cl The line's free now. I'll put you through.
Ca Thanks.

Call 6

Cl Good morning, Baker and Kerr. Can I help you?
Ca Hi. It's Fiona again. We were cut off.
Cl Oh, sorry about that. I'll try to reconnect you. Hold the line.
Ca Thanks.

Listening 2

Cl = Clare   D = David

Cl Good afternoon. Baker and Kerr. Can I help you?
D Good afternoon. Can you put me through to Sharon Thomson, please?
Cl I'm afraid she's out of the office at the moment. Can I take a message?
D Yes, my name's David Whelan from the Health and Safety Council.
Cl I'm sorry. Could you spell your surname, please?
D W-H-E-L-A-N.
Cl And it's the Health and Safety Council. Right. And what's the message,

please?

D I'm calling about the First Aid course Ms Thomson's is arranging with us. I'd like to confirm the week beginning 13 May but I'm not ...

CI Sorry, did you say the thirteenth or thirtieth?

D The thirteenth, 13.

CI OK ... yes ...

D Yes. The date's fine, but we can only take 25 participants, not 29.

CI So that's the First Aid course for the week commencing 13 May and you can only take 25 people.

D That's right, yes.

CI Right. I'll give her the message.

D Thanks.

CI You're welcome. Bye.

Unit 4b: Internal communication

Listening 1

H = Henry Wallace S = Sarah Longman

H Hello, Henry Wallace speaking.

S Hello, Henry, it's Sarah Longman from Accounts.

H Oh hello Sarah. What can I do for you?

S I'm calling all of the heads of department about expenses. I just wanted to remind you that if someone claims any expenses, they must enclose receipts with the claim.

H OK. I'll send a memo to remind my salespeople.

S Thanks, Henry. Bye.

Listening 2

K = Karen J = John

K Hello. Karen Mitchell.

J Hello Karen, it's John.

K Oh hi John. How are you?

J I'm fine thanks. Look, I got your note yesterday about the meeting. I'm sorry I didn't get back to you.

K That's OK. But I'm flying out to Paris next week and we need to meet before I leave. Is Thursday all right for you?

J Not really, no. How about Tuesday?

K Fine, I've got to be in the office on Tuesday morning anyway. How about lunchtime?

J Well, that's fine by me, but we should find out if Steve's available then, as well.

K That's true. I'll send him an e-mail and see if lunchtime's OK for him.

J If it's OK with Steve, let me know and we can fix a time.

K I'll e-mail him now. Thanks John. Bye.

J Bye.

Unit 5b: Performance

Listening 1

Good afternoon. My name is Juliet Sharman and I'm here to talk about Great Eastern's performance. As you all know, Great Eastern has only been a private company since it was bought by FirstGroup as part of the privatisation of the national railway network in 1997. In the years before privatisation, the company made a lot of changes to prepare it for the free market. I'd like to tell you a bit about those changes and show you how they've affected the company's performance since 1993. To do this, I'd like to draw your attention to figures three and four on page eight of your information brochures.

I'd like to begin with a look at the bar chart, which shows annual growth in passenger revenue from 1993 to 1997. As you can see, growth slowed from 2.4% in 1993/94 down to just 1% in 94/95. However, reduced costs and more efficient sales practices resulted in growth reaching 9.9% in 1995/96. This was followed by 7% in 1996/97. The bar chart clearly shows that the changes have made a big difference financially and have improved customer satisfaction, as we'll see.

I'm sure you've all read newspaper stories about bad service on the privatised rail network, so I'd like you to look at figure four, which shows Great Eastern's reliability and punctuality figures. As you can see from this graph, the company has an excellent reliability record. Reliability improved steadily from 99.1% in 1993 to 99.3% in 1995, where it has remained. Punctuality also rose steadily, going from 90% in 1993 to 91% in 1995. You'll notice the drop to 88% in 1996, which I'll explain later. Although we haven't received the final figures yet, I can tell you that punctuality improved in 1997 and has continued to improve this year as a result of further investment.

Listening 2

I = Investor J = Juliet Sharman

J So, that's the end of my presentation. Does anyone have any questions?

I Yes. Earlier you mentioned the drop in punctuality in 1996. What was the problem?

J Sorry, I said I'd explain that, didn't I? Well, it was mainly because of problems with the railway track. As you know, we have to lease both the track and our trains from other companies. The track belongs to a company called Railtrack. Although we receive penalty payments from them for any delays due to the track, it doesn't help our reliability figures. We don't like the situation but we can't change it. Next question, please.

I2 Could you tell us a bit about the company's future investment plans?

J Of course. At the moment Great Eastern is investing £9m in upgrading its stations. This includes facilities, information systems and security. We're also investing in new trains, which will lead to improved reliability levels. The gentleman at the back, please ...

I3 With the Government reducing its financial support to the company each year, how do you hope to improve profits in the future?

J That's a good question. The Government is going to give us less and less money over the next few years. And, as I said, we have to lease both the track and our trains, so our biggest costs are fixed. The only way the company can improve profits is by increasing passenger volumes. That's why we're spending so much on improving customer satisfaction. Next question, please.

Unit 7a: Product description

Listening 1

Morning everybody. Now, as you know, this morning we're going to talk about our latest products in our range of games. Before we talk about the selling points of each game, I'd just like to describe them briefly. I'll begin with this general knowledge game called Mindtwist, which comes in two versions: a standard size and a travel size.

As you can see, the differences are size, weight and, of course, cost. The standard version has a normal size board, two packs of cards, six wooden playing pieces, a timer and two dice. The travel size, Mindtwist Travel, is obviously smaller: it has a thin, light-weight, magnetic board which measures just 23cm square. The cards are smaller and the four playing pieces are magnetic counters which are made of coloured plastic. The total weight is only 300 grammes. The standard version will retail at £17.99 and the travel size at £10.99.

And now I'd like to show you another new game called Collect. This is a *card game for three to six players ...*

Listening 2

R = Robert S = Sophie

R *So Sophie, how are our products selling?*
S *Board games are the big seller at the moment. They're selling better than ever before?*
R *Good, so you might be interested in having a bigger range of our board games then.*
S *Yes, if there's anything different.*
R *We've got Mindtwist. It's our newest board game. The game itself comes in two versions: standard and travel. The games are basically the same but the travel version's lighter and smaller. There are also fewer playing pieces.*
S *I stock several general knowledge games already, but I don't have a travel size. I might be interested in that.*
R *Right. This is it. You can see it's nice and compact.*
S *Mmm, it looks interesting. Are the instructions easy to follow? Some of your games have very complicated instructions.*
R *Yes, other customers have told us that as well. So we've made the instructions easier. But I have another travel size game, called Collect. It's even easier to play. Let me show you. It's a card game based on the television programme Collectables. You know, antiques.*
S *Oh yes.*
R *And it isn't as big as the board game either.*
S *Hmm, well, it sounds different, but I'm not sure it'll sell as well as the board games. Not everybody's interested in antiques. Anyway, what's the recommended retail price for the Mindtwist travel version?*
R *£10.99.*
S *That sounds reasonable. And what would you be willing to sell it to us for?*
R *£9.99.*
S *Would there be a discount on large orders?*
R *Not on Mindtwist on its own, no. But if you were to buy both versions of Mindtwist, I could give you 5% on both games.*
S *OK, I'll take them both, but I'll order just a few to start with.*
R *Good. I'll get an order form.*

Unit 7b: Product development

Listening

J = Journalist M = Marketing Manager

J *So, you're launching a new product for arthritis - Arthran. Who is Arthran for exactly?*
M *Anybody who suffers from the condition.*
J *And how soon is this product going to be on the market?*
M *Well, we're launching it in five weeks' time, on 25 May, but obviously we're starting the publicity campaign before then.*
J *And is it going to be available from the chemists' as well as doctors?*
M *No, it's a powerful drug and will only be available in hospitals or on prescription from doctors - not over the counter.*
J *I see. And what are the side effects?*
M *The main one is tiredness. Doctors need to advise their patients not to drive while they're taking this drug. Of course, we're going to give doctors and patients all the necessary information about the drug and how to use it.*
J *And how are you going to do that?*
M *Well, at the beginning of May we're visiting doctors in hospitals and surgeries. But we're sending them detailed information packs at the end of April so they can read all about the drug and prepare for our visits.*
J *And what information is there for patients?*
M *Well, about a week before the launch, we're going to give general information posters to doctors for them to display in their waiting rooms.*
J *What's the purpose of those?*
M *To make patients aware of the new drug so they'll ask their doctors about it. And we're also producing information leaflets at the moment for patients who'll take the drug. They'll be available just after the launch on 25 May.*

Unit 8a: Business equipment

Listening

B = Becky A = Anna

B *Purchasing.*
A *Hi Becky. It's Anna from Accounts here.*
B *Hi.*
A *Becky, you know that shredder we've just bought?*
B *Yes?*
A *Well, everyone keeps asking how to use it and I can't find the operating instructions.*
B *Ah! Now I think they may still be here. Hold on a second ... Yes, I've got them here, Anna. What do you want to know?*
A *Well, what to do if it doesn't work. You know, things like that.*
B *Well. It says here that the machine jams if you insert too much paper into it. If that happens, press the red button, remove the excess paper and start again with less paper.*
A *Right. Are there any other possible problems?*
B *The motor overheats sometimes. If that happens, it switches off automatically. Just leave it for 15 to 30 minutes before you switch it on again.*
A *OK, I've got all that. Is there anything else I should know?*
B *Yes, there are a few things to be careful about - like never put your fingers in the shredder.*
A *That's a bit obvious, isn't it?*
B *And be careful with long hair and loose articles of clothing like ties. And that's it.*
A *Thanks, Becky. I'll put a notice with the instructions on the wall next to the shredder.*
B *Good idea.*

Unit 10a: Business hotels

Listening 1

I = Interviewer K = Kevin

I *So, what special needs do business travellers have?*
K *One of the most important things is a quick check-in and check-out. After a long trip it's annoying to have to wait at the hotel reception for five minutes. Room service is also very important. Guests often stay in their rooms working and don't have the time to go out to a restaurant, so they want their meals to be served in their rooms.*
I *And what facilities are there in the rooms?*
K *Well, nowadays communication facilities are essential, so things like a modem socket, where guests can plug their modems in, and a fax are very important.*
I *Yes, of course.*
K *The lighting is also very important. We've just spent a lot of money upgrading the lighting in our rooms. As I said, guests often spend their evenings preparing work, so they need good lighting at their desks.*
I *And what about facilities in the hotel in general?*
K *The bars are important. Corporate guests tend to spend more time in*

the hotel bars than tourists. It's very important to provide a business centre, too.

I What services does the business centre provide?

K Basic secretarial services such as photocopying and typing. It also co-ordinates conferences and any catering which is included in them. Clients always find it helpful to have these kind of things organised for them.

I Right, and what about distance to the airport and city centre? Is that important?

K Yes. We're in the east of London so we're near City Airport. A lot of our guests have meetings in this area, so they don't want to be near Heathrow airport or right in the city centre. But it is easy to get to the centre of London from here. It only takes about 15 minutes with our courtesy bus. And there's a river taxi, as well.

I Are your corporate guests interested in using your fitness centre or swimming pool?

K Not really. They're more popular with tourists. Our corporate guests are more interested in getting in and out of the hotel as quickly as possible and working while they're here.

Listening 2

R = Reception M = Montse

R Good morning. Can I help you?

M Yes. Could you tell me the best way of getting into the centre of London, please?

R Well, there is a courtesy bus, which leaves every 20 minutes during the rush hour, or the river taxi service to London Bridge.

M And when is the rush hour?

R It's between seven and nine in the morning and five and seven in the evening.

M And after nine in the morning?

R After nine the courtesy bus service runs every 40 minutes.

M Ah ha. And how long does it take?

R The bus takes about 15 minutes, depending on the traffic.

M And which way does it go?

R Here, I'll show you on the map. From the hotel it goes along the river bank and then on to Brunel Road. It crosses the river at Tower Bridge and then stops just after Tower Bridge at Tower Hill Underground Station.

M And what about the river taxi, does that change after rush hour?

R Yes, it's a half hourly service during rush hour and after that it runs to a timetable. It takes about 15 minutes. It's a really nice trip. You go across to Canary Wharf Pier first, then you go along the river, under Tower Bridge and you stop at a pier just before London Bridge. The only thing is, it costs £1.80 each way.

M OK. Thanks very much.

R You're welcome. Bye.

Unit 10b: Commuting

Listening

1 I think it's a stupid idea. The motorways are already too full and now they're going to stop cars using one of the lanes. It's crazy. The traffic'll be twice as bad and there'll be a lot more accidents as well. People will spend hours and hours stuck in traffic jams and be late for work all the time.

2 OK, I know cars are bad for the environment and all that, but big increases in petrol prices aren't going to make any difference. What about industry? Higher petrol prices are only going to increase companies' costs and put jobs at risk.

3 It's about time! When I go shopping there are thousands of people all on a narrow little pavement trying to walk along. It's impossible to relax. Car drivers should use park and ride schemes and leave their cars out of the city centre. Shopping should be fun and not stressful.

4 It's difficult to say, really. Paying every time you use a road might be a good idea. I suppose some people might leave their cars at home a bit more often, which would be good. But there isn't any public transport where I live, so it would be more expensive for me personally.

5 How am I going to get to work if I can't leave my car there? It takes twice as long to get to work on the bus and it costs twice as much, as well. So, of course I'm not going to use public transport.

6 I think it's a good idea. I hate it when you don't have the right money on the buses. They don't accept notes so you need a pocket full of change all the time. I like the idea of a plastic card - especially if it makes them cheaper to use as well. Nobody liked phone cards at first, did they? And now, look: everyone uses them.

Unit 11a: Arranging a conference

Listening 1

R = Rachel Day D = Daniel Black

R Good morning, Europa Events. Can I help you?

D Good morning. My name's Daniel Black from Amtech. Could you give me a quotation for the organisation of a marketing conference, please?

R Yes, of course. I'll need to take some details first. So, it's Daniel Black from Amtech. Can you spell the company name, please?

D Yes, it's A-M-T-E-C-H.

R And what's the address?

D Westbourne Business Park, Brighton, BN2 3EQ and the phone number's 01273 485 671.

R 01273 485 671. And it's a marketing conference. How many delegates will there be?

D Between thirty-five and forty.

R Do you have a preferred location?

D Yes. Well, we're thinking of Prague, if it's affordable.

R That's always the big question, isn't it? Could you tell me what your budget is, please?

D £20,000 maximum.

R OK. And when do you want to hold the conference?

D In September or October.

R How long would you like it to last?

D A weekend. We'd like the delegates to arrive for dinner on the Friday evening and leave after lunch on the Sunday.

R Will you want to have the delegates in one room for the whole conference or will you need seminar rooms?

D Well, we plan to break into two discussion groups during the day, so we'll need one seminar room in addition to the main conference room.

R Right, Mr Black. That's all I need to ask you for the moment. I'll look at your requirements and make a written proposal before the end of the week.

D Fine. Thanks very much.

Listening 2

R = Rachel Day D = Daniel Black

D Good morning. Daniel Black.

R Hello. This is Rachel Day from Europa Events.

D Hello. How are you?

R Fine thanks. I'm phoning about the marketing conference. I'd like to check some details before I send you the letter of confirmation.

D Sure, go ahead.

R So, the conference will be held on September 25 to the 27 for 37 delegates and all of the delegates will require accommodation for two nights. You will have the use of one conference room plus a smaller seminar room. Is that correct?

D Yes, that sounds right.

R Now there's just one thing I'm not sure about. Did you say that you want the delegates to pay their own bar and phone bills before they depart?

D No, just their phone bills.

R So all drinks should go on the master account?

D That's right, yes.

R Fine. That's all I need to know, thanks.

D And are you going to be in the hotel at the time of the conference?

R No, it won't be me as I'll be at another conference then. One of my colleagues will be waiting for you at the hotel when you arrive. I'll be able to give you the name of your contact person in a few days.

D Great, thanks.

R So, I'll confirm the whole thing in writing. You should receive the letter before the end of the week.

Unit 11b: At a conference

Listening 1

Good morning everybody. Welcome to the 7th Annual International Sales Conference. It's great to see so many of you - old faces and new ones! Now we're going to have two very busy days as usual, but I am sure you'll enjoy them. As soon as I finish, which won't be long, I promise you, we'll begin with our first session, which is our Sales Managers giving their National Sales Reports for their own countries.

We'll stay together for that session as I feel it's useful for everybody to see the overall picture. Then, after we've had lunch, we're going to divide into groups to discuss our targets for next year and how to reach them. At four o'clock we'll come back together again when Amy Carter, our guest speaker, gives her presentation. As you all know, the consultants Allman & Partners have been looking at the way we answer the telephone throughout the group and Amy is going to give a short report on their findings. Her presentation will probably finish just before 5.30.

Dinner this evening is at eight o'clock. We'd like everyone to meet in the bar for drinks from about seven o'clock. That way we can enjoy a drink together until the coach leaves for the restaurant at 7.45.

Tomorrow morning we're starting at nine o'clock with a look at ways of marketing the new product. This'll also be a workshop session. Then there'll be a coffee break before we come back together again and share our ideas with a feedback session. And that will bring us to the end of the conference and a farewell lunch. So, that's enough from me. I'd just like to wish you all an enjoyable and successful two days and hand you over to Jodie Cox, who's going to start with a look at Canadian sales.

Listening 2

C = Colleague J = Jodie

C So how did the conference go, Jodie?

J Oh it was good. All the sessions were interesting and all the speakers were really good. The organisation was a lot better this year as well. I think having a smaller number of people there made a big difference. You know, you could actually get things done in the workshops and make decisions a lot more quickly. There were about 30 delegates altogether, which was just perfect.

C And how was the hotel?

J Fine. The conference rooms were a good size and the hotel rooms were clean and very comfortable. I really liked the hotel a lot. I think we should go there again next year.

C And how was dinner on Saturday?

J Ah, that was probably the only thing that people really complained about. The food wasn't very good and the service was slow. If we go back to the same hotel again, we'll have to find another restaurant.

Unit 12: Exam focus

Part One: Questions 1-8

For Questions 1-8 you will hear eight short recordings. For each question, mark A B or C for the most suitable picture or phrase. You will hear each conversation twice.

1 What is Maria's job title?

A So, you work in Sales, don't you, Maria?
B Sort of, I'm actually in the Marketing Department.
A Oh I see. And what do you do there?
B I'm the Manager.

2 Where are they taking the visitors?

A Where should we take the visitors this evening?
B Good question. What kind of food will they like?
A I know a place that serves great Asian food.
B Not everyone likes spicy food, though. I know a place that does great pasta. Why don't we go there?
A OK.

3 What was the final decision about the meeting?

A Did you see the memo about tomorrow's meeting?
B Yes, I saw it was postponed until next week.
A Well, forget the memo. It's back on again at the same time.

4 Which part of the job offer was George unhappy about?

A Are you going to take the job, George?
B I don't know. The salary was OK.
A What about the hours?
B They were long but I don't mind that. I'm just a bit worried about the amount of paid leave, that's all.

5 Which graph is the Head of Department talking about?

A So, as you can see, sales rose at the start of the year and then levelled off in the summer. But I'm happy to say there was a big increase in orders for toys at Christmas.

6 When are the visitors arriving?

A Oh you stupid machine!
B Hey. What's all the excitement for?
A Because it's already half past ten. I've got visitors arriving in half an hour. I need to photocopy some reports and this stupid machine isn't working!

7 Which photocopier do they decide to buy?

A So which of these photocopiers should we buy?
B This one looks nice, the X40.
A Hmm. Bit expensive. The RX200 looks fast. It does 25 copies a minute.
B So does the BT100. And it's cheaper and smaller.
A But it hasn't got many functions, has it?
B That's true. OK, we'll get the bigger one.

8 Which part of the factory does Alan want to change?

A How can we increase production, Alan? Should we buy some more machines for the production line?
B That's not necessary. The real problem is that we can't store any more raw materials. We need to increase storage space.
A Hm. And the packing area, is that OK?
B For the moment. As I said, storage is the problem.

Part Two: Questions 9-15

You will hear two people discussing an invoice. Listen to the conversation and write the missing information in the spaces. You will hear the conversation twice.

A Hello, Accounts. How can I help you?
B I'd like to check an invoice please
A Certainly. Can you give me the invoice number please?
B Of course, it's HP420Y.
A HP420Y?
B That's right.
A OK, that invoice is dated 15th February, what seems to be the problem?
B I just wanted to check the details, my copy isn't very clear.
A Right, go ahead.
B Well, can you confirm that we ordered nine boxes of paper for the photocopier?
A No, you ordered ten boxes of paper at nine pounds ninety-four each.
B OK. That's ninety-nine pounds forty, isn't it?
A Yes, but that price is exclusive of VAT, which is 17.5%.
B Oh, how much is the actual total then?
A That's one hundred and sixteen pounds and eighty-eight pence to pay.
B Eighteen pence?
A Eighty.
B Oh, right and that needs to reach you by the 17th?
A Please.
B OK. Can I have your name in case I have any more problems?
A Of course, it's Marjorie Wilkes.
B Wilkes, how do you spell that?
A W-I-L-K-E-S.
B And have you got a direct line?
A Yes, the number is 01623 688 820.
B 688 120?
A 688 820.
B Great thanks, thanks for your help.
A You're welcome. Bye.

Part Three: Questions 16-22

You will hear a woman talking to some journalists about a new product range. Listen to the talk and write one or two words or a date in the spaces. You will hear the talk twice.

Good morning ladies and gentlemen. My name is Jade Ritchie and today I'd like to introduce you to our new range product range, but first let me welcome you to JollyGood. I hope you all had a pleasant journey here to our Head Office. Although we have a sales office in London, JollyGood Skincare has made its home here, in York, for the past fifty years. During this time we have built up a loyal base of housewives who appreciate our products for their high quality and no nonsense packaging. However, as we move into the new millennium, we felt it was time to broaden our appeal and move into new markets and so we have developed our "Feel Good" cosmetic range. As I said earlier, Feel Good is aimed at a different type of consumer but of course we are not going to abandon our traditional, more mature market and will continue producing all our original ranges. The Feel Good consumer is a modern, professional lady who expects the quality enjoyed by previous generations but wants a fresh looking product. This brings me to what we believe to be Feel Good's unique appeal - the price. What we have achieved is a serious quality product which won't break the bank.

If you look in your welcome pack you will see we have included some samples for you to try, but when will the general public be able to test our claims for themselves? Well, as I'm sure your must be aware, we have already started to run advertisements in some women's magazines. Our celebrity party, with special guests Vicky and Veronique from the TV series Little Sister, is September 11th, with products going on sale to the public the following day. We will also be running a number of nationwide promotions all based on the Feel Good promise "Look Great". All that remains is for me to thank you for coming here today.

Part Four: Questions 23-30

Listen to the conversation between a head of department and an employee. For Questions 23-30 mark the correct phrase to complete the sentence. Mark one letter, A, B or C for the phrase you choose. You will hear the conversation twice you have 45 seconds to read through the questions.

A Come in Sharon and take a seat.
B Thanks.
A So, where do we start? Should we begin with a look at last year and then go on from there?
B Fine.
A So, how do you feel you've done in your first full year with the company?
B Overall, I think I've done quite well. I feel quite confident now about what I do.
A And are you happy with your duties?
B Well, the job is exactly as it was advertised in the paper, so there have been no surprises. I like dealing with customers and I don't mind answering the phone and preparing invoices. Sometimes it's a bit boring typing long price lists, but then everyone has to do it.
A That's true. Does anything make your job difficult?
B The computer. To begin with, I was slow because I didn't know the program, but now I get annoyed when the computer just stops working for no reason. I often sit looking at the monitor for minutes, not sure whether it is still working or not. I think the network is too old for our software and we need some new machines.
A But apart from the computer, is there anything else you would like to change?
B Erm, let me see. I'd like the authority to issue credit notes without having to ask you first. You're often away on business and sometimes customers ring up with a complaint. And if we can't contact you, then we can't deal with the complaint properly. It's a bit embarrassing at times.
A Yes, but some of our customers always find something wrong and try and get a credit note with every order. You can't believe everything they say, you know. What about your objectives for the future?
B Well, I need to get to know the customers a bit better and maybe try to make fewer mistakes. But I think the most important thing is to increase my product knowledge, so I don't get embarrassed when customers make enquiries.
A Don't worry, you'll learn all that in time. What I'd like to ask you about now is ...

That is the end of the Test.

Unit 13a: Production

Listening 1

B = Brian V = Visitor

B So, this is a diagram of the bakery. Now it all begins with the main ingredients - those are flour and water. They're weighed and fed automatically into mixers. Yeast and additives are then added by hand and everything is mixed together for twelve minutes to make the dough.

V What are the additives for?
B They're just to increase the shelf-life of the baguettes. The dough is then divided into pieces. And after the weight is checked, the dough enters the first prover for ten minutes.
V The first what?
B Prover.
V What's a prover?
B I can tell you haven't baked bread before.
V No, that's very true!
B Well, you can't bake the dough straight away. You have to let it stand for a while so the yeast can react before you form it. This is called proving. Well now, the yeast makes the dough rise, and gives the bread shape and volume.
V Oh, right. I see.
B So, the dough is then formed into a baguette and dropped onto trays, which then continuously go round a circuit. The trays take the baguettes into another prover for 60 minutes. The temperature in the prover is perfect for the yeast to make the bread rise even more.
V 60 minutes, that long?
B Well, the prover stage is very important. If the bread doesn't prove properly, you can't bake it. Now the trays then continue around the circuit to the oven, where the bread is baked for ten minutes. And after leaving the oven, the trays enter the cooler. That's where cool air is blown over them for 40 minutes. The baguettes are then taken off the trays and dropped into plastic baskets for packaging. And the trays continue around the circuit and go back to the start again.
V And what happens to the baguettes?
B They're taken to the packing hall, where they're wrapped, boxed and despatched.
V And how long does the whole process take?
B From flour to boxed products takes about two and a half hours.

Listening 2

B = Brian V = Visitor

V So, Brian, what problems do you have with the production line?
B Well, we have a lot of problems with sensors. These are electronic sensors that tell the computer when a tray enters or leaves a prover or oven. The computer monitors the circuit and controls the speed of the trays. The computer stops the whole process when a sensor stops working properly - a complete shutdown.
V Really?
B Well, you have to remember that the line produces 6,000 baguettes an hour. The timing has to be perfect or the system stops. The sensors have to be set up exactly right. If they aren't, the computer won't start the system.
V What other problems do you have?
B Well, sometimes we have problems with the mixers. If the computer gets the mix wrong, we have to clean out the whole mixer.
V Do you have any problems with your workers?
B Not often, no. The system produces a new mix every 12 minutes, so it is possible that a mixerman can forget to put in the yeast and additives. If he forgets the extra ingredients, we lose the whole mix.
V Any other kinds of problems?
B Occasionally we have mechanical problems. Like when an old tray loses its shape, it can jam in a prover or oven. That can be a big problem because it can damage a machine and jam the whole system.
V So how much time do you lose a day on average?
B That's difficult to say, really. On a good day maybe 6 minutes. We can lose up to an hour and a half of production if we have a really bad day. And that means nearly 10,000 baguettes.

Unit 13b: Quality control

Listening 1

V = Visitor P = Pauline

V Could you tell me a bit about quality control at the factory?
P Well, there are four main quality control inspection points. We begin by visiting our suppliers to make sure we are happy with their quality control. Next, we inspect all goods in on arrival at our factory and the third inspection point is during production. And the final stage is chemical analysis of our finished goods.
V And what do you look for at each of the four inspection points?
P Well each stage is different. With our suppliers, for instance, we inspect their QC processes and, even more importantly, their factory hygiene. If we're not happy with their hygiene, we'll cancel the supply contract. At the goods in stage we make sure that order quantities are correct and the quality is OK. We also check the transport packaging. If the packaging is damaged, the warehouse shelf-life can be reduced.
V And what quality checks do you run during production?
P We take samples to check there isn't too much cooking oil on the snack and that each snack has the minimum amount of flavouring. We also check the size of the snacks and their crispness. If the snacks are too oily, they go soft.
V So that leaves the finished goods. What do you check for at the final QC stage?
P We check individual bags to make sure that the packet weight is above the acceptable minimum and that the packet is sealed properly. We also check the taste.
V And how do you do that?
P Well, we eat them. How else? We also do chemical analysis to check things like fat levels and other information that we have to put on the packets.

Listening 2

J = Jack K = Keith P = Pauline

J OK, so we all know there's a problem with reject levels, but before we look at ways of dealing with it, what I'd like to know is why don't we find the rejects sooner. How can they get all the way to the finished goods chemical analysis before we find them? Keith?
K Well, Jack. The problem is the oil temperature in the cookers. It keeps falling or rising suddenly. And that's why the samples don't always pick up high fat levels. The problem is worse when demand is high and we're running at full capacity, well, like we are at the moment.
J So what can we do about it?
K Well I think the first idea on your memo is the best one. We should increase the sampling rate. You see, if we take samples more often, we'll pick up the rejects sooner.
P That's true, but if we do that, we'll need extra human resources in the QC department. I prefer the second idea. I'd rather just change the temperature sensors in the cookers.
K We've already tried that, but it didn't make any difference. The problem is the oil in the cookers. When it gets dirty the temperature sensors don't work properly.
P So why don't we change the oil more often?
K Well it would help, but we have to stop production to change the oil. We're going to lose production capacity if we stop the line more often. And the extra oil will increase our costs, of course.
J Hmm. That's a point.
P Yes, but if it reduces the reject levels, a bit of lost production won't be a problem.

K It might not be a problem if we can reduce reject levels to zero, but I don't think that's possible.

J OK let's try it anyway. Keith, I'd like you to change the oil more often and monitor the sensors. Pauline, I'd like you to increase the sampling rate by just 10 per cent. That means you won't need extra staff. Let's do that for the next two weeks and see what happens. OK?

P Right.

Unit 14a: Direct service providers

Listening 1

J = Journalist G = George

J Direct Line was the first direct provider of insurance in the UK when it started 13 years ago. How many call centres does the company now operate?

G We have 6 regional centres which employ between 300 and 700 people each. In total we have about 3,000 staff in our centres.

J Why did the company decide to offer its products directly by phone and Internet rather than the usual way through insurance brokers or high street shops?

G Well, the major reason was probably cost. You see with a call centre you don't have to pay high rents for good high street locations or pay commission to brokers and agents. You can then pass on these cost savings to your customers through competitive pricing of your products.

J Right. And how does a call centre affect the quality of service a customer gets?

G When a customer calls, they get an instant response. The computer database shows all the customer's details, which saves a lot of time. This means we can offer our customers good products, quick service and lower premiums.

J And what products does Direct Line offer?

G Our insurance policies include motor - we're the UK's biggest direct motor insurer - house, travel and life. We also offer financial services such as mortgages, personal loans, savings and pensions. We've also recently started to offer a vehicle breakdown service.

J Gosh, so many. Are your operatives able to deal with all these different products?

G Some operatives only deal with one product, whilst multi-skilled staff can deal with 2 or 3 products. But the system is programmed to guide operatives in dealing with 80 - 90% of enquiries and claims, so they don't have to make any decisions themselves. Unusual or large risks are assessed by supervisors. The important thing is to get as much information at your operative's fingertips as possible. The more information they have in front of them, the less training they need.

J How do you see the future for call centres?

G They're definitely here to stay. But as more and more new call centres are set up, it'll probably become harder to find good staff, so companies'll have to offer better conditions. In the future, staff might even work from home on closed computer networks.

Listening 2

J = Journalist G = George

J George, we sometimes read negative stories about working conditions in call centres. Is it true, for example, that you know exactly where workers are for every minute of their shift?

G Yes, the computer system does monitor whether operatives are at their desks, but we make sure that they get an hour for lunch and plenty of other breaks.

J Does the monitoring affect their pay?

G Yes, but in a positive way. Operatives receive bonuses based on the number of calls they take, the products they sell and the mistakes they make. This way we reward good work.

J So what kind of hours do the operatives work?

G They work flexible shifts of 35 hours a week. Plus overtime if they want it.

J What do you mean by flexible shifts?

G Well, the computer system works out a shift plan based on the calls it expects and plans exactly the right number of operatives for each time of day. So shift times are flexible.

J So, do the operatives also work evenings?

G We're open from 8 till 8 Monday to Friday and from 9 till 5 on Saturdays. A lot of our operatives are young mothers or students, so they're happy to work evening shifts.

J And what about job satisfaction?

G Some people believe that working in a call centre isn't the most exciting job in the world - so it's very important to remember that your operatives are human. So we organise them into teams. The team that sells the most policies, for example, wins a prize. We also organise fun competitions during big sporting events like the World Cup or the Olympics.

Unit 14b: The banking sector

Listening 1

Cl = Clerk Cu = Customer

Cl Hello. Can I help you?

Cu Yes, I'd like some information on your telephone banking service.

Cl Certainly. Do you have an account with us?

Cu Yes, I do. This is my home branch.

Cl Well, with our telephone banking service you can do all your day-to-day banking over the telephone at any time of day or night.

Cu How does it work?

Cl All you do is ring up, key in your PIN number, choose the service you want and then just follow the instructions. It's as easy as that.

Cu And what can I actually do over the phone?

Cl You can check your balance, pay bills, order a statement or transfer money. All your normal day-to-day banking.

Cu Does it cost anything?

Cl No. The number is a freephone number, so you don't pay for your calls and the service is part of your normal bank account.

Cu Oh right. And can I phone at any time of the day?

Cl Yes, you can. There's an automated answering machine and staff are available 24 hours-a-day, seven days a week.

Cu Could I fill in a form now?

Cl Certainly. One moment, I'll just get an application form ...

Listening 2

Cl = Clerk Cu = Customer

Cl Right, could I have your full name, please?

Cu Yes, it's John Peter Barnard.

Cl And your address, Mr Barnard?

Cu 24, Manor Road, Winchester.

Cl And the postcode?

Cu SO23 9DY.

Cl Could I have your date of birth, please?

Cu Yes, it's 31 October 1968.

Cl Thank you. And your daytime phone number?

Cu 01962 866 155.

Cl And all I need now are your account details. Would you like the telephone banking just for your current account or for more than one account?

Cu Just for my current account, please.

Cl OK. So, the sort code is 77 25 08 and could I have your account

number, please?
Cu 60877422.
Cl 60877422.
Cu That's right.
Cl If you could sign the form here, Mr Barnard, and then that's it. I'll register you and then we'll send you your information pack and membership number.

Unit 15 contains extracts from a Speaking Test.
No tapescript is provided.

Unit 16b: Trading

Listening

J = Journalist R = Mr Rauch

J Could you tell me about Raupack and its activities?
R We're an agent for German manufacturers of packing machinery. We provide them with a British sales network and translate their documents, specifications and parts lists into English. We also deal with the British customers and all their enquiries and correspondence. And we arrange customers' visits to Germany.
J Mm, that's very interesting. How did this company begin?
R Before I started Raupack, I worked in sales for eight years for an international company here in the UK. We had to use some small suppliers of packing machinery to complete our product range. But working with both large and small suppliers caused problems. The smaller companies wanted someone to sell only their products, so in 1982 I left and set up my own company, Raupack Ltd.
J That was a big step. And how has this company developed since then?
R Well, I began selling to the drinks industry. Our suppliers began developing excellent new machines that were technically more advanced than our competitors'. These machines helped us to expand into the food and pharmaceutical industries. And our sales people were very good at understanding and selling these new machines so Raupack got a name for delivering excellent products and providing a service that was fair to both customers and suppliers. Since then turnover has grown to nearly £10m a year and our customers now include companies such as SmithKline Beecham, Boots and Glaxo. We moved into these new offices last year and at the moment we're looking for new staff to help the company grow further.
J Very good. And the future? How do you see the future?
R I think technical development is the key to the industry. Companies have to produce and pack more and more specialised goods to satisfy their customers. So, in future, our suppliers'll have to develop their machines technically but without losing any reliability. Our job, of course, is going to be to sell these new machines and continue to provide the best possible support for both our customers and our suppliers.

Unit 17a: Recruiting staff

Listening

R = Rick P = Patricia

R So Patricia, have you given any more thought to taking on an assistant in marketing?
P Yes and I'm still not sure about it. If we decided to take someone on, where would we advertise the vacancy?
R Well, I guess we'd advertise the position internally as we always do.
P But if we advertised the job internally, we'd have the same old problems - not enough applicants and lots of internal political problems. Couldn't we advertise the job outside the company for once?
R Well I suppose we could. But if we did, a lot of people wouldn't be very happy about it.
P So? Would that be a problem?
R Well, yes. I mean, the company always talks about how we like to promote our own people and how you can develop a career with us. So it'd look a bit funny if we didn't advertise it internally first.
P But even if we promoted one of our own people, the other internal applicants wouldn't be happy anyway. So what's the difference? Why couldn't we just advertise it in the national papers?
R But it's company policy. You know that. We always advertise internally first.
P Yes, I know. But why can't we try something different for a change? If we took someone on from outside the company, we'd bring some new ideas into the department. It's what we need, Rick.
R Look, why don't we just advertise it internally as we always do, right? That'll keep everyone happy and then, after a couple of weeks, we can put an advert in the paper as well. What do you say?
P Oh all right. But I'm not going to do the interviews. You can. I had to do the interviews last time and the people who didn't get the job didn't speak to me for weeks afterwards.

Unit 17b: Applying for a job

Listening

I = Interviewer A = Almudena Ribera

I So, Ms Ribera, I'd like to ask you a few questions about your professional experience and qualifications, if I may?
A Sure.
I Now your CV says that you've experience of dealing with clients from different countries. Could you tell me which countries you've dealt with?
A My department publishes translations of foreign books. Most of them are English language books so I deal with America a lot and Britain. And sometimes Italy, too.
I So, America, Britain and Italy. So your English is obviously very good and you speak Italian too. Could you tell me how good your French is?
A It's OK. I did French as part of my degree but it isn't as good as my English or Italian.
I So, that's reasonable French. Now, on your CV you say you have good keyboard skills. Could you tell me how many words a minute you can type?
A About 50. I learned to type as part of my studies but I need to practise a bit more.
I You're not the only one. I still use two fingers! And what about computers? Could you tell me a bit about which programs you use?
A At the moment I use Microsoft Word as I only need the computer for correspondence. In my last job I also used Powerpoint for our presentations.
I You used Powerpoint? Did you design the presentations yourself?
A The Training Director planned them but I had to do the actual computer work and make sure it worked properly during the presentations.
I So that was at Informática. But it says here in your CV that you left in 1996. Could you tell me why you left?
A I think the main reason was languages. I liked my job at Informática but all our clients were Spanish so I never got to use my languages. Then one day I saw the advertisement for the job at Ediciones Gómez and I'd always been interested in publishing, so I applied.
I So why do you want to change jobs now?
A Well, I still feel that I don't get enough practice with my languages...

Unit 18: Exam practice

Questions 30-37

For Questions 30-37 you will hear eight short recordings. For each question, mark A, B or C for the most suitable picture or phrase.

30 ***What does Alison order?***
A *So, Alison. Do you know what you want?*
B *I'm not sure. The chicken sounds nice, but so does the fish. What about you?*
A *Well, I think I'm going to have the fish.*
B *OK. I'll have that, too.*

31 ***Which is the flight to Sydney?***
Would all passengers for flight LH4521 to Brisbane please go to gate number 40. Flight LH4152 to Sydney is now also boarding at gate number 42.

32 ***Which hotel does Graham's colleague recommend?***
A *Have you booked a hotel room yet, Graham?*
B *No, I'm just looking at the brochure now.*
A *Well, don't go to this one here.*
B *Why? What's wrong with the Grand?*
A *It's too expensive. So's this one, the Orion. I'd go to the Plaza if I were you.*

33 ***Which machine are the people talking about?***
A *Karen. Could you help me for a moment?*
B *Sure. What's the problem?*
A *I'm not sure how to use this machine.*
B *It's very simple. Just insert the paper, key in the number and press the send button.*

34 ***What happens to the phone call?***
A *Hello, North Seas Shipping. Can I help you?*
B *Hello. Could I speak to Amanda Collins, please?*
A *One moment please, I'll just try her office. Hello, I'm afraid she's in a meeting. Can I take a message?*
B *It's OK. I'll try again this afternoon.*

35 ***How much does the retailer pay for each game?***
A *The games look interesting, but how much do they cost per unit?*
B *The unit price is $8.*
A *And are there any discounts on large orders?*
B *We could give you a dollar off per unit on orders over 500 units.*
A *Hm. Then I'll just take 200 units to begin with.*

36 ***How long will the order take to arrive?***
A *When are those samples arriving?*
B *Well, they sent them on Friday and it normally takes 4 working days.*
A *But Monday was a bank holiday.*
B *Oh yes. So they should be here on Friday then.*

37 ***What is wrong with the printer?***
A *Oh! The stupid machine isn't working again!*
B *What's wrong with it?*
A *Oh I don't know. I think it needs some more paper or it's run out of ink or something*
B *No, look here. There's some paper stuck in it.*

Questions 38-45

Listen to the manager talking to staff about the way they answer the telephone. For Questions 38-45, mark the correct phrase to complete the sentence. Mark one letter, A,B or C for the phrase you choose. You will hear the conversation twice. You have 45 seconds to read through the questions.

So, if everyone is here, I'll make a start. Now, as you might know, a few months ago we asked some consultants to take a look at the way we answer the telephone across the group. They telephoned our offices and made enquiries as customers normally would. They recorded information such as how quickly the call was answered, how friendly people were and how efficiently they dealt with the enquiry.

So, I'll begin with what they found out. Right, now, first of all, they found out that on average we answer the phone after four rings, which isn't bad, but we can still improve on it. Secondly, friendliness. Now, although some offices scored as high as 8 out of 10 for friendliness, the consultants only gave the company as a whole 6 out of 10. Once more, this wasn't as good as it should be. The consultants said that 7.5 is the minimum we should be aiming for throughout the group. And finally, efficiency. Now here, we did quite well. It seems that the people who normally answer the phone can either deal with enquiries themselves or put the caller through to the right person. However, there were one or two negative points which we still have to work on, such as always remembering to ask the caller's name before putting them through. So, as you can see, we need to do a lot of work.

Going back to the first point, about the phone ringing four times, everyone will now be responsible for answering the phone after the third ring. This way there is no excuse for keeping a caller waiting. The point about friendliness, however, is the most important. People want to hear a cheerful voice when they call the company and feel good when they do business with us. So we're going to choose some new hold music and the consultants have given us some good phrases to use on the phone. They're on the handout I gave you at the beginning. Does everyone have copy? Right, good.

So, moving on to efficiency ...

That is the end of the Test.

Answer key: Self-study

Unit 1a: Job descriptions

Ex ❶: 2 provide a service
3 interview an applicant
4 deal with a problem
5 attend a meeting
6 keep a record
7 organise a conference

Ex ❷: 1 give a presentation
2 provide support
3 interview a candidate
4 deal with people
5 attend a training session
6 keep a diary
7 organise a holiday

Ex ❸:

product	**produce**
sale	**sell**
organisation	organise
interview	**interview**
applicant	**apply**
advertising	**advertise**

Ex ❹: 1 interview 2 organise
3 advertise 4 applicants
5 products 6 discussion
7 sales

Ex ❺: 1 A 2 C 3 B 4 A 5 A 6 A
7 B 8 A 9 C 10 C 11 A 12 B

Unit 1b: Working conditions

Ex ❶: *Suggested answers:*
- paper, stationery, supplies, time, money
- holidays, overtime, salary, problems
- holidays, overtime, orders, stock
- computers, telephone calls, customers

Ex ❷: 1 with 2 about 3 at 4 of 5 of
6 in 7 at/in 8 with 9 in 10 with

Ex ❸: *Suggested answers:*
I rarely work 35 hours a week.
I usually work overtime.
I get 21 days leave a year.
I wear a suit but employees in the factory wear overalls.
There is a health and safety representative in every department.

Ex ❹: 1 Jason Martin
2 32
3 29/11/01
4 Leave
5 Production

Unit 2a: Company history

Ex ❶: 1 tried 2 visited 3 found
4 were 5 decided 6 sold
7 expanded 8 began 9 had
10 bought 11 had 12 set up
13 went 14 announced

Ex ❷: IN: December, 1992, summer, the 1980s
AT: 10.30, Christmas, the weekend (UK)
ON: Friday, 23 July, Tuesday morning, the weekend (US)

Ex ❸: 1 stop 2 produce 3 make

Ex ❹: 1 E 2 C 3 A 4 F 5 D

Ex ❺: *Suggested answer:* (35 words)
Copies of the new company brochure have just arrived from the printers. Could you collect your copies as soon as possible, please? You'll find them in John's office in the marketing department. Thanks.

Unit 2b: Company activities

Ex ❶: 1 is/are building 2 are developing
3 are growing 4 are modernising
5 is investing 6 are earning

Ex ❷: 1 are working 2 spends
3 are thinking 4 doesn't earn
5 are building 6 isn't investing
7 are growing 8 think, are taking
9 want, are offering 10 are climbing

Ex ❸: 2 Nokia is a Finnish electronics company.
3 Reuters is a British press agency.
4 Timberland is an American clothes manufacturer.
5 ABN Amro is a Dutch bank.
6 Daewoo is a Korean car manufacturer.
7 Godiva is a Belgian chocolate manufacturer.
8 Swatch is a Swiss watch manufacturer.
9 Softbank is a Japanese software distributor.
10 Danone is a French food group.

Ex ❹: 1 C 2 B 3 B 4 A 5 B 6 A
7 C 8 C 9 A 10 C 11 A 12 B

Unit 4a: Telephoning

Ex ❶:

[11] Right Mr Abraham. I'll give Mr Green the message.
[3] I'm afraid the line's busy. Can I take a message?
[13] You're welcome. Bye.
[1] Good morning, Priory Hotel.
[7] And what's the message, please?

5 Could you spell your surname, please?
9 Did you say 7:15 or 7:50?

4 Yes, please. Could you tell him Alan Abraham called?
12 Thank you very much.
8 Could you tell him I've booked a table at Marcel's restaurant for 7:15 this evening and I'll meet him there?
6 A-B-R-A-H-A-M.
2 Hello, could you put me through to Mr Green in room 105, please?
10 7:15. Quarter past seven.

Ex ❷: *Suggested answers:*
1 Can I take a message?
2 Could you spell your surname, please?
3 Sorry, did you say
4 I'm calling about
5 Could you tell her
6 I'll give her the message.

Ex ❸: 1 C 2 B 3 A 4 A 5 C

Unit 4b: Internal communication

Ex ❶: *Suggested answer: (35 words)*
We're having a meeting on Tuesday 21 Jan to discuss the new training schedule. Could you prepare your proposals by 18 Jan please, and can you give everyone a copy before the meeting. Thanks.

Ex ❷: *Suggested answer: (32 words)*
There will be a meeting on 21 January at 10.45 in the boardroom to discuss the new brochure. Could all staff please attend. The meeting is scheduled to last approximately one hour.

Ex ❸: *Suggested answer: (37 words)*
Elizabeth Sharp, the new Human Resources Manager, will be visiting us on Tuesday 11 April. The aim of her visit is to learn more about the company so please make sure that you introduce yourselves to her.

Unit 5a: Facts and figures

Ex ❶: A fall B rise C level off
D remain steady E recover F peak

Ex ❷:
1 Last year there was a drop **in** net sales **of** 9%.
2 Market share increased **by** 3%, up to 8%.
3 Net sales peaked **at** £22m in 1997.
4 European sales went **from** £4.2m to £3.0m.
5 Sales levelled off **at** £5m in 1998.
6 Costs rose **by** £3.3m. This was a rise **of** 10%.
7 Office software sales fell **by** 10% in 1997.
8 A strong pound meant a fall **in** exports in 1998.

Ex ❸: 2 product launch 3 net income
4 top-selling brand 5 annual report

Ex ❹: *Suggested answer:*
The most successful product was adventure games. Sales increased steadily from 30% to 45% in the period from 1995 to 1998. There was strong growth in action games for the first three years of the same period. They peaked at 25% in 1997 but dropped sharply in 1998. Sales of sports games fell from 25% to 15% in 1996 then levelled off in 1997 and rose to 20% in 1998. Sales of other computer games remained steady at 10% in 1995 and 1996, fell slightly in 1997 and then recovered in 1998.

Ex ❺: 1 F 2 H 3 G 4 C 5 A

Unit 5b: Performance

Ex ❶:
2 I'd like to begin with a look at
3 As you can see
4 The graph clearly shows
5 I'd like you to look at
6 I'd like to draw your attention to

Ex ❷:
1 has been 2 has already achieved
3 have worked 4 has performed
5 had 6 were
7 did not look 8 made
9 were not 10 has improved

Ex ❸:
2 New trains have **resulted in/led to** more reliable service.
3 The number of delays increased **because of/due to** track problems.
4 We can't raise prices. **That's why/Therefore**, we have to increase volumes.
5 Customer satisfaction has improved **due to/because of** better facilities.
6 Reduced ticket prices have **resulted in/led to** an increase in passenger volumes.

Ex ❹: 1 D 2 A 3 G 4 H 5 E

Unit 6: Exam focus

Part One: 1 C 2 A 3 B 4 B 5 A

Part Two: 6 G 7 D 8 C 9 H 10 F

Part Three: 11 G 12 C 13 E 14 A 15 D

Part Five: 16 C 17 C 18 B 19 C
20 A 21 A

Part Six: 22 A 23 B 24 B 25 B 26 B
27 C 28 B 29 C 30 A 31 B
32 A 33 C

Unit 7a: Product description

Ex ❶:

2	short	How long is the board?
3	cheap	How much does the game cost?
4	size	How big is Collect?
5	easy	How difficult are the instructions?

Ex ❷: Suggested answers:

2 The Extra is 2 kilos **heavier than the Super.**
3 The Extra is more **expensive than the other display panels.**
4 The Super is not as **heavy/big/expensive as the Extra.**
5 The Standard is the least **expensive of the display panels.**
6 The Standard is the **lightest/cheapest/smallest of the display panels.**

Ex ❸: 1 B 2 B 3 A 4 A 5 B
6 A 7 C 8 C 9 B 10 A
11 B 12 C

Unit 7b: Product development

Ex ❶: 2 After that/then 3 then/after that
4 When 5 while

Ex ❷: 2 are you going to do/are you doing
3 are starting
4 are using
5 Are you going to use/Are you using

Ex ❸: 1 A 2 C 3 B 4 A 5 B

Ex ❹: 1 B 2 B 3 A 4 B 5 C

Unit 8a: Business equipment

Ex ❶:

fax machine	printer	photocopier	shredder
dial	jam	jam	jam
jam	press	enlarge	press
press	print	reduce	insert
print	insert	press	shred
insert	switch on	insert	switch on
switch on	overheat	switch on	overheat
overheat		overheat	send
send		copy	
copy		print	

Ex ❷:

Noun	Verb
insertion	**insert**
operation	**operate**
reduction	reduce
copy	**copy**
printer	**print**
removal	**remove**

Ex ❸: Suggested answers:

2 Open the paper tray and insert more paper.
3 Press the red button. Remove the excess paper. Start again with less paper.
4 Open the door of the machine. Remove any jammed paper.
5 Switch it off. Leave it to cool. Try again.
6 Check there are staples in the machine. If there aren't, insert some.

Ex❹: 1 C 2 A 3 C
4 C 5 C 6 B

Ex ❺: 1 C 2 E 3 D
4 A 5 G

Unit 8b: Correspondence

Ex ❶: 2 enclosed 3 department
4 note well (from the Latin: nota bene)
5 regarding 6 week 7 excluding
8 including 9 extension

Ex ❷:

1	Dear Ms Rees	Yours sincerely
2	Dear Paul	Regards
3	Dear Sir/Madam	Yours faithfully
4	Gentlemen	Yours truly*

* *Gentlemen* is the US equivalent of *Dear Sirs* (UK). *Yours truly* is used in the US but rarely in the UK.

Ex ❸:

1	A spoken	B written or spoken
2	A spoken	B written
3	A spoken	B written
4	A written or spoken	B spoken
5	A written	B written or spoken
6	A spoken	B written or spoken

Ex ❹: Suggested answer: (66 words)

Dear Ms Daley

I am writing to enquire about your latest photocopiers. We are currently renting a model from you however we would now like to purchase one.

I would be very grateful if you could send us a copy of your brochure and any relevant product literature. Would it also be possible for you to send us a current price list?

I look forward to hearing from you.

Yours sincerely

Ex ❺: Suggested answer: (76 words)

Thank you for your letter of 5th April.

As requested I am sending you a copy of our brochure and some additional literature about our range of photocopiers. I am also enclosing an up to date copy of our price list which includes details of discounts available for customers who currently rent machines from us.

If you have any questions please do not hesitate to contact me.

Ex ❻: *Suggested answer:* *(38 words)*

Party

As you all know Friday 23rd will be Simon's final day with us at Sonitech. In order to wish him well in his new job there will be a farewell party in Reception at 5.30. Everyone is invited.

Unit 9: Exam focus

Left Column

Part One

Suggested answer: *(38 words)*

I'm in a meeting with one of the suppliers. I'll be back at about 12.30. If Mr Jablonski calls for me, could you explain where I am and ask him when I can call him back?

Thanks

Part Two

Suggested answer: *(78 words)*

With reference to your letter of 24th September I am writing to confirm your travel and accommodation arrangements. I have reserved you a hotel room from the 24th to the 28th of October however the company can only pay for the first four nights. If you let us have your flight details we can arrange for someone to meet you at the airport and take you to your hotel.

I look forward to hearing from you.

Yours sincerely

Right Column

Part One

Suggested answer: *(33 words)*

I am currently out of the office. I will be back on Thursday 23rd. If you have any urgent questions or problems before then please contact my colleague Andrea in our Bristol office.

Part Two

Suggested answer: *(77 words)*

As you know we have been having a lot of problems with our current photocopier (paper jamming etc.). I've seen an advert for a newer version, the TX200 Officepro which can also print excellent quality colour pictures and scan A4 colour documents. It's smaller than the present machine too so we would have more space in the corridor.

I think we should consider buying one, it costs £1,000 plus VAT and they can deliver in two weeks.

Unit 10a: Business hotels

Ex ❶:
1 *rooms (informal, well-equipped, comfortable)*
2 *service (efficient, friendly)*
3 *buildings (elegant, centrally-located, quiet)*

Ex ❷:
2 *modem socket* — 3 *fitness centre*
4 *courtesy bus* — 5 *single supplement*
6 *express check-in* — 7 *rush hour*
8 *health club*

Ex ❸:
1 *hotel parts (lounge, health club, fitness centre, restaurant, swimming pool, dining-room, bar)*
2 *facilities in rooms (desk, communication facilities)*

Ex ❹: *Suggested answer:* *(78 words)*

Further to your letter of 18 June I am writing to confirm the availability of four double rooms for 9-11 July. All our rooms are equipped with telephones and modems, the cost is $400 a night. Our business centre provides a number of facilities including Internet access twenty-four hours a day. Please find enclosed a copy of our brochure for more details.

If you require any further information, please do not hesitate to contact me.

Unit 10b: Commuting

Ex ❶:

1 C	O	2 M	M	U	T	E	3 R
		O					O
4 L	A	T	E				A
		O			5 A		D
6 P	A	R	K		C		
E		W			C		
7 T	R	A	F	F	I	C	
R		Y			D		
O					E		
8 L	A	N	E		N		
					9 T	A	X

Ex ❷:
2 *Public* ***transport*** *is very good in the city where I live.*
3 *The Government's new* ***transport*** *policy won't change anything.*
4 *Sorry I'm late. I was stuck in* ***traffic*** *for hours.*
5 *There's always a* ***traffic*** *jam on the motorway in the morning.*
6 *City centre* ***traffic*** *was reduced by the park and ride scheme.*
7 *There isn't any alternative* ***transport*** *where I live.*
8 *With* ***traffic*** *growth of over 2% a year we need more roads.*

Ex ❸: 1 C 2 A 3 B 4 B 5 A

Unit 11a: Arranging a conference

Ex ❶:
2 *decide on a budget/details/a proposal*
3 *ask for a quotation/details*
4 *make a proposal*
5 *invite delegates*
6 *finalise details/a budget/a proposal*

Ex ❷:
1 *proposal* — 2 *location*
3 *arranging* — 4 *requirements*
5 *quotation* — 6 *confirmation*

Ex ❸: *Suggested answers:*
2 *Do you have a preferred location?*
3 *Could you tell me what your budget is, please?*
4 *When do you want to hold the conference?*
5 *How long would you like it to last?*
6 *How many rooms will you need?*

Ex ❹: *Suggested answers:*

to organise a conference — *conference organiser*
to hold a conference — *conference programme*
conference package
conference centre
conference booking

Ex ❺: *Suggested answer: (77 words excluding salutation and closing phrase)*

Further to our telephone conversation, I am writing to confirm the Amtech marketing conference arrangements. The conference will be held at the Karoliny Conference Centre, Prague. The 37 delegates will arrive for Friday dinner on 25 September and depart after Sunday lunch on 27 September. We will provide a conference room and a seminar room. I enclose a copy of the conference programme and will confirm the name of the Europa Events contact person as soon as possible.

Ex ❻: *Suggested answer: (22 words)*

The marketing conference is from 25 to 27 September at the Karoliny Conference Centre, Prague. You should arrive in time for dinner on the Friday evening. Please confirm if you will be able to attend or not.

Unit 11b: At a conference

Ex ❶: *Suggested answers:*

2 we know the number of delegates.
3 you arrive at the conference.
4 we have had the feedback session.
5 the guest speaker arrives.
6 I have finished it.

Ex ❷:

2 badly-prepared	3 negative
4 useless	5 unproductive
6 boring/dull	7 unrewarding

Ex ❸:
2 *The conference was* **easy** *to organise.*
3 *She gave a* **brief** *(or* **short***) sales presentation.*
4 *Some of the sessions were too* **short**.
5 *The hotel beds were very* **soft**.
6 *The journey to the restaurant was* **short**.
7 *The speaker was* **easy** *to understand.*

Ex ❹: 1 C 2 A 3 B 4 A 5 C

Unit 12: Exam focus

Part One:

1 B	2 A	3 A	4 C	5 A
6 C	7 C	8 B		

Part Two:

9 HP420Y	10 15th
11 10	12 17.5%
13 £116.80	14 WILKES
15 688820	

Part Three:
16 York
17 housewives
18 Feel Good
19 modern professional
20 price
21 12th September
22 Look Great

Part Four:

23 B	24 B	25 C	26 B
27 B	28 A	29 C	30 C

Unit 13a: Production

Ex ❶:
2 *The ingredients are fed into the mixers.*
3 *The baguettes are dropped onto a tray.*
4 *The baguettes are baked for 10 minutes.*
5 *Cool air is blown over the baguettes.*
6 *The baguettes are packed into boxes.*

Ex ❷: *Suggested answer:*

First of all, the production line and sensors are checked before the line is started. If the line does not start, the sensors are re-set and the line is started again. After the line has started, the ingredients are fed into the mixers. If the mix is not correct, the mixer is cleaned out and the ingredients are fed in again. If the mix is correct, the dough is sent to the divider.

Ex ❸: *Machines: cooler, oven, divider, packing machine, former*
Processes: mix, divide, form, bake, prove, cool, wrap, box, despatch
Ingredients: water, yeast, additives

Ex ❹: *Suggested answer: (21 words)*

We have experienced some problems in the packaging department. The 82K machines have not all been set correctly for the new packaging. Please ensure you check all settings before using the new packaging.

Unit 13b: Quality control

Ex ❶:

2 inspection points	3 shelf-life
4 finished goods	5 goods in
6 chemical analysis	

1 finished goods	2 inspection points
3 quality control	4 shelf-life
5 goods in	6 chemical analysis

Ex ❷:

2 goods in	finished goods
3 rise	fall
4 reject	accept
5 reduce	increase

1 demand
2 goods in
3 finished goods
4 increase
5 suppliers
6 fall
7 rise
8 reject
9 reducing
10 accept

Ex ❸:

2 change — won't make/isn't going to make
3 doesn't make — 'll talk
4 increases — 'll have to/'re going to have to
5 'll happen/'s going to happen — keep
6 'll have to/'re going to have to — want
7 don't arrive — 'll look/'re going to look
8 won't be/aren't/isn't going to be — increase

Ex ❹: 1 H 2 A 3 E 4 B 5 C

Unit 14a: Direct service providers

Ex ❶: house, life, travel - **insurance**

insurance - policy, line, company

Ex ❷:

1 memorandum	(the others are all types of agreement)
2 claim	(the others are all something the customer pays)
3 location	(the others are all something you pay)
4 exciting	(the others are all to do with speed)
5 loan	(the others are all lines of insurance)
6 quality	(the others are all quantity)
7 provider	(others are all financial services)

Ex ❸: 1 premium 2 loan
3 broker 4 commission
5 enquiry 6 monitor
7 claim 8 policy
9 supervisor

Ex ❹: 1 A 2 C 3 B 4 B 5 C 6 A
7 A 8 C 9 C 10 B 11 C 12 A

Unit 14b: The banking sector

Ex ❶:

1 S	T	2 A	T	E	3 M	E	N	T		
		C			E					
		C		4 B	R	A	N	C	H	
5 S		O			G					
6 E	M	U			E					
C		N			R	E	D	U	8 C	E
T		T		9 S					U	
O				T					R	
R		10 S	M	A	R	T	C	A	R	D
				F					E	
	11 P	R	O	F	I	T			N	
	C							12 I	T	

Ex ❷: 2 transfer money 3 pay bills
4 order a statement 5 sign a form
6 follow instructions 7 key in a PIN number

Ex ❸: 2 deal with problems
3 invest in new technology
4 pay for a service
5 fill in a form
6 note down some details

Ex ❹: 1 Accounts 2 Andy Smith/The bank
3 386SX or higher 4 4MB
5 Windows 3.0 or higher

Unit 15: Exam focus

Reading Part Seven
Questions 1-5
1 CLOSE & SONS
2 TIM NICHOLLS
3 10 DEC 1998
4 TEK 200
5 £3495

Writing Part One
Suggested answer: (32 words)
I'm working from home tomorrow so that I can finish preparing my presentation for the meeting on Friday. If anyone needs to contact me my home phone number is 020 8767 9289

Writing Part Two
Suggested answer: (73 words)
I think I have found a suitable hotel for the trade fair in Barcelona. It's called the Hotel Gaudi and it has special business traveller rooms with communication facilities. Moreover it is in a good location, in the city centre but only 35 minutes from the airport and 25 minutes from the exhibition centre.
If you agree, I think I should book rooms as soon as possible.
Could you confirm the dates please?

Unit 16a: Quality control

Ex ❶: 2 in/within 3 on 4 in/within
5 until 6 on 7 by 8 until

Ex ❷: 1 documents 2 charge/rate
3 vehicles 4 urgent
5 rate/charge 6 destinations
7 packages 8 weight

Ex ❸: 1 B 2 A 3 C 4 C 5 A

Unit 16b: Trading

Ex ❶: 1 *enquiries, correspondence*
2 *documents, specifications, a parts lists*
3 *a sales network, a service, support*

Ex ❷: 2 *C* 3 *H* 4 *B* 5 *A*
6 *E* 7 *F* 8 *D*

Ex ❸: 1 *Thank you for your enquiry.*
2 *We are pleased to quote as follows.*
3 *Our standard terms and conditions apply.*
4 *The price is quoted in euros.*
5 *The price does not include VAT.*
6 *We look forward to hearing from you.*

Ex ❹: 1 *C* 2 *G* 3 *A* 4 *E* 5 *F*

Unit 17a: Recruiting staff

Ex ❶: 1 *applicants*
2 *an application form*
3 *appointed*
4 *vacancy*
5 *recruit*
6 *candidates*

Ex ❷:

1 ***to fill***
to advertise — *a vacancy*
to apply for

2 ***internal***
external — *applicants*
to recruit

3
recruit — ***a candidate***
internal applicants
workers

4
advertise — ***a vacancy***
jobs
a position

Ex ❸: *Suggested answers:*
2 *you would have to advertise.*
3 *I'd look for a different kind of work.*
4 *I'd miss my family.*
5 *the job was offered to you?*

Ex ❹: 1 *D* 2 *E* 3 *F* 4 *B* 5 *C*

Unit 17b: Applying for a job

Ex ❶: 2 *Could you tell me where you work at the moment?*
3 *Could you tell me if the position includes a pension?*
4 *Could you tell me how you heard about the vacancy?*
5 *Could you tell me if there is any training?*
6 *Could you tell me what your present salary is?*

Ex ❷: *Personal qualities: flexibility, enthusiasm, motivation, communication skills.*
Skills: word-processing, language, presentation, keyboard.

Ex ❸: 1 *Please find enclosed a copy of my CV.*
2 *I am very interested in the position because ...*
3 *Since 1996 I have been working as ...*
4 *I am writing with reference to your advertisement ...*

Ex ❹: 1 *B* 2 *B* 3 *A* 4 *C*
5 *A* 6 *C* 7 *B*

Unit 18: Exam focus

Reading Questions 1-5
1 A *2 C* *3 C* *4 A* *5 B*

Reading Questions 6-10
6 D *7 F* *8 C* *9 H* *10 G*

Reading Questions 11-20
11 A *12 B* *13 C* *14 B* *15 A* *16 A*
17 C *18 A* *19 A* *20 B* *21 A* *22 C*

Reading Questions 23-27
23 Buddy Holly *24 Palace Theatre* *25 3 July*
26 20.00 *27 6*

Writing Question 28
Suggested answer: *(36 words)*
The company will be closed for the Christmas period from Wednesday 25 December to Thursday 2 January. If you want extra holiday please confirm the dates and fill in the holiday forms by Friday 15 November.

Writing Question 29
Suggested answer: *(71 words)*
I am very sorry that I have had to cancel our meeting on Friday at such short notice. This is due to the fact that my boss is off sick all week and so I am unable to leave the office.
I would like to suggest that we reschedule the meeting for next Tuesday at the same time, 10.45. Could you let me know if that would be convenient for you?

Listening Test 30-37
30 A *31 B* *32 C* *33 A* *34 C*
35 B *36 C* *37 B*

Listening Test 38-45
38 C *39 B* *40 A* *41 A* *42 A*
43 B *44 C* *45 B*

Essential vocabulary

1a: Job descriptions

Jobs

accountant
consultant
human resources (HR) manager
marketing manager
production manager
sales executive

Work

to work as (+ job)
to work for (+ company)
to work in (the food industry)

Duties

to attend (a meeting)
to deal with (a problem)
to discuss (problems)
to give (advice)
to interview (applicants)
to involve (+ -ing)
to keep (a record)
to organise (a conference)
to provide (a service)
to be responsible for (+ -ing)

General

to advertise
applicant
to be based on
department
financial products
head
personnel

1b: Working conditions

Frequency

annually
daily
monthly
rarely
weekly

Working conditions

at (the current) rate
bonus
break
day off
employment
equipment
health and safety
leave (holiday)
line manager
overalls
overtime
regulations
salary
shift
supplies

General

annoying
to arrange
to break down
to consult
efficient
in operation
instead of
to review
to run out of
stationery

2a: Company history

Companies

holding company
joint venture
parent company
public limited company (plc)
subsidiary

Activities

to buy
to expand
to export
to found
to manufacture
to own
to produce
to register
to set up
to take over

General

facilities
partnership
plant
stake
to survive
turnover

2b: Company activities

Addition

also
furthermore
moreover
not only ... but also

Contrast

although
however
in spite of

Activities

assembly
to build
to develop
to grow
to invest
investment
to modernise

General

to attract
attraction
to climb
costs
to earn
flexible
low
model
to receive
van
wages

4a: Telephoning

Telephone phrases

Can I speak to ...?
Can I have extension 204, please?
Is Keith available?
Who's calling?
Hold the line, please.
I'll put you through.
I'm afraid the line's busy.
I'm afraid he's not available.
Do you know when he'll be free?
Can I take a message?
I'm calling about ...
I'm returning his call.
I'll call back later.
I'll give him the message.
Could you repeat that?
Could you spell that?
Did you say ...?
We were cut off.
Thank you for calling.

4b: Internal communication

Paperwork

brochure
diary
memo
note
notice
proposal
receipt
schedule

General

appointment
boardroom
to cancel
to claim
essential
expenses
head office
obligation
prize
quarter
request
requirements
to take place

5a: Facts and figures

Describing trend

to increase/increase
to rise/rise
to grow/growth
to improve/improvement
to recover/recovery
to peak/peak
to level off
to remain steady
to decrease/decrease
to drop/drop
to fall/fall
sharp(ly)
strong(ly)
steady/steadily
slow(ly)
slight(ly)

General

annual report
brand
income
product launch
range
retail

7a: Product description

Describing products

length (long/short)
to be made of ...
to measure
size (big/small)
to weigh
weight (heavy/light)

General

board game
complicated
difficult
discount
general knowledge
instructions
reasonable
retailer
to stock
version

8a: Business equipment

Office equipment

to copy
to dial
to enlarge/enlargement
envelope
eraser
fax machine
guarantee
to jam
operating instructions
to overheat
photocopier
to print
printer
reduction
to remove/removal
scissors (pair of)
shredder
stapler
to switch on/off
warranty

General

to be careful
convenient
feature
special offer
to rent

5b: Performance

Giving reasons

because of
due to
to lead to
to result in
that's why
therefore

Presentations

as you can see
bar chart
to draw attention to
figure (Fig 3)
graph
the graph clearly shows
to make a presentation

General

customer satisfaction
customer service
delay
to lease
penalty
performance
privatisation
to promote
punctuality
to reduce
reliability
revenue
track
to upgrade
volume

7b: Product development

Product development

to approve
authorities
average (on average)
development
to monitor
to reach (the market)
research & development (R & D)
stage
to take (+ time)
to test

Drugs

chemist
disease
healthy
over-the-counter
patient
prescription
safe
safety
side-effects

General

advertising campaign
information pack
leaflet
poster

8b: Correspondence

Formal letter phrases

Thank you for your letter of ...
With reference to ...
I am writing to ...
I am pleased to ...
I am afraid that ...
I would be grateful if you could ...
I enclose ...
If you require any further information, please do not hesitate to contact us.
I look forward to hearing from you.
Yours sincerely
Yours faithfully
Best wishes/regards

Abbreviations

ASAP (as soon as possible)
Dept (department)
enc (enclosed)
excl (excluding)
incl (including)
ext (extension number)
NB (note well)
re (regarding)
wk (week)

General

enquiry
quotation
seminar

10a: Business hotels

Hotel

business centre
catering
check-in
communication facilities
courtesy bus
fitness centre
guest
health club
room service
supplement
swimming pool

Directions

along
to cross
near
next to
opposite
past
straight on

General

centrally located
comfortable
desk
lighting
modem socket
rush hour
well-equipped

11a: Arranging a conference

Conference

to arrange (a conference)
to hold (a conference)
to ask for (a quotation)
to decide on (a budget)
to finalise (details)
to invite (delegates)
to make a (proposal)

conference booking
conference centre
conference organiser
conference package
conference programme
conference room

General

access
accommodation
to confirm
duration
location
projector
suitable
workshop

13a: Production

Process

to bake
to box
to check
to collect
to cool
to despatch
to divide
to feed
to form
to mix
to weigh
to wrap

General

circuit
to damage
dough
electronic
human
production line
ingredients
mechanical
oven
sensor
shape
tray

10b: Commuting

Transport

accident
commuter
fuel
lane
motorway
pay-as-you-drive
park and ride
pedestrian zone
petrol
public transport
stuck in traffic
traffic jam
traffic lights

General

to affect
effect
affordable
government
note
change
pavement
policy
to share
smart card
tax

11b: At a conference

Conference

delegate
feedback
guest speaker
report
session
venue

Adjectives

brief
busy
exciting
hard
heated
helpful
intelligent
interesting
positive
productive
professional
rewarding
serious
useful
well-prepared

General

to last
to perform
target

13b: Quality control

Quality control

to analyse
analysis
to inspect
to reject
to sample

Factory

capacity
finished goods
goods in
packaging
shelf-life
supplier
warehouse

General

demand
flavouring
hygiene
quality
quantity
soft
taste
workforce

14a: Direct service providers

Insurance
- broker
- claim
- commission
- policy
- premium

General
- call centre
- competitor
- competition
- direct provider
- loan
- mortgage
- operative
- response
- supervisor

16a: Delivery services

Delivery service
- aircraft
- carrier
- charge
- delivery
- document
- electronic tracking
- express
- network
- package
- parcel
- shipment
- vehicle

General
- commitment
- to rely on
- urgent
- worldwide

17a: Recruiting staff

Recruitment
- application (form)
- to apply (for)
- to appoint
- blue-collar worker
- white-collar staff
- clerical job
- curriculum vitae (CV)
- employment agency
- external
- internal
- to fill (a vacancy)
- to place (an advertisement)
- position
- to promote
- to recruit
- recruitment
- to get rid of
- to take on
- vacancy

14b: The banking sector

Banking
- balance
- bank account
- bank statement
- branch
- current account
- PIN number
- sort code
- to transfer money

General
- to compete (with)
- date of birth
- Emu (European monetary union)
- to fill in (a form)
- to follow (instructions)
- to finance
- IT (information technology)
- merger
- Millennium Bug
- PC (personal computer)
- postcode
- redundancy
- sector
- to warn

16b: Trading

Import agent
- ex works
- invoice
- packing
- to quote
- parts list
- spare parts
- specifications

General
- availability
- fair
- receipt
- skill
- technically advanced
- to translate

17b: Applying for a job

Applying for a job
- degree
- experience
- graduate
- to graduate
- higher education
- marital status
- nationality
- permanent
- temporary
- qualifications

Skills & qualities
- bilingual
- communication skills
- enthusiastic
- keyboard skills
- motivated

General
- honest
- to lie
- software package
- weakness
- words per minute (wpm)

Irregular verbs

become	became	become
begin	began	begun
break	broke	broken
bring	brought	brought
build	built	built
buy	bought	bought
catch	caught	caught
come	came	come
cost	cost	cost
cut	cut	cut
drink	drank	drunk
drive	drove	driven
eat	ate	eaten
fall	fell	fallen
feel	felt	felt
find	found	found
fly	flew	flown
forget	forgot	forgotten
get	got	got
give	gave	given
go	went	gone
grow	grew	grown
hear	heard	heard
hold	held	held
keep	kept	kept
know	knew	known
leave	left	left
lend	lent	lent
lose	lost	lost
make	made	made
mean	meant	meant
meet	met	met
pay	paid	paid
read	read	read
rise	rose	risen
say	said	said
see	saw	seen
sell	sold	sold
send	sent	sent
show	showed	shown
shut	shut	shut
sleep	slept	slept
speak	spoke	spoken
stand	stood	stood
take	took	taken
tell	told	told
think	thought	thought
understand	understood	understood
win	won	won
write	wrote	written

***PASS Cambridge BEC* Series**

Preliminary Level
Student's Book, ISBN: 1-902741-25-0
Teacher's Book, ISBN: 1-902741-26-9
Workbook (with Answer Key), ISBN: 1-902741-29-3
Class and Exam Focus Audio 2 CD Pack, ISBN: 1-902741-28-5
Self-Study Practice Tests with Answer Key (+ FREE CD), ISBN: 1-902741-40-4

Progress to Vantage
Student's Book, ISBN: 1-902741-43-9
Teacher's Book, ISBN: 1-902741-44-7
Workbook (with Answer Key), ISBN: 1-902741-47-1
Class Audio 1 CD Pack, ISBN: 1-902741-46-3

Vantage Level
Student's Book, ISBN: 1-902741-30-7
Teacher's Book, ISBN: 1-902741-31-5
Workbook (with Answer Key), ISBN: 1-902741-34-X
Class and Exam Focus Audio 2 CD Pack, ISBN: 1-902741-33-1
Self-Study Practice Tests with Answer Key (+ FREE CD), ISBN: 1-902741-41-2

Higher Level
Student's Book, ISBN: 1-902741-35-8
Teacher's Book, ISBN: 1-902741-36-6
Workbook (with Answer Key), ISBN: 1-902741-39-0
Class and Exam Focus Audio 2 CD Pack, ISBN: 1-902741-38-2
Self-Study Practice Tests with Answer Key (+ FREE CD), ISBN: 1-902741-42-0

To accompany the Student Books, **multilingual essential vocabulary lists** are freely available in several languages from our website.

For more information please visit our website or contact your local ELT stockist.

www.summertown.co.uk